The Development
of Language and Reading
in the Young Child

The Charles E. Merrill
Comprehensive Reading Program

Arthur Heilman
Consulting Editor

The Development
of Language and Reading
in the Young Child

Susanna Whitney Pflaum
*The University of Illinois
at Chicago Circle*

CHARLES E. MERRILL PUBLISHING COMPANY
A Bell & Howell Company
Columbus, Ohio 43216

75008

Published by
CHARLES E. MERRILL PUBLISHING COMPANY
A Bell & Howell Company
Columbus, Ohio 43216

International Standard Book Number: 0-675-08879-8

Library of Congress Catalog Card Number: 73-86011

4 5 6 7 8 9—78 77

PRINTED IN THE UNITED STATES OF AMERICA

Preface

This book is intended for future teachers or those who are already working in the field of early childhood education in child-care centers, nursery schools, kindergartens, and primary grades. It presents information about the development of language in young children and suggestions for classroom procedures to maximize that development. Since language is viewed here as the primary basis for reading acquisition, the chapters on beginning reading stress use of child language as a means toward that end.

The first part of the book is devoted to language development. Reference is made to theories of language and cognition in Chapter 1. These theoretical considerations become the basis for a description of specific aspects of language growth in Chapter 2 which also contains references to studies by developmental psycholinguists who have been strongly influenced by the theory of generative grammar in recent years. Every attempt has been made to explore this area without undue complexity for the nonlinguistically oriented reader. Chapter 3 analyzes the issues and evidence surrounding language differences found in the speech of young children, while Chapters 4 and 5 review major implications drawn from the previous chapters and translate them into specific classroom activities. Part II is concerned with reading; the reading process discussed in Chapter 6 sets the focus for discussion of prereading needs in Chapter 7 and the beginnings of reading acquisition discussed in Chapter 8. Chapter 9 summarizes major concepts and presents a workable classroom program to ready children for reading instruction and for initiating the first stages of reading. Thus, the book essentially describes the growth toward literacy in children from about the age of three to approximately the age of seven.

In a small book of this nature, it is not possible to pursue the critical areas discussed as thoroughly as one might want; however, it is hoped that this survey of research, the synthesis of ideas gleaned from others, and the suggestions for classroom implications will begin the reader's quest for more information and for better ways to expand children's growing ability to understand their world through language.

My appreciation for help received in the writing is limitless. I am especially grateful for Sandy Dellutri's patience with the manuscript typing. My colleague Anna Marie Larson gave me excellent suggestions. Other helpful readers of parts of the material were William Whitney, my father; Babette Holliday, and Jack McFadden. And special thanks go to my children Melanie and William Pflaum for their support.

Susanna Whitney Pflaum

Contents

vii

Part II: Preparation for Reading and Beginning Reading 109

The Development
of Language and Reading
in the Young Child

PART I

Language Growth during the Preschool Years

CHAPTER 1

Language and Thinking: Motivation for Language Growth

The extensive and profitable study and analysis of language *development* by psychological and linguistic researchers in the past decade enables us to apply significant findings to the concerns of teachers in day-care centers, nursery schools, kindergartens, and the primary grades. It is not wise to discuss the *language* of young children in isolation since language develops in concert with cognitive growth; language both reflects and promotes thought. The interplay between language and cognitive development is our first and, probably, our most important concern. Therefore, we will concentrate in this chapter on the intersection of language and cognitive growth and, specifically, on the work of Piaget, Vygotsky, and Bruner. While there are differences in the interpretations these psychologists give to the role of language in cognitive development, there are enough similarities in their observations to provide a framework for subsequent analysis.

The first section of this chapter will include discussions of the work of Piaget, Vygotsky, and Bruner and will concentrate on the following questions: Does the development of language stimulate the development of thought? What strategies are used by children in their acquisition of cognition and language? What roles do adults play in language development? Having established some awareness of the role of language in thinking, we will turn in the second section to a more detailed analysis of what motivates language growth. Such an analysis should increase awareness of the role the environment plays in language development.

3

LANGUAGE AND COGNITIVE DEVELOPMENT

Before beginning the main body of the discussion in this chapter, we should try to examine thought and language separately. By so doing, we will make clearer the role of language in human life and will be able to outline the boundaries of the following discussion. But it is extremely difficult, if not hazardous, to try to separate language from thought. Since most adult Western thought is verbal in orientation, it is difficult to imagine nonverbal thinking; nonetheless, even as adults, we do have nonverbal thoughts. Fleeting, unremembered dreams are nonverbal. The reaction to speeded-up visual displays seen on television may be nonverbal. Certainly our affective reaction to many of our perceptions is nonverbal. Even some types of complex thought are nonverbal. Many artists, for example, would find it difficult (and unnecessary) to try to verbalize their thinking, for they can "think" directly onto their canvases, into their musical scores, through their choreography, or in their sculptures without the need of mediating language.

There are few other examples of complex thinking which are not verbal in Western society; indeed, our society prizes the ability to be verbal as a mark of education and success. Because of our strong verbal orientation, it is difficult to recognize nonverbal characteristics which, as we will see in the following discussion, probably mark many children's early cognitive activities. However, if possible, we should try to abandon for the time being our predilection for verbal translation of thought so that we can begin discussion of the tremendous insights into the intersection of thought and language in young children which Piaget, Vygotsky, and Bruner offer us.

Piaget

The most influential and compelling theory of cognitive development comes from the work of Jean Piaget *(20, 21)* and his colleagues *(14).* We will review a few major Piagetian concepts of children's cognitive development before analyzing his position on language. For Piaget, cognitive development, from the very beginnings of life through adolescence, is marked by individuals' active and unconscious structuring of the input they perceive in the environment. That is, children deal only with those aspects of their world out of which they can make sense. In Piaget's terminology, children *assimilate* environmental input into their present cognitive structure. If the input is new and adds a new dimension to their thinking, their thought patterns are modified or changed by *accommodation.* Assimilation and accommodation are the basic processes by which individuals learn.

Even before language is acquired, during the first year of life (the *sensori-motor stage*), children begin to figure out their own reality for themselves. Infants' thoughts during this stage are tied to actions or specific sensory qualities of stimuli. The first words spoken by children also are tied to the actions they perform or observe. By the end of the period, at about eighteen months, children have arrived at a point where they think of themselves as separate objects in a world made up of permanent objects and can perform simple problem-solving tasks. By this age, children no longer perceive the existence of events and objects only in relation to themselves *(21).*

After the start of the *preoperational period,* which begins at about eighteen months and continues to about age seven, a number of important changes occur in children's cognitive development. The new *cognitive* abilities acquired during this period are determined largely by children's ability to symbolize. Children in the sensorimotor stage learned that objects have permanence; at the beginning of the preoperational stage, they master use of objects to represent other objects and situations in play and thinking. When children pretend that blocks of various sizes "stand" for a family, their symbolic play demonstrates their representation of familiar family groups in another medium. Children at this stage of development also begin to make drawings which are helpful in organizing their thinking. Although the drawings may not appear to be realistic to the adult observer, they are intended to be. Drawings help children develop mental images of objects. Finally, during the early part of this stage, children develop the ability to form real mental images of objects not present. Once children have formed mental images and once they have labels for these images, they comment on and describe absent objects and past events *(21).*

Piaget has been concerned with the role of language in the development of thought for many years. In 1926, he published a book entitled *The Language and Thought of the Child (20)* which examined the function of the speech of children at play with other children. He found a great preponderance of *egocentric speech* among preschool children, with a greater amount of *socialized speech* emerging in children over the age of seven. Egocentric speech is centered essentially on one's own actions; children talk aloud to and about themselves even when in the presense of other children. Socialized speech involves real dialogue; information and questions are provided in an interactive situation. Piaget's later studies *(21)* have shown that the amount of egocentric speech in the preschool child diminishes under certain circumstances; for example, this often occurs when children converse with adults. Generally, though, children appear to talk for and to themselves about their play and own activities. It is important to note that, according to Piaget, the egocentric speech of young children does not determine their behavior; it is a *verbal accompaniment to behavior.* Piaget's work suggests that language in its functional use appears to be limited to a level of sophistication which has already been achieved in cognitive development. In his theory, cognitive development determines the course of language growth.

During his forty-five years of study of cognitive growth, Piaget has not changed his position on the role of language in thinking drastically. He continues to believe that language ability is generally determined by the level achieved in cognitive development; however, there are points where language does stimulate cognitive growth to a certain extent. For example, language enables children to detach thought from action at the start of the preoperational stage. Thus, thought becomes symbolic and, because language too is inherently symbolic, it becomes the natural medium for representing absent objects and past events. This ability to represent is a hallmark of the beginning of the preoperational stage, and language is one important source used by children as they move into this stage.

Piaget has found in experiments with older children *(21)* that language does not play an important role in the development of logical behavior. Deaf-mute children do not experience as much delay in their cognitive development in experimental tasks as do blind children of the same age. According to Piaget, the absence of vision appears to slow growth more than does the absence of language. He further believes, "Language does not constitute the source of logic but is, on the contrary, structured by it."[1]

However, even if language does not contribute to the development of logical behavior, it is recognized as a tool of instruction in cognitive development for children who are in transition to the *concrete-operational period* of development. In a study conducted by four of Piaget's colleagues in Geneva *(14)*, the effect of language training on success in conservation tasks was examined. Experiments examin-

---

[1]Jean Piaget, *The Language and Thought of the Child* (New York: Meridian Books, 1955), p. 90.

ing the influence of language and other factors on the achievement of conservation of children between ages four and eight showed that:

> First, language training, among other types of training, operates to direct the child's interactions with the environment and thus to "focus" on relevant dimensions of task situations. Second, the observed changes in the justifications given (by the subjects) for answers in the conservation task suggest that language does aid in the storage and retrieval of relevant information. However, our evidence offers little, if any, support for the contention that language training per se contributes to the *integration and coordination* of "informational units" necessary for the achievement of the conservation concepts. Language learning does not provide, in our opinion, a ready-made "lattice" or lens which organizes the child's perceptual world.[2]

The authors of this study agree with an American interpretation of Piaget's work that language does not play a major organizing role in determining intellectual development until children achieve formal, mature thought during adolescence. Furth *(12)* further asserts that because of the rather minor role language plays in cognitive growth during the preschool and primary years, verbal output (oral, read, and written language) should not be emphasized in schools until well after the normal age for initial literacy training.

In answer to the question, "Does the development of language stimulate the development of thought?" Piaget would assert that except as an aid in stimulating symbolic thought and in focusing on concrete operations, language does not stimulate intellectual development strongly until adolescence. Indeed, language development *is stimulated by* cognitive growth rather than the reverse. In answer to the question of which strategies children use to acquire cognition and language, Piaget would contend that the strategies used in learning language are not used to create new thinking abilities. Instead, language services thought.

The classroom implications of Piaget's work are far-reaching. For example, Kamii's *(15)* analysis of the implications of Piaget for preschool education describes the adult role in the classroom as one of establishing an atmosphere which offers children activities and objects which will stimulate them toward optimum growth. Not only should adults provide objects and produce events designed to pro-

---

[2]B. Inhelder; M. Bovet; H. Sinclair; and C. D. Smock, "On Cognitive Development," *American Psychologist* 21 (1966):160–64.

mote thinking, but they also should use both their and the children's language to probe and discuss the problems the children encounter with concrete objects. Teachers who are sensitive to Piaget's work can probe in such a way as to both discover the children's present levels of functioning and also provide the children with activities, objects, and questions to help promote cognitive growth. Furth *(12)* is an excellent source for teachers to use in acquiring these skills.

Vygotsky

In 1934, a few years after Piaget's *Language and Thought* first appeared, the work of a Russian psychologist named Lev S. Vygotsky was posthumously collected and published as *Thought and Language (24)*. Vygotsky's work had little impact on psychology in Western Europe and the United States until relatively recently when it was reissued and translated. Since Vygotsky offers an alternative interpretation of the role of adult language in the development of the young child's thinking and his use of language, a summary will provide a good contrast with the work and conclusions of Piaget.

In Vygotsky's work, dialogue between adult and child is of major importance, is a critical factor influencing language development, and is a stimulation to cognitive growth. Thus, children learn names and language structures from this dialogue. Although it takes many years of growth to reach mature conceptual levels, the beginning of language and thought comes from the model provided by adults. The development of concepts is initiated by adult models and structured by the individual with further dialogue as a source. According to Vygotsky, when a mature concept expressed in qualitative language is finally and independently organized by the individual, the final product of cognitive and language development has been achieved.

To continue, we will look first at Vygotsky's position on the function of communication in childhood development and then turn to his powerful description of the growth of concepts. In order to summarize Vygotsky's analysis of early communication, we must first define his terms *external speech* and *inner speech*. *External speech* is that which can be heard both in dialogue with others and in monologue. Adults provide very young children who are just beginning to talk with language models in dialogue. As children imitate, begin to respond to the dialogue, and later produce monologues, external speech is evident. Through imitation, response patterns become the habitual patterns which are present in external speech and which are used to structure children's inner speech. Thus, external speech is prerequisite to the inner speech which precedes mature thought. Vygotsky describes *inner speech* as a sort of silent speech which occurs before real thought begins. In fact, inner speech leads to thought.

Thus, for Vygotsky, the model provided by adults is necessary to teach names, to demonstrate language structures to young children, and to provide practice. From the adult model, children acquire form and structure which are then the organizing sources for the structuring of thought.

An example might help to indicate the contrast between Vygotsky's and Piaget's analyses of the role of language and learning strategies in the development of thought. Those interested in child language and cognition frequently point out that children use words without mature meanings or with missing attributes. When a youngster of five, let us say, uses *because* and *although* without full conceptual understanding, Piaget would say that they are largely meaningless terms. In addition, he would contend that until the child acquires the complex significance of these terms, no amount of use in speech will help him to learn their meanings. On the other hand, Vygotsky's analysis would hold that these words are used in speech with partial understanding of position but without the mature idea of coordination. Vygotsky would also contend that an individual child's understanding increases gradually as he uses the terms in his everyday speech *(7), (10), (22)*.

Another major point of contrast between the two theories is the analysis of children's use of speech to communicate. According to Piaget, children's speech with others is partially, though not exclusively, egocentric in orientation until the children have reached the age of seven or eight and attained the concrete operational stage of development. The adult role in providing language models exists, of course, but it does not expand children's thinking beyond the limits which they have constructed for themselves. However, in Vygotsky's theory, the role of adult language is clearly critical for all language and thought development. The dialogue and monologue which adult language provide are forms of external speech which are necessary to prepare for inner speech and for real thinking.

We must not conclude from this discussion that children were viewed by Vygotsky as passive learners who absorbed only the models provided them. More analysis of his position is needed. We have stressed the modeling role of adult language, but it is also true that for Vygotsky, the acquisition of concepts and the structuring of experience occurs as an active process. In this respect, Vygotsky is much closer in his views to Piaget than appears from the earlier discussion. Vygotsky *(24)* identified three stages in children's conceptual development which are not unlike Piaget's.

Heaps During infancy and before language begins, children group objects haphazardly without perceiving stable relationships among objects. Fleeting images characterize their organization of the world.

Complexes Complexes are formed early and are observable throughout the preschool period, during which they become increasingly stable. The stage of complexes is comparable to Piaget's preoperational stage. In the beginning, children may perceive attributes which are shared among objects in a group even though attributes may differ among some of the objects. When children achieve what Vygotsky calls the *pseudo-concept,* conceptual thinking begins, as they are able to group objects according to consistently shared attributes. But to accomplish this kind of grouping, children must acquire concrete and functional attributes from the adult model. Adults must help children to form this pseudo-concept which is a necessary factor for dialogue and monologue. Dialogue and monologue are, in turn, prerequisites for inner speech.

Concepts Finally, during adolescence, individuals develop the ability to abstract attributes of groups independently. As mature thinkers, they are no longer either tied to concrete, functional attributes or dependent on adult naming as they were as children.

In terms of the two questions asked at the beginning of this chapter, Vygotsky's position is clear. First, language is a major stimulant for conceptual growth; however, conceptual growth is also dependent on interaction with objects in the environment. Second, the strategies used in learning language become a major means for acquiring thought processes. Mature thought is achieved only after acquired language forms have provided children with labels and structures to use as they interact with objects. In contrast to the preschool curriculum designed to realize Piaget's work, a preschool curriculum intended to follow Vygotsky's theory would define carefully the language terms and activities provided for children to maximize their cognitive growth.

Bruner

In his brilliant initial chapters of *Studies in Cognitive Growth (6)*, Jerome Bruner discusses his view of the interrelatedness of language and cognitive development. In some respects, Bruner's analysis lies between Piaget's and Vygotsky's, for he believes that language plays a stronger role in stimulating thought than does Piaget but does not give it as preponderant a role as does Vygotsky.

Bruner holds that language serves in two respects as a stimulant for general cognitive growth during the preschool years. However, before language can play this role, children must have had sufficient developmental opportunities and successful experiences so that their acquisition of language can proceed normally. During these initial stages of cognitive growth before language begins, children perceive the world in terms of undifferentiated relationships which correspond to Piaget's sensori-motor stage and Vygotsky's heaps.

Language becomes a major stimulant to cognition once language acquisition begins, according to Bruner, because the quite sophisticated strategies used by children as they acquire language (which will be discussed later in this chapter and in greater detail in Chapter 2) become available for cognitive learning in general. Children's first language structures are rule-governed. With age and experience, children begin to use sentences based on more specialized rules. These rules are not taught directly from outside sources but are developed gradually through the children's experiences. Bruner has suggested that the strategies children acquire as they develop language rules are crucial to cognitive development. Bruner, Oliver, and Greenfield's studies *(6)*, which have shown that the ability to achieve symbolic behavior after school entrance is more apparent in developed, verbal-oriented societies than in primitive ones, suggest that when abstractions described through language are valued—as they are in Western society—language does indeed interact positively with thought.

Language helps in general cognitive development because of its abstract nature. Children begin to be able to perceive object groups during the first years, but this perception is only in terms of superficial appearances. Gradually, children acquire the ability to look beyond the surface and to group objects in terms of inherent characteristics. There is a parallel in language growth: In the beginning of vocabulary learning, the *word* appears to be equivalent to the object. Later, children learn that the word is a *name* for the object. To explain, let us imagine a child who says "ball" for his one red ball. "Ball," to him, means that round thing he can hold. In time, he notices that lots of other round things are called "ball," too. If all those round bouncy things are balls, than "ball" must be a name for round things like that and not just his nice round red thing. This is, of course, a vast simplification of the process, but it is intended to illustrate how *naming,* which is necessary to the establishment of groupings, appears through children's language experience.

Of course, Bruner recognizes the great impact on language which comes from the development of cognition. During the preschool years, language stimulates thought by providing children with a complex structure which helps in organization of general cognitive structures. However, there is an active relationship between the development of language and thought which continues beyond the preschool period. Later, language helps older children attain the achievement of mature thought of individuals who use language to abstract the features of experience and reorganize them into a rational system.

In answer to the two questions raised at the start of the chapter, Bruner indicates that language does stimulate cognitive development in certain respects. Further, he believes that strategies used in language acquisition serve as stimulants to the development of thought. Bruner's view of language provides us with an acceptable guideline for planning instruction of young children, while findings from Piaget's work and Vygotsky's insights extend Bruner's framework. For example, we recognize that children must have active involvement with concrete objects if they are to develop the thinking strategies which will, in turn, increase language ability. But if we were to follow Piaget's theory as the exclusive source for our curriculum, we might deemphasize the educative role of adult language except as a probing mechanism into children's thinking as implied by Kamii *(15).* We might also deemphasize the educative value of children's verbal output except as an indicator of cognitive level as suggested by Furth *(12).* On the other hand, if we were to follow Vygotsky exclusively, we would stress adult language.

We believe that a good curriculum combines elements from the views of all of these theorists. A good school program should provide children with plenty of independent activity, as would a Piaget-based program, in order to ensure active structuring and involvement in events. In addition, this program should include many opportunities for children to hear and interact with adults and each other in dialogue as Vygotsky would recommend. Finally, as Bruner *(5)* suggests, a program of merit encourages children to describe their experiences in their own terms and to build on the language forms used.

It is clear that why language develops as it does influences how the classroom environment should be organized. We turn in the following section to this question of "why" or motivation for language acquisition and to the environmental influences for language growth.

MOTIVATION FOR LANGUAGE GROWTH

In this section, we will still be concerned with theoretical matters; however, there are more specific implications and applications for the classroom to be drawn from the following discussion than was true in the preceding material. We have already learned that language acquisition appears to stimulate general cognitive growth to some extent. However, we still have not discussed what motivates the beginning and continual growth of language ability in children; nor have we looked into the factors existing in the children's environment which are instrumental in acquisition of language. Therefore, there are two questions to be answered in the following discussion: What motivates the start of language acquisition and continues to motivate its growth throughout the preschool years? In what ways does adult language influence growth of child language?

In order to explain what motivates the beginning of language acquisition, we need to examine what it is that is unique about human language. Why is it man acquires a system which provides us with the means to produce completely novel sentences (9)? Is it because we have a special neurological apparatus for language learning as the biologist Lenneberg (17) maintains? Or is our language simply an illustration of the human ability to accumulate learning quantitatively (rather than a different kind of learning) as some behaviorally oriented psychologists would say? [See Athey (1) for a good review of the various views on language growth.] If the human ability to communicate were simply a greater accumulation of knowledge than that of lower animals, then it ought to be possible to train higher primates to begin a primitive form of language. In contrast to earlier unsuccessful attempts, a recent effort (13) to teach a chimp sign language shows the beginning of one-word sign language. However, the chimp's sign language lacks the inventiveness true of all human language.

Rather than present an extensive account of the different positions on the motivation for language learning, we will accept the biological, cognitive position that man has a neurological preference for language. Evidence for this position will become apparent as we review some facts about child language learning. At the same time though, we recognize the role of imitation in vocabulary acquisition as an important element in language development.

If language is specific to the species, then it is not illogical to expect all children to learn to talk. And, indeed, this is usually the case. Most children learn some language without any overt training on the part of adults. At this point, the reader probably is thinking of children who cannot talk and is doubting this claim that all children learn language. There are, of course, a very few children who do not learn much language because of severe neglect and some others who do not develop much language because of a physical disorder or a severe nervous disability. However, these groups are a distinct minority when compared with the number of children who learn language quite normally. Even in the case of many disabled children, it is often surprising how much language is acquired; except for severe cases, handicapped and retarded children do learn some language. It appears from study that comprehension and oral ability do not need to go hand in hand. Lenneberg *(17)* has reported a case of a nonverbal boy studied from age four to age nine. At four, he could not even babble; he was totally inarticulate. At nine, after intensive training, the best he could do was to say a word with great difficulty and then only if an adult said it with him. However, tests of understanding of language indicated that he had near normal passive comprehension of language and its structure. Apparently, language comprehension develops even under most difficult situations and speech is not even necessary for its growth.

Psycholinguists and others who claim that children have an inherent propensity for language have found that language generally begins within a regular range of time regardless of the individual child's environment. Lenneberg *(17)* has also reported instances of hearing children born to deaf parents, who cannot reinforce the speech they do not hear, begin to speak at about the same time as children growing up in a normal family. Lenneberg's studies also indicate that position in the family does not appear to affect the time when language begins; the findings show that second and third children begin to speak at the same age as did the first children in spite of the fact that parents of first children often show more interest in their language beginnings. First children may learn more language once they begin, but, according to Lenneberg, all normal children appear to begin to acquire language at approximately the same time.

From a brief study of the literature on the subject, it becomes apparent that children's language growth is marked by points of significant change which occur regularly for all children. (In Chapter 2, the characteristics of this growth are described.) These points in language growth are related to certain milestones in motor development. While this does not mean that certain motor skills must be achieved for language to grow, both language and motor skill are controlled by maturational factors. For example, just as it is not possible to train a child to walk who is not ready, it is also not possible to teach a six-month-old infant to say words. Further, even though there is a relationship between the two, the developmental character of language growth is separate from that of motor acquisition. To illustrate, there are a few children whose motor development is quite normal but whose language development is significantly slowed. These children, if they have no discernible physical or emotional disorder, usually learn language, although their acquisition occurs later than with normal children. The maturational schedule for language is independent of that for motor development *(17)*.

Lenneberg offers still another piece of evidence for the inductive character of language development in young children in his finding that when language changes noticeably, the environment does not appear to change drastically. In other words, it is impossible to find factors in the environment of the young child which will account for language change. The home does not provide situations which specifically propel the child into new language forms *(17)*. The child's readiness and the provision of language models about him appear to be enough to precipitate language acquisition. In Lenneberg's view, the motivator for language acquisition is inside the child; it is his natural language learning ability.

Since language learning ability appears to be inherent in very young children, there must be an unspecified neurological structure in the infant. Of course, we cannot determine exactly where this structure is and how it works, for the language component of the brain defies such specificity. However, there has been speculation on how such a structure might work. Linguists such as Chomsky *(7)* and psycholinguists such as McNeill *(18)*, *(19)* have hypothesized a construct, which they call the Language Acquisition Device (LAD), to represent language learning children. Bear in mind as we discuss this "device" that it does not exist to any observable degree; it is only a hypothesis. But, as McNeill *(18)*, *(19)* points out, what happens with LAD may well be what happens with children.

In the diagram, LAD receives the input from the language of the environment. LAD analyzes this input in such a way as to produce a language rule system. (By rules, we mean an implicit sense of how to organize words in sentences. In fact, LAD was proposed as a way of accounting for the developing rule system underlying the language of children.) The rule system then becomes the basis for the form of the speech which is produced. Only the language LAD "hears" and the speech "produced" are observable. The hypothesis lies within the large closed box.

Children appear to do what LAD does. Children hear the observable language around them. When they are ready, they organize that language input and simplify its complexities so that they unconsciously form a system which is the underlying basis for their produced language. As children mature, they are able to receive more complex input. The new input is also organized and the rule system adjusted to new complexities. As a result, the speech produced reflects the new rules and increased understanding of syntactic forms.

Although the concept of LAD is a hypothesis, it does demonstrate the relationship between language heard and language produced by children. It stresses the following concepts about language acquisition: Language growth results from children's growing ability to hear language forms; children make sense of language input in terms of their level of maturity; they form rules to account for the input; finally they produce speech based on the rule system.

Although we cannot pinpoint exactly how children hear and process the structure of adult language, it is clear that this data is absorbed somehow, for as children make comparisons between their primitive expressions and the complex ones of adults, their language grows. If we knew exactly how adult language is used by children, we would be able to provide valuable instructional input in classroom programs. Unfortunately, we have no such exact knowledge, although researchers have looked at possible kinds of adult-child interaction and offer some probable methods which children use.

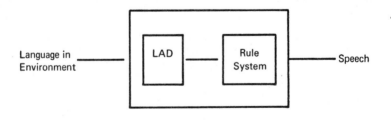

FIGURE 1

The Language Acquisition Device

One possibility is that children simply imitate the sentences adults use and learn language forms through this imitation. However, if this were the major source for language learning, LAD would not be needed since learning by imitation is simpler than the form of learning described in LAD. Sometimes children do imitate adult sentences, but they reduce the number of words adults use to a few essential ones which they can handle. The question about imitation is whether, in fact, the apparent imitations children make are just that—imitations—or whether they are based on children's rules for language. Ervin's *(11)* study of the complexities of children's spontaneous imitations has revealed that children's imitations are never more advanced in syntactic structure than are their other nonimitative sentences. Further, she found that there are relatively few direct imitations and therefore concluded that there must be other methods for children to acquire their language.

Before we turn to other possibilities, we should recall that language learned by imitation should not be discounted altogether. Certainly, without imitation, there would be no learning at all at the level of vocabulary acquisition. Children must be exposed to adult names for objects, actions, etc. in order to acquire a vocabulary. The process may work in this manner: When a toddler is playing with a toy, a pail for instance, an adult or older child will name that toy. The child associates the word "pail" with the object. After associating it, he may imitate the spoken word "pail." It is likely that in some way he will be reinforced for saying "pail." Thus, imitation is crucial for word learning; however, it does not appear to be a very productive process in acquiring syntactic rules.

Another possible source of help for children who are learning language may come from adult correction and/or reinforcement of their speech. However, Brown and Hanlon *(3)* have found that parents seldom react to the "correctness" of children's speech. Instead, they comment on the truth factor of their children's utterances. That is, parents are apt to agree with a child who makes a relevant comment, even if it was stated in an obviously immature fashion. On the other hand, they may disagree with the child's perfectly well-formed utterance because of the content. As a result of this tendency by parents, the importance of parental correction of sentence structure as a source of language acquisition may be diluted.

Still another source for language learning may be by a process of imitation in reverse. Brown and Bellugi *(2)* have suggested that adult *expansion* may provide important data for the language learning child. An expansion occurs when a child's statement such as "here sock" is repeated by an adult in his form as, "Oh, here is the sock." Thus, the adult displays quite naturally to the child how his idea is described in mature language. Possibly, the child learns more mature structures by comparing his own sentence with that of the adult. Two empirical studies of the influence of expansion on children's language maturation show opposite effects. Cazden *(7), (8)* has reported that deliberate expansion after each comment by the child in short daily sessions is not particularly helpful in advancing syntactic ability when the child is compared with a group of children not treated in this manner. On the other hand, McNeill *(18)* has reported a study which shows expansion to be very effective for language growth. The main difference in the design of the second study is that *only* the child's sentences which were comprehensible to the adult were expanded. Thus, the authors of the second study avoided probable confusion resulting from misunderstandings of child utterances. We cannot be absolutely sure of the role of expansion since we have contradictory evidence, but because of the more natural situation in the second study, it seems safe to assume that deliberate, meaningful expansion will not harm language growth and may help it. The second study also demonstrates that some training does speed children's syntactic learning.

It is also possible that children learn simply from adult comments on the truth of what they say. This possibility has also been put to test with equivocable results. Cazden's *(7), (8)* study shows strong positive growth from many adult comments, while McNeill's *(18)* shows less. Still, natural comments on the truth factor, which comprise the majority of adult remarks in adult-child dialogue, probably do have some salutory effect on the development of language.

According to Brown, Cazden, and Bellugi *(4),* an additional source for the language learning child may be the prompting by an adult. For example, if a child were to say, "I ate (word lost)," the adult might try to increase his understanding by prompting, "What did you eat?" Prompting thus isolates the noun in the child's utterance and also demonstrates the past tense equivalence of "ate" and "did eat" in the statement and question forms. Prompting has not been empirically examined to find out if it, in fact, does offer children language data.

Having considered a variety of alternatives, we are left with the possibility that expansion, comments on the truth factor, and prompting may provide language learning children with the sources they need to compare mature and immature structures. In spite of the fact that we have no neat research results, it seems that we can assume from this discussion that interactive dialogue between adults and children is essential for language growth. Thus, the school language program we propose will emphasize adult-child and child-child dialogue. Specifically, we will provide for natural, informal use of expansion, comments on the truth factor, and prompting.

In answer to the questions raised at the beginning of this section, the motivation for the start of language in young children is controlled largely by maturational factors. Since children have a natural ability to learn language, all that is needed at the start is the presense of language around them. Language will naturally continue to grow, but it will develop more quickly under optimal conditions of adult-child interaction. We cannot answer the second question as decisively, since there are few specific data to help us. But adult use of expansion, comments on truth, and prompting are possible ways for adult language to provide data for the child to process and accommodate to his rule structure.

Earlier in this chapter, it was stated that children may acquire a valuable tool for the promotion of their general intellectual development as they acquire the rule system underlying language production. The ultimate goal for education is to promote effective thinking, of course, and by maximizing the language acquisition process through dialogue we may be enhancing children's general intellectual growth.

REFERENCES

1. Athey, I. J. "Synthesis of Papers on Language Development and Reading." *Reading Research Quarterly,* 7 (1971): 16–110.

2. Brown, R., and Bellugi, U. "The Processes in the Child's Acquisition of Syntax." *Harvard Educational Review,* 34 (1964): 133–51.

3. Brown, R., and Hanlon, C. "Derivational Complexity and Order of Acquisition of Child Speech." In *Cognition and Development of Language,* edited by J. R. Hayes. New York: John Wiley & Sons, Inc., 1970.

4. Brown, R.; Cazden, C; and Bellugi, U. "The Child's Grammar from One to Three." In *The 1967 Minnesota Symposium on Child Psychology,*

edited by J. P. Hill. Minneapolis: University of Minnesota Press, 1968.

5. Bruner, J. "Poverty and Childhood." In *Preschool in Action: Exploring Early Childhood Programs,* edited by R. K. Parker. Boston: Allyn & Bacon, Inc., 1972.

6. Bruner, J.; Oliver, R. R.; and Greenfield, P. M. *Studies in Cognitive Growth.* New York: John Wiley & Sons, Inc., 1966.

7. Cazden, C. *Child Language and Education.* New York: Holt, Rinehart, & Winston, Inc., 1972.

8. _____. "Subcultural Differences in Child Language: An Interdisciplinary Review." *Merrill-Palmer Quarterly,* 12 (1966): 185–219.

9. Chomsky, N. *Aspects of a Theory of Syntax.* Cambridge: The M.I.T. Press, 1965.

10. Dale, P. S. *Language Development: Structure and Function.* Hinsdale, Illinois: The Dryden Press, Inc., 1972.

11. Ervin, S. "Imitation and Structural Change in Children's Language." In *New Directions in the Study of Language,* edited by E. Lenneberg. Cambridge: The M.I.T. Press, 1964.

12. Furth, H. *Piaget for Teachers.* Englewood Cliffs, New Jersey: Prentice-Hall, Inc., 1970.

13. Gardner, R. A., and Gardner, B. T. "Teaching Sign Language to a Chimpanzee." *Science,* 165 (1969): 664–72.

14. Inhelder, B.; Bovet, M.; Sinclair, H.; and Smock, C. D. "On Cognitive Development." *American Psychologist,* 21 (1966): 160–64.

15. Kamii, C. "An Application of Piaget's Theory to the Conceptualization of a Preschool Curriculum." In *The Preschool in Action: Exploring Early Childhood Programs,* edited by R. K. Parker. Boston: Allyn & Bacon, Inc., 1972.

16. Kohlberg, L.; Yaeger, J.; and Hjerlholm, E. "The Development of Private Speech: Four Studies and a Review of Theories." *Child Development,* 39 (1968): 691–736.

17. Lenneberg, E. *Biological Foundations of Language.* New York: John Wiley & Sons, Inc., 1967.

18. McNeill, D. *The Acquisition of Language: The Study of Developmental Psycholinguistics.* New York: Harper & Row, Publishers, 1970.

19. _____. "Developmental Psycholinguistics." In *The Genesis of Language: A Psycholinguistic Approach,* edited by F. Smith and G. A. Miller. Cambridge: The M.I.T. Press, 1966.

20. Piaget, J. *The Language and Thought of the Child.* New York: Meridian Books, 1955.

21. Piaget, J., and Inhelder, B. *The Psychology of the Child.* New York: Basic Books, Inc., 1969.

22. Smith, E. B.; Goodman, K. S.; and Meredith, R. *Language and Thinking in the Elementary School.* New York: Holt, Rinehart, & Winston, Inc., 1970.

23. Van Lawick-Goodall, J. *In the Shadow of Man.* Boston: Houghton Mifflin Co., 1971.

24. Vygotsky, L. S. *Thought and Language,* edited and translated by E. Haufman and G. Vakar. Cambridge: The M.I.T. Press, 1962.

CHAPTER 2

How Language Grows

This chapter provides an introduction to *child language* and describes how child language normally begins and grows during the preschool years. The chapter is organized into three parts which correspond to the three major components linguists use in analyzing language. The first section describes the *syntactic* component, which includes the initial growth of single words and their later combination into sentences. *Syntax* is the term used to describe how words are organized into sentences. In English, word order and, to a lesser extent, the endings on words are important ingredients which indicate to us the role of the words we use. The second section describes the acquisition of what linguists call the *phonological* or sound system of language. The third section presents a brief review of how understanding of meaning develops in the preschool child. Linguists refer to this meaning component of language as *semantics*.

The following questions help to focus on the main ideas of this chapter: What are the general characteristics of the language of the young child? What strategies are used by the child in acquiring the language spoken by the people around him? From the discussion on these questions will come specific implications for classroom programs which will be explored to a greater extent in the material in Chapters 4 and 5.

THE ACQUISITION OF SYNTAX

The following section is organized to reflect the developmental stages of language growth in children. It is important to note at the start that both the age boundaries and the changes described at each stage will vary from child to child and that even when a discernible change has taken place, children do not stop using the language forms of the preceding stages. However, age boundaries do help us to understand the general order and pattern of language acquisition even if they do not apply to an individual child's exact development.

One-Word Utterances

Language really begins with the child's first meaningful words. This fact seems simple enough, but, in reality, it is often difficult to determine exactly when this important event occurs. When, for example, do an infant's babbling syllables take on meaning? When does "pa-pa-pa" begin to mean "Daddy"? To complicate matters further, infants usually understand words before they use them (e.g., "no-no") and understand the *intonation,* or the rise and fall of the voice, used by others before they say real words. In any case, by about the end of the first year or the beginning of the second, most children do use a few words meaningfully. Very gifted infants may say words as early as eight months, while handicapped children may not say their first recognizable word until as late as three years and two months (3.2) *(21).*

During the six months following initial vocabulary acquisition, there is relatively little change, but after this period, the growth of vocabulary increases dramatically. At age 1.0, the average number of words used meaningfully by a child is three; at 2.0, it is 272 *(20).* From this point on, vocabulary grows even more quickly. It is difficult to gauge the extent of vocabulary beyond this point, but estimates of the child's understanding at age six of the words others use run as high as 24,000 words *(18).*

Common first words are "pa-pa," "da-da," "ma-ma," "no-no," "byebye," and some infantile word for milk. In most cases, the words are repeated syllables composed of a consonant and a vowel (sometimes called an *open syllable* because of the consonant-vowel combination as in *pa, ma,* and *no). Infantile single words, like these open syllables, have been called *holophrases,* or single words which express vague, sentencelike meanings. Early in this period, children's words (or holophrases) are usually related to the action the child or someone around him is performing. Children seldom use verbs to express an action; instead, nouns are often the first words learned. A noun-like word also is often used to show emotion; for example, the word for milk may be used to express desire. Sometimes children simply name objects *(23)*. An illustration is a child who says his word for *dog* when he is loosely naming the dog as well as associating an act which he has noted the dog perform. He is unlikely to refer to *dog* without a picture of the animal, an object associated with it, or the presence of a dog. Because the child can be using a word in any of these ways in order to paraphrase a holophrase (and understand what the child means), adults need to know the context of its use.

Two- and Three-Word Utterances: Ages 1.6 to 2.6

Between the age of 1.6 and 2.6, children begin to combine words. In Chapter 1, it was stated that the stages of acquisition of language overlap and vary. However, according to Lenneberg *(19)*, it is consistent among normally developing children, regardless of their language environment, to begin combining words between the ages of 1.6 and 2.6. Table 1 shows representative examples of these "early sentences" taken from one study which examined this particular stage in detail.

Two and three-word utterances have been described by Brown and Bellugi *(4)* as *telegraphic speech,* and as you read the examples in Table 1, you find that the sentences do indeed resemble telegrams. There are fewer function words (articles, prepositions, conjunctions,

TABLE 1

Examples of Two- and Three-Word Utterances[1]

all broke	bye bye papa
I see	mail car
no bed	*papa away*
see train	all gone juice
more hot	fall down there
more walk	airplane all gone
other shoe	outside more
dry pants	there bye bye car
boot off	it doggie

[1]M. S. Braine, "The Ontogeny of English Phrase Structures: The First Phase," *Language* 39 (1963): 1–13. Reprinted by permission of the journal.

and *auxiliary* verbs, such as *have, be, is,* etc.) than there are nouns and verbs in both the sentences in Table 1 and in telegrams. Only essential words are used. For example, "airplane all gone" probably means *The airplane has gone away.* Since children can handle only a few items in their memory at a time, Brown and Bellugi *(4)* feel that only the most important, meaning-bearing words are retained for communication. Another way to explain these emerging primitive "sentences" is to classify the words children use into groups or classes.

McNeill *(23)* and Braine *(3)* have analyzed this type of utterance and divided the words into two classes. One class is called *pivot* and consists of only a few members which are never combined with each other but are combined with the members of the other class. The *open class* has more members, many of which are nouns and adjectives. Words in the open class can be combined with each other. Table 2 illustrates these two classes.

Comparison of Table 1 and Table 2 reveals that the first word of a two-word utterance is usually a pivot. But a word which is a pivot for one child can be an open word for another. In Table 2, *pretty* is such a word. As child language matures during the next two or three years, these classes will be subdivided again and again until the word classes resemble those of adults.

The possibility that these two-word utterances may simply be imitations of adult sentences which have been reduced to a few essential words relates to a discussion in Chapter 1. While it is true that many of the utterances in Table 1 are reduced imitations of adult sentences ("Papa away" for *Papa has gone away,* for example), something else is also occurring. It is difficult to imagine adult sentences for which the following child utterances are imitations: "outside more," "there bye bye car," and "allgone juice." "Outside more" may be used by the child as he explains that he wants to stay outside longer. An adult would not use the word *more* in expressing the same desire. It could be that just as adults produce an infinite number of new sentences based on a *grammatical rule system,* children's utterances are based on a rule system, too. The novel, nonimitative child sentences listed in Table 1 result from children's applications of their system. This interpretation of child language demonstrates that it is quite correct and based on a growing and developing language rule system rather than being incorrect according to adult rules. When a child's rule systems are made explicit, as they are in Bloom's extensive study of the early stages of acquisition *(2),* the rules appear to vary somewhat from individual to individual; how-

TABLE 2

Pivot and Open Classes from Three Studies of Child Language[2]

Braine		Brown and Bellugi		Miller and Ervin	
Pivot	*Open*	*Pivot*	*Open*	*Pivot*	*Open*
allgone	boy		Adam		arm
byebye	sock		Becky		baby
bit	boat		boot		pretty
more	fan	my	coat	{this that}	dolly's
pretty	milk	that	coffee		yellow
my	plane	a	knee		come
see	shoe	two	man		doed
might-	vitamins	the	mommy		•
night	not	bit	nut		•
hi	mommy	green	sock		•
	daddy	poor	stool		
	•	wet	tinker-	{the a}	other
	•	dirty	toy		baby
	•	fresh	•		dolly's
		pretty	•		pretty
			•		yellow
					•
					•
					•
				{here there}	arm
					baby
					dolly's
					pretty
					yellow
					•
					•
					•

[2]D. McNeill, "Developmental Linguistics," in *The Genesis of Language: A Psycholinguistic Approach*, ed. F. Smith and G. A. Miller (Cambridge: The M.I.T. Press, 1966), p. 26. Reprinted by permission of the publisher.

ever, there are some common traits found in the sentence structure of various primitive two- and three-word utterances in the many studies of beginning language *(2), (3), (5), (7), (22), (23), (24)*. It is clear from all the studies of language learning that children are learning basic grammatical elements even though their expression is very incomplete from an adult point of view (see more extensive reviews of this point in References *11* and *12*.)

Some children show an early use of the subject and object in their sentences. That is, children sometimes produce the subject part of the sentence and the object of the *predicate*. (Predicate refers to the nonsubject part of a sentence.) "Airplane all gone" and "it doggie" are examples of subject plus object sentences. Another early structure includes verb and object ("see train," for example). Sometimes, too, children say the subject and verb part of the sentence (for example, "I see"). In these examples, subject, verb, and object elements are being acquired but are not all combined in one structure. And at the same time, children are also apt to be combining words to indicate modification ("more hot"), conjunction, and genitive and locational structures *(2)*.

In summarizing this stage, we can say that the term telegraphic speech *describes* early child sentences. When the words of two-word sentences are classified into pivot and open classes, we can see that children are really producing utterances from an immature language system, but that the sentence elements the children first use are also the most essential parts of mature language. As children mature during the year following this phase, more and more of the other structures in the adult language system are acquired in very rapid succession.

Further Development of Child Grammar: Ages 2.6 to 3.6

Much syntactic acquisition occurs in children during the year from age 2.6 to 3.6. At age three, the average length of sentence is about 4.1 words, while a year later, it is about 4.7 words per sentence *(28)*. Even more important than the increase in the length of sentences during this year are the particular additional words acquired and the function they play in children's sentences. In order to trace this process, the discussion here will concentrate on the development of verb forms, negative sentences, questions, and rules called *transformations*. In addition to these new developments in children's language, we will briefly review the growing ability of children to use word endings.

In the development of verb forms, two major events occur early in this period. First, the ending *-ing* appears in such statements as "I making coffee." The emergence of *-ing* is one example of a group of verb forms called *auxiliary verbs* (AUX). Auxiliary words in adult language accompany verbs to express tense, to indicate questions and negatives, and to show passive voice; some examples are *have, will, been, -ing*. Not only are auxiliary verb forms realized in the use of *-ing* at this early period, the AUX also appears in past tense forms in such statements as, "He feeled it." *Gonna, wanna,* and *hafta* also may appear in children's speech, and in the next months, more mature AUX forms are learned.

The acquisition of the *copula* (the verb *to be*) is the second major growth factor in the development of verb forms during this period. Sentences like the following may occur: "Doggie is here." "That's a clock." "Doggie here." Brown and Fraser's study *(5)* illustrates that even after it is acquired though, the copula is not always used by the child in his speech as in "Doggie here."

After this initial appearance of new verb forms, most children's sentences have the subject as well as the full predicate. In diagram form, the acquired sentence structure appears to be the following:

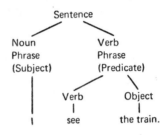

FIGURE 2

The additions made to the verb precipitate other changes during this stage.

One of these additions occurs in *negative* sentences. During the two-word stage, negative sentences such as "no bed" occur. In these cases, the word *no* functions as a pivot word. During the stage discussed here, the negative word is placed within the sentence's structure and is combined with AUX. Table 3 illustrates some negatives used by children of this age.

The sentences in the first column of Table 3 were spoken at the beginning of this stage; sentences in the second column appeared at the end. In the first sentences, the *no* is occasionally used as a tag word at the end but more often is incorporated into the middle of the sentence just as it is in adult sentences (for example, "He no bit you"). In the second column, the fact that many auxiliary forms appear *(do, will, am)* shows that AUX has now become a definite part of the grammar. And because AUX is present, the negative element *not* can be attached to *do* as it is in adult grammar; for example,

TABLE 3

Illustrative Negative Sentences[3]

I can't catch you.	I didn't did it.
We can't talk.	I can't see it.
You can't dance.	I don't want cover on it.
I don't like him.	You didn't caught me.
Book say no.	Donna won't let go.
Touch the snow no.	I am not a doctor.
That no fish school.	This not ice cream.
He no bit you.	I not crying.
That no mommy.	That not turning.
I no taste them.	They not hot.
	It's not cold.

[3]E. S. Klima and U. Bellugi-Klima, "Syntactic Regularities in the Speech of Children," in *Modern Studies of English*, ed. D. Reibel and S. Schane (Chicago: Aldine Publishing Co., 1969). Reprinted by permission of the publisher and Edinburgh University Press.

did is attached to *not* in "You didn't caught me." At times, the copula is still optional, as in the sentence, "I not crying." However, by the end of this stage of development the child is using more than one AUX in the same sentence. In fact, the past tense form of the verb is often used twice. The past tense rule is often *overgeneralized* as in "I didn't did it" and "You didn't caught me."

The development of questions during this stage, which is shown in Table 4, parallels the kind of change we have traced in negatives. During the earlier two-word stage, question meaning was realized by rising pitch. A child would say "ball go" with questionlike rising pitch or intonation. This question would mean "Has the ball gone?" The intonation was used very much like the *no* tag in the early negatives. In the next column of Table 4, there are many questions beginning with a wh-word *(who, where, why)* which clearly ask for a missing object, location, or even a cause. The ability to ask these questions indicates a new awareness of sentence function. With the beginning questions, there are also sentences with *-ing.* In the last column, however, even more learning has taken place. The most important change is indicated by the word order inversion of newly acquired AUX forms and the subject. For example, in the last column, one child asked, "Does lions walk?" In this question, he places the AUX *does* first and the subject *lions* next. The inversion of AUX and subject may be one of the first adultlike word order, or transformational, rules that children learn. Transformations enable children to change words around and put sentence parts together. For

TABLE 4 [4]

Illustrative Questions[*]

Pivot Stage	Beginning Questions	More Advanced Questions
Who that?	See my doggie?	Does the kitty stand up?
Ball go?	Dat black too?	Does lions walk?
Fraser water?	Mom pinch finger?	Did I saw that in my book?
Sit chair?	Where my sleep?	Can I have a piece of paper?
I Have it?	Where my mitten?	Where small trailer
	What my dollie have?	he should pull?
	Why not me drink it?	Where the other
	Why you smiling?	Joe will drive?
	Why you waking me up?	Where my spoon go?
		What I did yesterday?
		What you had?
		What you doed?
		Why he don't know
		how to pretend?
		Can't you work this thing?

[4] E. S. Klima and U. Bellugi-Klima, "Syntactic Regularities in the Speech of Children," in Modern Studies of English, ed. D. Reibel and S. Schane (Chicago: Aldine Publishing Co., 1969). Reprinted by permission of the publisher and Edinburgh University Press.

example, when children learn to put the auxiliary verb form *can* in front of the subject as in *Can you swim?*, they have acquired one of the many transformational rules in our language. Because of the inversion transformation, the first four questions in the last column are remarkably similar to adult questions, and as Klima and Bellugi-Klima *(17)* point out, the child's comprehension of adult questions is increasing. What is still lacking, though, is subject-verb agreement and the elimination of double past tense forms. The wh-word questions in the last column seem immature by comparison with the first four yes/no questions, since inversion of subject and AUX has not yet occurred in the wh-word questions. This transformation is acquired in the next few months by most children.

Thus, in about eighteen months, children acquire an amazing amount of syntactic knowledge. For example, in asking questions during the two-word stage, children can question only generally a thought or an action. Soon after this point, however, they can ask for a specific missing object, person, location, or cause. By the age of about 3.6 years, children are nearly as specific in their questioning as adults. Of course, they still have not learned all the rules the adult knows; for example, they have not mastered the wh-word question inversion and use of the indefinite *any,* as in the sentence, *Don't you want any?*

Another striking development during this period is the acquisition of the word parts which make nouns plural and which produce noun-verb agreement. These forms are called *inflections.* Children first seem to learn noun plurals, then possesives, and finally verb inflections, even though the same ending is applied to all these structures *(10).* This order of acquisition suggests that children find the meaning associated with noun inflections more important than that of verbs. How children use their new inflections shows us their general strategies about language acquisition. Cazden's study *(9)* found that irregular forms were often used correctly at first but later were used "incorrectly." In other words, children at the beginning of this stage might say "He ran," "I did," and "We came" as adults do. A few months later, the same children might say, "He runned," "I doed," and "We comed." This phenomenon occurs because in the beginning, the children are using *ran, did,* and *came* as memorized items and not with understanding of the past tense idea. Later, they learn the past tense concept as shown in the example above: "He feeled it." When they learn the general rule for an inflection (in this case *-ed* at the end of a verb), they apply it to all verbs, whether or not adults use that general rule or a rule for a variant ending. Thus, children generalize about the formation of inflections and apply the generalization to all members of that class. Later, over time, they learn the rules which apply to smaller and smaller groups of words in that class. Overgeneralized learning also occurs in the acquisition of noun plurals ("Wash my feets") and with possessive pronouns ("That's mines").

The learning of inflections is a very efficient process and shows the use of sophisticated strategies. Categorization of items in a class occurs first; in the instance above, for example, a verb class was formed. Then comes the formation of a rule which works in most instances; the addition of *-ed* to verbs when past tense is intended illustrates this point. The rule is then applied to all members of the relevant category. Only much later and with much experience will children become aware of the idiosyncratic rules of their language. For example, the reader has probably heard youngsters of six and seven saying "brang" for *brought* even though *brought* is the form consistently used by adults around them. A moment's thought will show that such children are sensibly associating *bring* with *ring;* if the past of *ring* is *rang,* the past of *bring* ought to be *brang. Bring* ought to belong to the subgroup of verbs with *ring, sing,* etc. Children are very efficient when learning rules.

In summary, this period is one of amazing language growth. In a period of about a year, children acquire many of the most basic grammatical rules of language. By the end of this period, at age 3.6, children's sentence structure is close to the adult form. The verb forms used are nearly mature and allow for questions and negative statements which resemble adult forms. Some transformational rules have been acquired and during the next stage, more transformations are learned so that children can state rather complex sentences.

Final Preschool Period: 3.6 to 6.0

Many of the recent studies on which the preceding discussion is based have examined language acquisition before the age of 3.6 or 4.0. There have been fewer recent studies of the language acquisition of older preschool and primary children. However, there are some studies of these older children which show us some of the boundaries of language change during these years.

Menyuk *(24), (25)* has studied the language of nursery school and first-grade children. Although she did not trace a sequence of acquisition of transformational rules, we can get an overview of growth between 3.8 and 6.5 by adapting some other data and comparing the two groups. Table 5 illustrates the number of instances in which certain transformations appeared in the speech of subjects during recorded sessions. Transformations within single sentences are generally more common than are rules which enable simple sentences to be combined into *conjoined* or *complex sentences. Conjoined sentences* are composed of two or more simple sentences joined by *and, but, or,* etc. *Complex sentences* have a main clause and one or more subordinate clauses and are also called *embedded sentences.* Embedding takes place when a simple sentence becomes a subordinate clause attached to a main clause; for example, *the dog was barking* is embedded in *The boy ran after the dog that was barking.* When two sentences are combined as they are by children of this age group, conjoined sentences occur more often than complex sentences.

In Table 5, relative clauses and *because* clauses are fairly common, but *if* and *so* clauses are not. These last two types of clauses are used more often by the first-grade group than by the nursery-school-aged groups, so they are probably learned sometime during

TABLE 5[5]

Subjects Using Selected Transformations and Sentence Embeddings

Transformations	Nursery School (N=48) (Age Range: 3.1–4.4) (Mean Age: 3.8)	First Grade (N=48) (Age Range: 5.11–7.1) (Mean Age: 6.5)	Examples
Contraction	48	48	didn't
Possessives	48	48	Mary's hat
Pronoun (Transformation)	48	48	...and *he* can...
Adjective	48	48	brown hat
Infinitive Complement	48	48	I wanted to do it.
Main Clause Conjunction	41	48	He sang and Mary danced.
Conjunction with Deletion (either Sub or VP)	40	47	Mary sang and danced.
Relative Clause	37	46	The man who sang is old.
Because Sentence Embedding	30	46	...because he said so.
Particle Separation	41	44	put down the box, put it down
Reflexive	29	44	I did it myself.
Imperative*	35	42	Shut the door.
Passive*	23	41	The boy was hit by the girl.
Participal Complement	19	31	I saw her washing...
If-Sentence Embedding*	12	30	...if you want to.
So-Sentence Embedding*	12	29	...so he will be happy
Compound of Nominals*	6	24	baby chair
Iteration	5	13	You have to clean clothes to make them clean.

[5] Adapted from P. Menyuk, "Syntactic Structures in the Language of Children," *Child Development* 34 (1963): 407–22. Copyright © 1963 by The Society for Research in Child Development: Reprinted by permission of the Society for Research in Child Development and the author.
*Numbers are significantly different.

33

this stage by many children. Although this information does not tell us exactly when and in what order sentence combining transformations are learned, it does show that many common transformations of this sort are learned during this period. Studies by O'Donnell, Griffith and Norris *(27)*; and by Hunt *(14)* show that oral and written language continue to develop during the school years in terms of the number of complex sentence embeddings.

Most common inflections are acquired by the time the child reaches the age for school entrance, although there are some words which are still imperfectly used (for example, *brang* for *brought*); these cases are still in the process of refinement. Some "errors" in inflections may be due to differences in dialect, a topic which will be discussed in Chapter 3. In her classic study on inflectional learning in children of nursery school and first-grade ages, Berko *(1)* found, while testing inflections (word endings) on nonsense words, that preschoolers of about 4.5 could often correctly use noun plurals and third person singular verb forms, but they did so without the degree of success of children of about 6.3. Generally, all children had more difficulty with the plural ending in words such as *glasses* than they did with the endings on *pictures* and *arms.* The younger children also had more difficulty than the older ones with the past tense form *rang.* The best performance for both groups came when the form was regular. In general, the differences between the younger and the older group were in terms of the number of errors rather than the kind of errors made. Thus, we find the same characteristic as in the previous stage of acquisition; as language is learned, rules are applied to general categories and then are redefined and applied to specific subgroups.

Brown and Hanlon *(6)* have suggested that the sequence of language structures acquired during the preschool years roughly parallels the hierarchical character of language in general as it is analyzed by generative grammarians. In other words, children first learn the subject and predicate, sentence elements which are the most important and are always needed. Children then learn sentence parts which make their simple sentences more like those of adults—AUX forms, negatives and question structures, and inflections. Then rules which allow for compound and complex sentences are acquired. Thus, psycholinguists who study language development have shown that the same structures which children learn first are the most basic elements of language.

Children learn an amazing amount of syntax during the short period from the time they first put words together at about eighteen months of age to kindergarten or first grade when their language structure is very much like that of adults. At no other point during life does one learn so much so quickly. In spite of this extensive learning, syntactic knowledge is not complete at age five or six. Children continue to learn other ways of combining sentences, and according to Chomsky's (11) study, they still have some specific syntactic rules which apply to special words yet to learn.

ACQUISITION OF THE SOUND SYSTEM

Learning the sounds of one's language is a rapid process, not unlike the learning of syntax, which is nearly completed during the preschool years. Similar to the hierarchical development of syntax, the growth of phonemic ability is characterized by initial acquisition of the most distinctive sounds in the language followed by rapid acquisition of less universal distincions.

In this section, we will be referring to the acquisition of *phonemes*. Phonemes are the smallest sound segments distinguishing one word from another. For example, *pig* and *dig* are different words in English and /p/ and /d/ are English phonemes. (Slash marks are generally used to indicate phonemes.) *Ring* and *bring* are differentiated by the phoneme /b/ in the second word. *Say* and *see* are separate words because of the different vowel phonemes. English has approximately forty-four different phonemes.

During the first year, infants make many different sounds. Although these sounds cannot properly be called phonemes, since an infant has not yet distinguished words, McNeill (22) has reported that nearly all the sounds which are possible for people to make are produced during the first year of life, even though all of these sounds will not be used in any one language. Once words are acquired, the sounds in the words truly become phonemes. In the first words only a few primitive phonemes can be distinguished, but when infants are playing with sounds or *babbling,* they continue to use all kinds of sounds. A number of years ago, Jakobson (15) proposed an explanation for this phenomenon. Jakobson showed that many children's first words were similar regardless of the language being learned. According to his theory, since the sounds of language are arranged so that some phonemes are far more distinct from each other than others, the most different sounds are learned first. Later, children learn to differentiate among less distinct phonemes. For example, the two phonemes /p/ and /a/, which Jakobson said would be the first learned, contain a basic distinction which exists in many languages. When producing these phonemes, one uses very different parts of the vocal machinery; /p/ is a consonant which is made at the front of the mouth with closed lips and with a slight explosive sound when it is the first sound in a word; /a/ is a back vowel made with open lips and open vocal tract. Jakobson has stated that, in time, children learn to make more and more differentiation of phonemes which have less and less variation. Thus, the child who has first acquired /pa/ might next acquire a nasal phoneme (/m/, /n/, or / ŋ /), so that /ma/ may be the second word. Next, there would be a division in the vowel system so that /a/ and /i/ (a wide back vowel and now a narrow high one) are differentiated and more syllables are possible. With continual splitting of these phonemes, the system gradually is acquired.

To the chagrin of many new mothers, some children seem to name their fathers before they do their mothers. Jakobson's *(16)* theory and evidence indicate that there is an explanation for this fact. The earlier appearance of /pa/ over /ma/ is based on the characteristics of language rather than parental importance. In fact, there is similarity in many different languages for the parental terms used by infants. Most father terms in many languages have one of the following phonemes for the initial consonant: /p/, /b/, /d/, or /t/. The latter three phonemes have characteristics similar to /p/. Most mother terms have one of the three nasal phonemes. Parental terms are the result of adult adaptation to the phonemic restrictions on infant language acquisition rather than of infant learning from adults.

While Velten *(29)* has offered some empirical verification for the main points in Jakobson's theory of the beginning of language acquisition, there is less data to support the theory during later development. This is due, perhaps, to the rapid learning which occurs after a beginning which is difficult to pinpoint. However, there is comparative data available on the phonemes acquired by age three and by six which shows the boundaries of phonemic growth. According to Carroll's *(8)* interpretation of a study by Templin, by the age of six, most children have nearly full mastery of the sound system of English. Even at three, most children have acquired many phonemes. Ninety percent of a group of sixty three year olds used the following phonemes clearly: /n/, /t/, /g/(the *g* in *goat*), /m/, /b/, /d/, /w/, /h/, /p/, /k/. Seventy to 80 percent could also use: /f/, / ŋ /(ŋ is the sound at the end of *rang*), /l/, /s/. Fifty to 60 percent had /v/, /r/, /s/(*sh* in *shut*), /ǰ/(*j* in *judge*), /č/(*ch* in *church*). Among the sounds which caused the most difficulty for children at age three were these: /z/, /ž/(*z* in *azure*), /θ/(*th* in *thick*), / ð /(*th* in *then*), and /hw/(*wh* in *which*). These more difficult phonemes are not present in some languages and show less sound distinction from each other than do those first learned. For example, the difference between /z/ and /ž/ is slight; some languages do not have either /θ/ or / ð /. These difficult language specific phonemes are learned late by children, but some adults who are learning English for the first time never are able to learn to use them correctly.

By the age of six, all of the above consonant sounds have been learned by 90 percent of the sample studied except /s/, /š/, / ð /, /z/, /ž/, /hw/, /č/. Some of these sounds cause difficulty for late-developing youngsters even after they reach the elementary grades. (Those children whose speech is developing slowly but in the normal sequence should not be confused with children who are unable to make some sounds which are acquired early by most children.) The main point of Jakobson's theory that phonemes are acquired in the order of their general applicability is correct during later development as well as in the beginning of phonemic acquisition.

In summary, there is rapid learning of phonemes after initial appearance of linguistically meaningful words. Not only does this development parallel the rapidity and onset of acquisition in syntax, but there is also another parallel between acquisition of these two aspects of language. Both show early learning of the most basic elements; in both we have traced the gradual differentiation into smaller and more specific cases. By the age of six, most of the basic sounds and syntactic rules have been acquired.

ACQUISITION OF THE MEANING SYSTEM

In this section, we will discuss the development of meaning in terms of vocabulary acquisition and concept extension. The reader should recognize that full meaning comes from use of words in the context of sentences and discourse. The course of language meaning development is very much related to cognition. The content of this section, therefore, relates directly to the concerns discussed in Chapter 1.

Leopold *(20)* has studied in great detail his daughter's language acquisition, and among his chief concerns was her learning of language meaning. He describes the early stages in the following manner:

> ... meanings are necessarily hazy and vague at first; (that) the dearth of vocabulary compels the child to use words for purposes to which they are not adapted from adult point of view; and (that)

meanings become progressively sharper and closer to the standard.[6]

What is meant by "hazy and vague" is illustrated in the following example. A small boy of 1.3 who had just learned to say "doggie" for *dog* went with his parents to an art museum. Because he had no name for other animals as yet, every time he saw a four-legged creature in a painting, he shouted "doggie." My daughter visited her grandparents after an eight month absence at the age of 1.6. She could not remember them and, at first, used one word for both of them. In other words, until she learned each of them as an individual, she named them as a set. These two examples illustrate with very young children some of the problems older children have in learning mature meanings of more complex words.

In the long process of acquiring a fixed meaning for a word, one must have a multitude of experiences with that word. For adults, these experiences need not be direct; for young children, they must be direct. In learning "doggie," for example, the young museum visitor had recognized some salient characteristics, or *attributes,* of the concept *dog.* He had learned some attributes for *dog:* dogs have four legs (or at least more than two); they are hairy, etc. However, he had not yet learned which animal attributes do *not* belong to *dog* but do belong to other animals. Gradually, as he acquired an understanding of the distinguishing attributes and names of other animals, he also learned more about *dog.* In other words, every child needs to learn which attributes are attached to a given word as well as which attributes belong not to it but to a similar word. Long after children first use a word, they are still acquiring attributes and experiencing the meaning of the word in various settings, and they continue in this process until a conventional meaning is achieved.

This kind of learning has been called *horizontal vocabulary expansion* by McNeill *(22).* Probably, most of the words which preschoolers use are learned in this way.

As a child learns the attributes of a concept, he comes into contact with other related words which he ultimately learns to group together. Thus, for example, as the child learns the correct limiting attributes for *dog,* he also acquires other animal names and forms a word group, or a *semantic cluster.* Once a semantic cluster has been formed in the child's mind, he adds new items to this cluster

---

[6]W. F. Leopold, "Semantic Learning in Infant Language," in *Child Language: A Book of Readings,* ed. A. Bar-Adon and W. F. Leopold (Englewood Cliffs, New Jersey: Prentice-Hall, Inc., 1971), p. 55.

with greater ease. If a child has some understanding of the cluster *animals* and has acquired the attributes and names of *deer, dog, cat, horse, cow,* etc., it is relatively easy to add *goat* to the cluster after the child has named it and has had direct or pictured experiences with it. In this case, the child learns *goat* with a fairly complete set of unique attributes because he already knows the other terms in the cluster. This experience is an instance of what McNeill calls *vertical vocabulary expansion (23)*. Vertical acquisition occurs faster than horizontal but probably involves the child's learning fewer words during the preschool and primary years.

Expansion of vocabulary obviously continues well beyond the early preprimary and primary years, since the sheer amount to be learned is so much greater than is required in learning a finite set of rules for syntax and a limited number of phonemes. This inherent difference between the learning of word meaning and acquisition of syntax and phonology has important implications for the classroom language program; as a result, the area of word and sentence meaning will probably be of more direct concern in the classroom than will the other components of language.

There is still another important distinction to be made in comparing acquisition of semantics with the learning of the other components of language. We have seen that in acquisition of syntax and phonology, the child appears to use the sophisticated learning strategies of categorization, generalization, and application to new instances quite efficiently. Our question now is whether the same strategies are used in acquisition of language meaning. Although categorization and application may help in learning vocabulary in some instances, (for example, experiences with various household *brushes* will help a child to learn that a painter's tool is also a *brush*), these strategies will not always work. We can imagine the confusion which a child meets in learning the names for the containers used in the home; some are bottles, some jars, some glasses, some pans, some pots. Some containers are made out of glass but not all glasses are made out of glass. Some pots are large, but there are also small pots such as the mustard pot. And what is the difference between a cooking pot and a pan? Because the strategies for acquisition which work in one semantic cluster may not work with many others, trial, comparison with adult use, correction when mistakes are made, and many direct experiences with objects are necessary before full acquisition of attributes, separation of items, and groupings of words in a cluster reach maturity. Consequently, during the preschool and primary years, there is apt to be some confusion in children's minds concerning the attributes associated with terms and the differentiation of one term in a cluster from others.

Ervin and Foster's *(13)* study shows how members of a cluster can be confused. Children of age six and older were shown pictures of faces which combined a number of factors: happiness, cleanliness, prettiness, goodness. The responses of the six year olds indicated that for them, *pretty* was highly correlated as a descriptive term with *happy; clean* was correlated with *pretty; good* with *pretty; happy* with *good.* Because these words are often used in similar contexts, the children probably had not yet sorted out the attributes which are unique to each one. Even though descriptive terms are often used in children's speech, there may be continual confusion as to the specific meaning of terms which appear to be used "correctly." Thus, it is difficult to determine whether children really do understand all the terms they use in everyday speech.

In this chapter we have differentiated among the three language components, syntax, phonology, and meaning. In so doing, we have found that a major difference exists in the extent and rapidity of language acquisition of these components. To be more specific, we have found that young children's syntactic structures are based on an unconsciously acquired rule system. With the acquisition of first primitive rules, children are able to produce "sentences" which are not merely reductions of adult speech but are often entirely novel. The complex rules not only are learned early, but the learned strategies used by children are also sophisticated. Recall, for example, that once children learn the rule that verb past tense is made by adding the ending *-ed* they use the rule for all verbs in the past tense. Further, when they acquire a new verb, children are able to consistently and immediately use it as a verb, and they are able to apply the past tense inflection to it from the very beginning. Thus, children seem to use categorization, generalization, and application with new items efficiently. In acquiring the phonological system, children also use sophisticated strategies; they learn the phonemic structure rapidly and have nearly completed its acquisition by the time they reach school age.

Conceptual development is different from that of syntax and phonology both in terms of the sheer amount to be learned and in the continuation of the process beyond early childhood. Although adults help children to learn vocabulary items by naming, it is obvious that development of meaning depends upon children's having many experiences. These experiences should ensure that both positive and negative attributes are acquired so that categorization of words occurs. As was stressed by Piaget, Vygotsky, and Bruner, development of language meaning cannot occur in isolation, although much of the motivation for growth of meaning does come from general language development as children use their knowledge of language to order their experiences.

REFERENCES

1. Berko, J. "The Child's Learning of English Morphology." *Word* 14 (1958): 150–77.

2. Bloom, L. *Language Development: Form and Function in Emerging Grammars.* Cambridge: The M.I.T. Press, 1970.

3. Braine, M. S. "The Ontogeny of English Phrase Structures: The First Phase." *Language* 39 (1963): 1–13.

4. Brown, R., and Bellugi, U. "Three Processes in the Child's Acquisition of Syntax." *Harvard Educational Review* 34 (1964): 133–51.

5. Brown, R., and Fraser, C. "The Acquisition of Language." In *Monographs of the Society for Research in Child Development,* edited by U. Bellugi and R. Brown 29 (1964): 43–79.

6. Brown, R., and Hanlon, C. "Derivational Complexity and Order of Acquisition of Child Speech." In *Cognition and Development of Language,* edited by J. R. Hayes. New York: John Wiley & Sons, Inc., 1970.

7. Brown, R.; Cazden, C.; and Bellugi-Klima, U. "The Child's Grammar from One to Three." In *Minnesota Symposia on Child Development,* edited by J. P. Hill. Minneapolis: University of Minnesota, 1968.

8. Carroll, J. "Language Development." In *Encyclopedia of Educational Research,* 3rd ed., edited by H. Chester, pp. 744–52. New York: The Macmillan Co., 1960.

9. Cazden, C. "The Acquisition of Noun and Verb Inflections." *Child Development* 32 (1968): 433–48.

10. ———. *Child Language and Education.* New York: Holt, Rinehart, & Winston, Inc., 1972.

11. Chomsky, C. *The Acquisition of Syntax in Children from Five to Ten.* Cambridge: The M.I.T. Press, 1969.

12. Dale, P. S. *Language Development; Structure and Function.* Hinsdale, Illinois: The Dryden Press, Inc., 1972.

13. Ervin. S., and Foster, G. "The Development of Meaning in Children's Descriptive Terms." *Journal of Abnormal and Social Psychology* 61 (1960): 271–75.

14. Hunt, K. W. "Syntactic Maturity in School Children and Adults." *Monographs of the Society for Research in Child Development* 35 (1970): 1–63.

15. Jakobson, R. "The Sound Laws of Child Language and Their Place in General Phonology." In *Child Language: A Book of Readings,* edited by A. Bar-Adon and W. F. Leopold. Englewood Cliffs, New Jersey: Prentice-Hall, Inc., 1971.

16. ———. "Why 'Mama' and 'Papa'?" In *Child Language: A Book of Readings,* edited by A. Bar-Adon and W. F. Leopold. Englewood Cliffs, New Jersey: Prentice-Hall, Inc., 1971.

17. Klima, E. S., and Bellugi-Klima, U. "Syntactic Regularities in the Speech of Children." In *Modern Studies of English,* edited by D. Reibel and S. Schane. Englewood Cliffs, New Jersey: Prentice-Hall, Inc., 1969.

18. Larrick, N. "How Many Words Does a Child Know?" *The Reading Teacher* 7 (1953): 100–04.

19. Lenneberg, E. *Biological Foundations of Language.* New York: John Wiley & Sons, Inc., 1967.

20. Leopold, W. F. "Semantic Learning in Infant Language." In *Child Language: A Book of Readings,* edited by A. Bar-Adon and W. F. Leopold. Englewood Cliffs, New Jersey: Prentice-Hall, Inc., 1971.

21. McCarthy, D. "Language Development." In *Encyclopedia of Educational Research,* edited by W. S. Monroe, pp. 165–72. New York: The Macmillan Co., 1950.

22. McNeill, D. *The Acquisition of Language: The Study of Developmental Psycholinguistics.* New York: Harper & Row, Publishers, 1970.

23. ———. "Developmental Linguistics." In *The Genesis of Language: A Psycholinguistic Approach,* edited by F. Smith and G. A. Miller. Cambridge: The M.I.T. Press, 1966.

24. Menyuk, P. *Sentences Children Use.* Cambridge: The M.I.T. Press, 1969.

25. ———. "Syntactic Structures in the Language of Children." *Child Development* 34 (1963): 407–22.

26. Miller, W., and Ervin, A. "The Development of Grammar in Child Language." In *Monographs for the Society for Research in Child Development* no. 92 (1964): 9–34.

27. O'Donnell, R. C.; Griffin, W. J.; and Norris, R. C. *Syntax of Kindergarten and Elementary School Children: A Transformational Analysis.* Research Report No. 8. Champaign, Illinois: National Council of Teachers of English, 1967.

28. Templin, Mildred. *Certain Language Skills in Children: Their Development and Interrelationships.* Minneapolis: University of Minnesota Press, 1957.

29. Velten, H. "The Growth of Phonemic and Lexical Patterns in Infant Language." *Language* 19 (1943): 281–92.

CHAPTER 3

Language Development across Social and Cultural Groups

The problems associated with the education of children of poverty have been with us since the beginning of our nation's history, but only in recent years have there been widespread attempts to improve and change programs for the education of poor children. Although there have always been individuals who have devoted themselves to the teaching of illiterate adults and poor children, the social unrest and subsequent governmental action during the 1960s have resulted in a great number of new educational programs for inner-city schools in the United States. These programs have attempted to counteract the overwhelming evidence that students from inner-city schools tend to be poorly prepared for performance of the tasks necessary in our technically oriented, urban society. Unfortunately, as Coleman's report *(12)* shows, no successful instructional system has yet been found to eliminate the inequality of achievement levels in basic reading and math skills between inner-city students and the students of middle-class urban and suburban communities.

Much of the special program development has been in the area of reading improvement. The depressed reading level of inner-city students has also motivated special language development programs to better prepare these preschool children for reading. The language development of preschool, inner-city children is the particular concern in this chapter. Later, we will make explicit the applications for reading instruction for inner-city children in light of the present discussion of language development.

One major concept included in the discussion of the characteristics and processes of learning language in Chapters 1 and 2 was that children have an innate ability for language learning; furthermore, as Lenneberg *(32)* showed, the beginnings of acquisition occur quite regularly regardless of language background. In spite of the fact that the subjects in most of the studies referred to in the previous chapters came from white middle-class homes, we cannot assume that children from diverse backgrounds will learn language by a different process. Nonetheless, while the process of learning will be similar, the result of that process may be quite different. In other words, we can assume that the processes of interaction and natural growth motivate language development for all children regardless of environment; however, we cannot assume that environmental differences will not cause differences in the language of children. We are then faced with answering these two questions: Since all children probably acquire language through similar processes, what is the effect of environmental difference on the quality and quantity of the emerging language? Do environmental factors influence children's language development enough to account for the widespread difficulty which poor children and those from minority groups have in school?

A group of studies published during the mid 1960s examined the question of whether or not there is a difference between the amount of language knowledge that middle-class children have and the language knowledge that lower-class, "disadvantaged" children have at various points during the elementary years. For many educators and psychologists, the resulting conclusion that a language deficit does exist in the language of disadvantaged children indicates a need to intervene in the educational process early in the preschool years to offer the child language experiences he would otherwise not receive at home. This conclusion has been reinforced by studies which have suggested there are specific areas of language dysfunction in disadvantaged children.

Another group of writers, mainly sociolinguists, have looked at the language of minority members from an entirely different viewpoint. These writers have compared the form of language spoken by various groups and found consistent points of contrast in these different forms of English. As a result, they recommend that educators perceive the language of disadvantaged children as being different from that of middle-class children rather than deficient. They further recommend to educators that attempts to change language structures will cause increased confusion for children at a point when they are still acquiring their basic language knowledge.

In this chapter, the empirical and linguistic sources for these two positions will be reviewed as a necessary background for a discussion of the development of an instructional program which reflects some of what is known about language development. There will also be an analysis of various forms which English takes in major minority groups in this country.

THE LANGUAGE-DEFICIT HYPOTHESIS

A common conception among in-service teachers, as reported in Shuy, Wolfram, and Riley *(37)*, is that the language knowledge of poor children, especially black children, lacks some essential characteristics which exist in the language of the middle-class, white children. One text written for preservice teachers even states that overcrowded, noisy homes prevent adequate language learning *(21)*. While more and more educators are accepting a less prescriptive attitude toward the language of various groups, there persists among many the idea that the language of disadvantaged children is deficient. For example, teachers in as diverse locations as Chicago, Memphis, Coney Island, and Michigan hold biased expectations for children's school success because of variations in dialect *(10)*. Before teachers accept the fact that such deficiencies exist, a close examination of the research which supports this view is necessary. If there is sufficient evidence for language deficiency, then we must develop a program to fill in the gaps, but if there is any doubt that such gaps exist, we must reexamine the thrust which language development programs should take.

In Chapter 1, we noted the behaviorist position that language is learned by imitation of structures. According to this position, reinforcement by adult speakers is crucial for continual growth and refinement of child language. The implication is that the quality and quantity of a child's language knowledge depends on the language models he has and on the amount of reinforcement he receives in his home. Thus, some homes may provide an impoverished background for language learning. Much of the language deficit hypothesis depends on this analysis of language learning. It is important to recognize that if the model which a child has for his language learning is viewed as being inferior, the language deficit position has more force than if the language model is viewed as being different but not deficient.

A series of studies in the early 1960s showed a language deficit in lower-class and in black children. Deutsch and Brown *(16)* found that when groups were equated by socioeconomic level the IQs of black children were lower than those of white children in both the first and the fifth grades. The difference between black and white children was greater at the higher socioeconomic levels than at the lower levels. Since IQ is dependent largely on verbal ability, M. Deutsch *(15)* analyzed language data at the first- and fifth-grade levels. He found that being poor and/or a member of a minority group resulted in a tendency to have poorer language functioning than being white and middle class. Although Deutsch found little difference between groups in the ability to label, the differences appeared in the ability to use language for abstract purposes and were greater at the fifth-grade level than at the first. This discrepancy led the author to assert that there is a cumulative deficiency in verbal development; in other words, as poor children grow older, their verbal functioning develops more slowly than that of middle-class children and the gaps get larger and larger. John's *(23)* study comparing first- and fifth-grade black children's performance on various standard measures of verbal fluency shows no difference between lower- and middle-class children at the first-grade level but does indicate a significant difference by the fifth grade. This study lends further support to the theory of cumulative language deficiency. Of course, it is possible to argue, as Baratz and Baratz *(5)* have done, that the cumulative nature of group differences results at least in part from inadequate schooling.

In addition to researchers who have outlined the extent of language deficiency, some have attempted to uncover the causes of such deficiency. John and Goldstein *(24)* have analyzed the influences which limit lower-class children's ability to categorize. Since verbal interaction was thought to be essential for building categorization ability in preschool children, John and Goldstein felt that lower-class homes would contain fewer opportunities for essential corrective feedback. Their study shows a difference by socioeconomic class in ability to categorize, but it does not give evidence for differences in verbal interaction. Nonetheless, if data were available concerning the amount of verbal feedback, John and Goldstein's conclusion in the above study might be supported. In another study, Hess and Shipman *(25)* analyzed verbal interaction between black mothers and their four-year-old children from four socioeconomic groups. They found that middle-class mothers used more verbal explanation and promoted problem-solving behavior in teaching a task to their children more often than did lower-class mothers. Although this study often is used to support the position that there is an insufficient verbal interaction between adults and children in poor families for full language development, the full implications of the Hess and Shipman work cannot be completely understood until there is certainty of the extent of the verbal deficiency in lower-class children.

The work of the English sociologist Bernstein provided the analytic framework used in the Hess and Shipman study and in many others. Bernstein's work has evolved over many years and is based on his observations of verbal difference by class in England. Bernstein hypothesized and had some supporting data *(7)*, *(8)* for the view that the lower-class member is more apt to use what Bernstein calls a "restricted language code" in contrast to a middle-class member who has both the restricted code and the "elaborated code" available to him. The restricted code is bound to context, stereotyped, condensed, and full of implicit meanings. Speakers using the restricted code are apt to make reference to outside authority to support their statements. The elaborated code, on the other hand, is marked by explicit meanings, few limits by context, more differentiated messages, more rational explanation, and support from within for statements. Bernstein himself *(9)* has repudiated the view that this distinction between codes refers to differences in language knowledge. Rather, he suggests that it refers to situational use of language. Despite this fact, a number of writers in the United States have used Bernstein's codes to support the language deficit position *(13)*. Another problem with the application of Bernstein's work is that there is great variance between language forms of class groups in England and in the United States.

Other explanations for a language deficit of minority groups and the poor have been offered. For example, since there is a correlation between good auditory discrimination (perception of phonemic differences) and success in beginning reading, C. Deutsch *(14)* felt poor auditory discrimination among poor black children might indicate a cause for the well-documented failures some of these children have in learning to read. Deutsch did find that in retarded readers in first grade poor auditory discrimination, as measured on a standard test, existed at a significant rate, but the same relationship was not found at the fifth-grade level. This latter finding is not surprising since sound/symbol relationship is less important at higher levels of reading. In the same study, Deutsch noted that a review of the literature in acuity, or ability to hear, among animals showed that hearing was damaged in experiments where excessive noise was consistently present. Deutsch suggested that noisy slum homes would contribute to inadequate development of hearing and could eventually depress ability to make discriminations. Although there appears to be support for the idea that the environment causes inadequate discrimination, there are a number of problems with this view. First, the relationship between loss of acuity and ability to discriminate has been questioned by Yoder *(39)*. Second, there was no evidence offered in Deutsch's study to show that the homes of those children who had poor auditory discrimination were excessively noisy. In fact, Friedlander's work *(20)* shows that excessive noise may be characteristic of many families regardless of socioeconomic level. Finally, the test for auditory discrimination may have been used inappropriately since the sounds which children were asked to discriminate may not be different phonemes in their dialect.

Although this last study does not argue convincingly for the existence of poor auditory discrimination among poor black children, the language deficit theory does appear to hold. However, other studies of the language knowledge of minority and majority groups raise questions about the extent of a language deficit. For example, Entwhisle's studies *(18)*, *(19)* of children's word associations show an entirely different picture from that seen thus far. According to her analysis, the ability to give a spontaneous word in association with a stimulus word which is of the same grammatical class and semantic cluster indicates language maturity. Surprisingly, at the first-grade level, white slum children were found to be superior to white suburban children in this respect. Even more surprising to those aware of the language deficit studies is the evidence that black slum children were also superior to white suburban children, even though they were behind the white slum children. But this superiority of both white and black slum children disappears over the school years. The depression of verbal ability with advance in school can support either the cumulative deficiency hypothesis or the effect of bad schooling on slum children. Entwhisle thinks there is a combination of causes. In any case, she believes that at the start of school, there are some strengths existing in the language of slum children.

Another study by Lacivita, Kean, and Yamamoto *(30)* tested elementary-school-aged children's ability to assign meanings to words in sentences made up of nonsense words. The only signals to meaning were inflections which indicated the grammatical classes of the words. The fact that there was no difference by social class in the children's ability to assign meanings of the same grammatical class as the nonsense words was interpreted as an indication that there is no difference in language knowledge of children by social class. In a similar way, Shriner and Miner *(35)* showed that white preschool children did not differ by social class in their ability to generalize morphological rules, and Cazden *(10), (11)* reported that very early growth in acquisition of language structures demonstrated that lower-class black children were undergoing the same sequence and kind of acquisition as middle-class whites. Ammon and Ammon *(2)* reported that training young speakers of black English in vocabulary has a more positive effect than training them in sentences. Cazden *(11),* too, recommends vocabulary training for all children, particularly for poor children.

When we assimilate this information, it appears that the evidence substantiating the view that social class and/or race adversely effects language acquisition is limited. Attempts to show environmental causes of deficiency in auditory discrimination have not been very fruitful. We are left with the information that there are differences in the verbal interaction among parents and children by social class, that IQ scores are depressed in poor and black children (a point which is explained by some writers as reflecting the unfairness of the tests used to determine IQ), and that ability to categorize is poorer in lower-class children. Thus, the language deficit theory does not appear to be completely correct. In fact, there are indications that basic language knowledge is at the very least comparable in all children at the age for school entrance, regardless of social or racial group, while the extent of vocabulary and categorizing may not be comparable. Yet as recently as 1970, comments such as the following appeared:

> The child of poverty has language problems. These are problems far more crippling than mere dialect problems . . . in brief, the child of poverty has not been taught as much about the meaning of language as a middle-class child of the same age.[1]

Some language development programs, such as that of Bereiter and Engelmann *(6),* are apt to reflect the language deficit theory. However, as teachers, we must ask ourselves what the effect of language training meant to overcome a deficiency may be in a young preschooler who, in fact, may not have such a deficiency. This training may not be harmful, of course; however, it is possible that in the effort to develop language skills, schools may be undermining the child's feeling of security in his own means of communication. If a

---

[1]S. Engelmann, "How to Construct Effective Language Programs for the Poverty Child," in *Language and Poverty: Perspectives on a Theme,* ed. F. Williams (Chicago: Markham Publishing Co., 1970), p. 102.

child feels that something is wrong with his way of talking, he may become less likely to talk and withdraw from verbal activity in school. Furthermore, attempts to change his language may cause serious confusion during the period of acquisition.

THE LANGUAGE-DIFFERENT HYPOTHESIS

Sociolinguists who advocate the *language-different position* come from a different academic background than do the advocates (this group does not necessarily include the authors of the studies referred to in the last section) of the language-deficit hypothesis. Sociolinguists have been trained by the linguistic school, the main concern of which has been to outline the grammatical systems of various language. In this school all languages, even diverse language of primitive peoples, are viewed as being equal in communicability. And when linguists of this background study variations within one language, they believe that one variation is equal to another. Sociolinguists study *dialects;* in the past, they have concentrated on study of dialects of culturally determined minority groups. A dialect is a variety of a language used by one group of people with differences in vocabulary, grammar, and pronunciation from other varieties of the language used by another group. Implicit in the definition given for dialect is another major concept basic to sociolinguistics; dialects exist on a continuum with the most different dialects in any language appearing at either end. The separation of dialects on the continuum is based solely on structural differences. For these writers, the model presented to a child by parents who speak any dialect is as adequate for language learning as any other.

Sociolinguists study a wide variety of language and speech characteristics—regional dialects, attitudes toward dialects, control of speech by situation, determinants of dialect by social class, and the relationship of dialect to cultural norms. The study of dialects has revealed some thought-provoking facts about English; for example, the language is characterized by a great number of dialects, and despite the extensive borrowing back and forth among the dialects, there are unique structures in dialect which have been maintained over a long period of time. Of great interest to sociolinguists during the last decade has been the dialect spoken by a large number of black people, which will be referred to here as *Black English* and which has been contrasted often with forms of Standard English spoken by members of more dominant groups. Contrasts between

Black and Standard English offer us information about the language-difference theory.

Stewart *(38)*, a dialectologist who ranks high among those who study Black English, has traced the history of the English spoken by slaves during the early history of the country. It is Stewart's thesis that many forms of Black English today reflect the early *creolization* of English by slaves. Creole languages are modifications by depressed minority groups of the dominant language. Creolization produces variations from the dominant language which are more extensive than variations by dialect. Apparently, slaves in the United States spoke a language similar to that spoken by slaves in Surinam and in the Carribean islands which reflected their West African origins. During slavery, those slaves who worked in the plantation house began to modify their speech toward the British-descended English fairly quickly, while the creolized form of English spoken by field hands changed more slowly. After slavery, continual modification of the language in the direction of the more socially prestigious Standard English continued. Despite the movement toward Standard English, such present-day Black-English forms as the absence of the verb *to be* when momentary action is meant, presence of *be* when habitual action is meant, lack of possessives in some instances, and uninflected pronouns are, in Stewart's view, all traceable to early creole language spoken by slaves.

However, the borrowing has not all been one way. Standard American English shows influences of Black English. For example, the common American use of *uh-huh* to indicate affirmation with rising intonation and to indicate negation with falling intonation has been traced by Abrahams *(1)* to language spoken in West Africa. There have been lexical borrowings from Black to Standard English of such terms as *man* in the sense of comrade, *the man* in the sense of white authority, *cool, hot, Charlie,* etc. Older jazz terms, such as *gig* and *pad,* existed in Black English before they became part of the white man's lexicon. Furthermore, just as the spirituals sung in slave times carried connotations for the slaves that the white owners did not understand, at least one investigator [Abrahams *(1)*] has suggested that modern rock songs as sung by blacks carry in-group meanings. Despite the borrowings back and forth, sociolinguists find many consistent structural characteristics in the speech of some blacks which are caused by dialect.

An important question to ask is how dialect variation is reflected in the process of acquisition. The most obvious fact is that black children whose parents speak Black English will learn to speak that dialect. The language norms which the black child is learning as he acquires language will be in the direction of his parents' speech. Unfortunately, there have been few cross-dialect studies of children's language during the preschool period, so there is little evidence of how children of Black English speakers acquire the unique characteristics of their dialect. However, by examining a few of the points of contrast between Black English forms and those of Standard English we can infer the process which is occurring.

There are a number of cautions which must be made before we turn to this discussion of Black English forms though. First, there are many more points of similarity between the dialects than there are differences, of course; otherwise, we would be discussing different languages rather than dialects. Second, many blacks do not speak or have never spoken Black English. Third, not all characteristics of Black English discussed here are in the speech of all speakers of Black English. Fourth, Black English is much closer to the Standard English spoken in the South than that spoken in the North; therefore, Black English in northern cities is at greater variance from Standard English than it is in the South. Fifth, many blacks speak both Standard and Black English. Sixth, there are many other dialects of English which are at variance with Standard; we are examining Black English here because it has been studied more closely than others.

There are a number of Black English grammatical factors found in the speech of speakers in cities such as Detroit by Shuy; Wolfram; and Riley *(37)* and New York by Labov *(27)* which are at variance with the forms of Standard English. Table 6 lists some main points of contrast. The first two contrasts illustrate a rule which does not exist in Standard English. In the first entry, "He going," the copula is deleted under certain conditions when momentary action is meant. It is present as "be" when habitual action is intended. Note that in Standard English the phrase "all the time" is necessary to translate the full meaning of the second entry. This structure is often used as an example to deny the assertion that Black English is a simplified version of Standard, since, in this case, Standard is simplified to a greater extent than Black English. Further characteristics of Black English are: optional deletion of the possessive marker ("John cousin"); deletion of the noun plural marker in some instances; ("I got five cent"); insertion of a pronoun after the proper noun ("John he live in New York"); alternate forms of variant verbs ("I drunk the milk"); different systems of noun-verb agreement ("Yesterday he walk home," "She have a bicycle," and "You go

TABLE 6 [2]

Syntactic Differences between Black and Standard English

Black English	Standard English
1. He going.	He is going.
2. He be here.	He is here *all the time.*
3. John cousin.	John's cousin.
4. I got five cent.	I have five cents.
5. John he live in New York.	John lives in New York.
6. I drunk the milk.	I drank the milk.
7. Yesterday he walk home.	Yesterday he walked home.
8. She have a bicycle.	She has a bicycle.
9. You go home.	You'll go home.
10. I ask did he do it.	I asked if he did it.
11. I don't got none.	I don't have any.
12. I want a apple.	I want an apple.
13. He book.	His book.
14. He over to his friend house.	He is over at his friend's house.

[2]Adapted from J. C. Baratz, "Teaching Reading in an Urban Negro School System," in *Teaching Black Children to Read*, ed. J. C. Baratz and R. W. Shuy (Washington, D.C.: Center for Applied Linguistics, 1969), pp. 99–100 by permission of the Center for Applied Linguistics.

home"); variant structure of embedded questions ("I ask did he do it"); different transformational rules for some negatives ("I don't got none"); indefinite article differences ("I want a apple"); possessive and other pronoun differences ("He book"); and prepositions which vary in some settings ("He over to his friend house").

William Labov *(28)* has argued that many of these dialect characteristics are related to differences in the sound systems of the dialects rather than in syntax. For example, one characteristic of the phonology of Black English is *r-lessness* (meaning a reduction of /r/ in some instances). Some other dialects, such as Bostonian, reduce the final /r/, but Black English speakers are also apt to reduce the medial /r/. Further, Black English is marked by *l-lessness* so that *toll* in Standard English may be pronounced *toe* in Black English. Thus, in the example "You go home" above, deletion of the /l/ in the Standard *you'll* may be due to a difference in sound rather than the form of the future tense. Labov has noted that the presence of *going to* and emphatic *will* in the future in Black English show that this tense is present in some instances.

Another characteristic of Black English is the reduction of a consonant cluster to a single consonant sound. Since Standard English has many final consonant clusters, this characteristic causes a very noticeable sound variation and may explain why there is no plural marker in the statement, "I got five cent." In fact, there is a general weakening of final single consonant sounds, especially /t/ and /d/. This characteristic may explain the absence of the past tense form in "Yesterday he walk home." Comparison of dialects indicates a number of phonological as well as a few syntactic differences between Black and Standard English. In the last section of this chapter, the reader will find further description of the characteristics of Black English in the hope that increased knowledge of this dialect will increase sensitivity to the language of some black children.

In terms of language acquisition, some of the structures which the child is learning are those represented in Table 5. For example, in acquisition of embedded indirect questions, the child acquiring Black English will not have the markers *if* or *whether*. This absence does not demonstrate lack of knowledge, according to the sociolinguistic framework, but instead shows simply a difference by dialect in the realization of the same underlying rules of language. In acquiring phonemes, the young Black-English speaker will learn only those which are present in his environment. One result is that there are a number of words which are homonyms in Black English (such as "bowl" and "bold") but which are distinguishable by sound as well as meaning in Standard English. Black speakers may still understand the various meanings, and use of the word in context will uncover its unique meanings. Sociolinguists have shown that a major environmental factor in the acquisition of language is not the extent of language knowledge in the child but the difference in the dialects being learned. And because they view each dialect as being equally utilitarian in terms of its power to communicate, the psycholinguists believe there will be no inherent difference in children's ability to communicate because of the dialect which is spoken.

The Question of Dialect Change

While linguistic science describes dialect differences and argues for acceptance of variant dialects, society at large still reflects a prescriptive attitude toward dialects, particularly toward Black English. Shuy *(36)* has reported that employers, even of nonskilled labor, react negatively to a Black English speaker, even though they disclaim any preference for "good" English. Consequently, many educators believe that at some point before the end of the school years, the student should have the opportunity to acquire Standard English so that he will not be discriminated against unnecessarily in adult life. The question educators ask is when such instruction should occur. Athey and Salzberg *(3)* have suggested that training in Standard English begin during early preschool, since this is the period of most rapid language growth. On the other hand, we would suggest delaying the addition of Standard English until much later in the school years for a variety of reasons.

Study of dialect offers some evidence to help make decisions concerning the question of when and how instruction in Standard English should take place. First of all, while it is true that the preschool period is the best time for learning a *new language,* this fact must not be confused with *dialect learning.* Acquisition of the first or even a second language presents the child with a very different learning situation from that required in sensing the much less obvious changes and using the slight phonological and syntactic distinctions required to speak two dialects of one language adequately. I think we must avoid confusing the learning of a first and a second language with acquisition of a new dialect.

Labov *(29)* has showed that not until just before or during adolescence do children become aware of and sensitive to dialect differences. Furthermore, there are stages through which youngsters pass in the acquisition of Standard forms. For example, Labov's *(27)* and Loban's *(33)* studies show a high incidence of Black English forms in children's speech at the start of adolescence. This presence may indicate a choice not to use Standard English forms by many youngsters, even though they may not be aware of the differences in the dialects.

Maturity and motivation are both important ingredients for acquisition of Standard English forms. Because it is crucial that students maintain the dialect of the significant people about them, we would probably be wise to avoid early drastic language change. When students show a desire to learn Standard English and the instruction takes advantage of this motivation, it would be best to consider these forms as additions to their existing English. Finally, because awareness of language differences comes later than the preschool period and because such awareness will facilitate learning, instruction in Standard English ought to be delayed until late in the elementary school years.

Beyond the Language-Deficit and Language-Different Hypotheses

The language-different hypothesis is based on linguistic analysis; the language-deficit hypothesis, on empirical study. In the previous section, we found that the language-deficit theory is weak in its fullest sense. The language-different advocates do not present much counteracting empirical evidence, but the consistency of dialectic structures lends convincing support to the concept that the major environmental factor in language acquisition for all children is the acquisition of the dialect of family and community. I believe that we must reject sweeping statements which claim that schools should provide language skills which are lacking in poor black children. As teachers, we must be sensitive to dialect and its power to communicate; however, we are still left with unanswered problems. For example, we do not know as yet the extent of the interference which non-Standard English dialects may cause in learning to read and write. It is difficult to isolate dialect interference from other possible explanations for lack of success in school learning, such as inequality of school programs, instruction, and materials. Another unanswered question is the effect of different kinds of interaction between parents and their children in different social classes and evidence of difference in ability to categorize and vocabulary acquisition in children from different social classes. Still another problem considered by Cazden *(10)* expresses concern that the deficit-different discussion obscures an important issue, the effect of the social context on children's speech performance.

Cazden *(10)* has reviewed a number of recent studies which examine the effect of situation on language behavior. The results of these studies have implications for our instructional program. For example, longer and more complex speech is manifested by children if they are asked to respond to real rather than pictured objects, if unconventional rather than conventional pictures are the stimuli, and if they are asked to tell a story from the memory of a series of pictures rather than with the aid of pictures that are present. Studies also show that even young children adjust their language behavior to their listener. They speak in longer, more complex sentences when talking to adults, especially if they have initiated the conversation themselves. In all, "the greater the degree of affect or personal involvement in the topic of conversation, the greater the likelihood of structural complexity."[3]

The situation or social context of speech affects speech behavior of children from different social classes somewhat differently. When the task in which they are involved is open and free, children of

---

[3]C. Cazden, *Child Language and Education* (New York: Holt, Rinehart, and Winston, Inc., 1972), p. 209.

higher socioeconomic groups are apt to use longer, more complex speech than lower-class children; however, this situation may be due to the sensitivity of the lower-class child rather than to a characteristic of language behavior. Although ability to use language to explain and to analyze also appears to be affected by class membership, Hieder *(22)* has indicated that when examiners direct lower-class children to do what is expected of them, they are nearly as analytic as middle-class children. Labov *(26)* has shown that the effect of listener and situation influences lower-class black children's speech to a considerable extent. To substantiate his view, he presents dialogues between a preadolescent boy in Harlem and a man who was raised in Harlem and is a skilled interviewer. When the topic was one of violence, there was minimal response; however when a friend of the boy was brought in and the interviewer sat on the floor and used taboo words, the boy responded with more involvement, longer responses, and greater interest. Labov's analysis illustrates the verbosity and logic of Black English speakers when the situation is favorable.

In comfortable street-talk, many Black English-speaking children learn to be competent in culturally preferred styles of oral language. In fact, verbal performance in indirect speech forms determines social status among some adolescent and young-adult, Black English-speaking groups. Ritual insults, embellished story-telling, nonverbal accompaniments, and the use of nonliteral meaning characterize the verbal games children learn from their older siblings. Expressive language may be highly advanced among these children *(10),* even though the unfamiliar functions of the content-oriented language required in school tasks may become personally threatening. Many such children respond to school language tasks by withdrawing verbally, even while oral language development in the socially preferred styles continues outside school.

One study reported by Cazden *(11)* shows that equalizing the situation for such children even has an impact on IQ performance. For this study, IQ tests were given to lower- and middle-class black children in New York. However, in contrast with most comparative studies, the tests were given only after many hours had been spent in establishing a rapport between the examiner and each child. Contrary to most results, there were no IQ differences by social class on this test. It may well be that the situational effect on speech and on cognitive performance is so important that it may have biased the results on numerous studies comparing disadvantaged and middle-class children. More unbiased research is needed, of course, but as educators, we must hold in abeyance our assumptions that lower-class children come to us with deficiencies. Instead, we must provide instruction which will maximize all children's strengths and be sensitive to the dialects and cultural values of our students.

Language Contrasts of Major Minority Groups

The following section includes a chart of the main characteristics of Black English and a list of the areas of difficulty which Spanish-speaking people experience in learning English. Although we have analyzed Black English in the previous section, a more complete list of the main points of contrast between Black and Standard English is also included.

The reader will recall the analysis of features of Black English that appeared in Table 6 on page 53. According to Labov *(28)*, however, the major differences between Black and Standard English are phonological, although there are also important syntactic differences. Chart 1 contains both phonological and syntactic features. The list is presented to show words which many Black English speakers treat as homonyms. The syntactic characteristics are written in contrast to Standard forms; they are the features from Table 6 which are not caused by phonological differences. Of course, not all speakers of Black English will use all these forms, but teachers should learn to listen to their children's speech for those which are used. They should listen for the appearance of dialect characteristics in order to gauge whether the child uses most or just a few of the above characteristics, whether there is a need to adjust prereading and reading activities, whether the majority or a minority of the class speaks Black English, and whether a child comprehends Standard English forms. The simple list of dialect characteristics given in Chart 1 can be translated into a checklist to use for diagnostic and subsequent planning purposes.

The language situation of our growing Spanish-speaking population is somewhat different from that of Black English speakers. Those children who grow up in a truly bilingual situation, where both English and Spanish are spoken as native languages, do not have the problems in school encountered by those who grow up in an environment where Spanish only is spoken. Truly bilingual children are relatively rare, however. Most children of Spanish-speaking communities—and there are thousands of Spanish-speaking children in our schools—have only a cursory acquaintance with English. These children will encounter problems in kindergarten

CHART 1[4]

Characteristics of Black English

I. *Sound System Homonyms*

r-/essness

guard = God	court = caught	terrace = tess
nor = gnaw	fort = fought	
sore = saw	Paris = pass	

l-lessness

toll = toe	all = awe
help = hep	Saul = saw
tool = too	fault = fought

Simplification of consonant clusters

rift = riff	box = bock	wind = wine
past = pass	mix = Mick	hold = hole
meant = men	mend = men	

Weakening of final consonants

seat = seed = see	feed = feet
bit = bid = big	road = row

Combination

picked = pick	raised = raise
miss = mist = missed	stream = scream
fine = find = fined	strap = scrap

Vowel sounds

pin = pen	find = fond	sure = shore
since = cents	peel = pail	boil = ball
beer = bear	poor = pour	

Th-sounds

Ruth = roof
death = deaf

II. *Syntactic Characteristics*

Black English	*Standard English*
He going.	He is going.
He be here.	He is here all the time.
I drink the milk.	I drank the milk.
She have a bicycle.	She has a bicycle.
I ask did he do it.	I asked if he did it.
He over to his friend house.	He is over at his friend's house.

[4] Adapted from W. Labov, "Some Sources of Reading Problems for Negro Speakers of Nonstandard English," in *Teaching Black Children to Read*, ed. J. C. Baratz and R. W. Shuy (Washington, D.C.: Center for Applied Linguistics, 1969), pp. 29–67 by permission of the Center for Applied Linguistics.

and the primary grades unless schools make provisions for their special needs. Many educators believe that as children learn to *read* English, they must have a good beginning in acquisition of *oral* English. Otherwise, as Modiano's study *(34)* suggests, it may be best to introduce reading in the first language. Although many schools are now recognizing the need for instruction in *oral* English, it is unfortunate that many school programs show a misunderstanding of the term *bilingualism*. Although some schools have effective bilingual programs in which both languages are used as the medium of instruction, others have so-called bilingual programs which teach only the majority language.

At the preschool level, less attention is needed to help the monolingual Spanish-speaking child learn English than is needed later. During the preschool years, children learn a *new language* easily. In fact, preschool children who have equivalent languages have an amazing ability to switch from one language to another to fit the person with whom they are speaking. I knew a two-year-old girl whose father always spoke Italian and whose mother always spoke Spanish. The child consistently spoke Italian to her father and Spanish to her mother. In addition, she knew some English and a little French. Other bilingual families have reported that there is some confusion of vocabulary items at the initial stage of acquisition but that once words are combined, the two languages are not confused. Guaranteeing the presence of a natural language environment in the preschool classroom seems to be provision enough for preschool children to learn English as a second language *if* they are required to speak English to communicate. To encourage second language acquisition, Cazden *(10)* recommends that schools create "an educational environment that reactivates the natural language-learning abilities which all children have."[5] Such an environment stresses rich, natural dialogue in the new language.

Preschool programs also should prepare children for reading. Because of the contrast of structures between Spanish and English, awareness on the teacher's part of areas of difficulty native Spanish speakers may encounter with English will help him to develop articulation and discrimination of sounds in English which may be lacking in a Spanish-speaking child. Once the teacher isolates a problem area, he can show the child how the sound is articulated in English and words which contain the sounds. The following list

---

[5]C. Cazden, *Child Language and Education* (New York: Holt, Rinehart, and Winston, Inc., 1972), p. 177.

shows major areas of difficulty for Spanish-speaking people who are learning English.

CHART 2

Problem Areas in Learning English[*]

Sound System

1. Spanish does not have some English phonemes:
   /ẟ/ as in *then*
   /θ/ as in *thing* (Except for Castilian Spanish)
   /z/ as in *zoo*
   /ž/ as in *pleasure*
   /š/ as in *shoe*
   /ǰ/ as in *jump*
2. Consonant clusters in Spanish are in medial position.

Syntactic System

1. Spanish modifying adjectives, pronouns, and articles have inflections which agree with the nouns; English adjectives are not inflected and English pronouns and articles are inflected differently.
   > *las palomas blancas* = the white doves
2. Spanish adjectives and nouns have a different order in some cases.

3. *Spanish subject pronouns* are not always realized; in English, they must be:
   > *Es un campesino* = He is a farmer.
4. Spanish verbs have inflections to indicate future, past, and conditional; English verbs have separate auxiliary verbs which are difficult to learn.
5. English third person singular verbs with *s* are difficult.
6. Spanish yes/no questions do not necessarily have inverted subject and verb.
7. Spanish does not have *do*-support necessary in many English questions and negatives. (e.g., Where *did* you go?)

Vocabulary

1. There are many Spanish/English cognates. Difficulty may arise in pronunciation.
2. Many words have different forms.
3. Idioms and alternate connotations can produce difficulty.

---

[*]Adapted from R. Lado, *Linguistics across Cultures* (Ann Arbor: University of Michigan Press, 1968). Reprinted by permission of the publisher.

Because of these problem areas, Spanish speakers may say /d/ for / ð / so that *them* is /dem/. Similarly, they may say /s/ for /θ/ so that *thing* is /siŋ/. Further, Spanish-speaking children may not hear such distinctive English phonemes as those in *Sue* and *shoe.* Learning the adjective/noun order and form will be difficult for these children. English sentences spoken by young Spanish children may appear immature because the subject pronoun which appears in English ("Is a farmer") is absent in Spanish. Other syntactic "irregularities" may occur in the child who is learning English and should be noted as developing bilingualism rather than immaturity.

CONCLUSION

As we have reviewed the empirical and linguistic sources for the language-deficit and the language-different positions in this chapter, it has become evident that neither position is a completely satisfactory explanation for the disparity of linguistic performance across social and cultural groups. The language-deficit position is unsatisfactory because it ignores the linguistic evidence of dialect differences. Recent research which accounts for language differences indicates little deficit in syntactic knowledge of young, poor children. The language-different position appears to be acceptable; however, it does not go far enough in explaining the language disparity found in school situations and the concomitant disparity which exists in school achievement. New work on the effect of situational control on language production probably will point to new directions for educators to take in setting up optimal environments for language development of all children. We will turn in the next two chapters to discussions of implications of the information presented so far for the preschool and primary classroom and of instructional matters in general.

REFERENCES

1. Abrahams, R. "Welding Communication Breaks." Paper read to Trainers of Teacher Trainers Conference on Language and Cultural Diversity, January 1971, at St. Cloud, Minnesota.

2. Ammon, P. R., and Ammon, M. S. "Effects of Training Black Preschool Children in Vocabulary vs. Sentence Construction." *Journal of Educational Psychology* 63 (1972): 421–26.

3. Athey, J. J., and Salzberg, A. "Language Development." Paper read at American Educational Research Association meeting, April 1972, at Chicago.

4. Baratz, J. C. "Teaching Reading in an Urban Negro School System." In *Teaching Black Children to Read,* edited by J. C. Baratz and R. W. Shuy. Washington, D.C.: Center for Applied Linguistics, 1969.

5. Baratz, S. S., and Baratz, J. C. "Early Childhood Intervention: The Social Science Base of Institutional Racism." *Harvard Educational Review* 40 (1970): 29–50.

6. Bereiter, C., and Engelmann, S. *Teaching Disadvantaged Children in the Preschool.* Englewood Cliffs, New Jersey: Prentice-Hall, Inc., 1966.

7. Bernstein, B. "Language and Social Class." *British Journal of Sociology* (1960): 271–75.

8. _____. "Social Class, Linguistic Codes, and Grammatical Elements." *Language and Speech* 5 (1962): 221–40.

9. _____. "A Sociolinguistic Approach to Socialization: With Some Reference to Educability." In *Language and Poverty: Perspectives on a Theme,* edited by F. Williams. Chicago: Markham Publishing Company, 1970.

10. Cazden, C. *Child Language and Education.* New York: Holt, Rinehart, & Winston, Inc., 1972.

11. _____. "The Neglected Situation in Child Language Research and Education." In *Language and Poverty: Perspectives on a Theme,* edited by F. Williams. Chicago: Markham Publishing Company, 1970.

12. Coleman, J. S., et al. *Equality of Educational Opportunity.* Washington, D.C.: U.S. Government Printing Office, 1966.

13. DeCecco, J. P. *The Psychology of Learning and Instruction: Educational Psychology.* Englewood Cliffs, New Jersey: Prentice-Hall, Inc., 1968.

14. Deutsch, C. "Auditory Discrimination and Learning: Social Factors." *Merrill-Palmer Quarterly* 10 (1964): 277–96.

15. Deutsch, M. "The Role of Social Class in Language Development and Cognition." *American Journal of Orthopsychiatry* 25 (1965): 75–88.

16. Deutsch, M., and Brown, B. "Social Influences in Negro-White Intelligence Differences." *Journal of Social Issues* 20 (1964): 24–35.

17. Engelmann, S. "How to Construct Effective Language Programs for the Poverty Child." In *Language and Poverty: Perspectives on a Theme,* edited by F. Williams. Chicago: Markham Publishing Company, 1970.

18. Entwhisle, D. P. "Semantic Systems of Children: Some Assessments of Social Class and Ethnic Differences." In *Language and Poverty: Per-*

spectives on a Theme, edited by F. Williams. Chicago: Markham Publishing Company, 1970.

19. _____. "Developmental Sociolinguistics: A Comparative Study in Four Subcultural Settings." *Sociometry* 29 (1966): 67–84.

20. Friedlander, B. Z. "Receptive Language Development in Infancy." *Merrill-Palmer Quarterly* 16 (1970): 7–51.

21. Greene, H. A., and Petty, W. T. *Developing Language Skills in the Ele. mentary Schools,* 3d ed. Boston: Allyn & Bacon, Inc., 1967.

22. Heider, E. R. "Style and Accuracy of Verbal Communications within and between Social Classes." *Journal of Personality and Social Psychology* 18 (1971): 33–47.

23. John, V. "The Intellectual Development of Slum Children: Some Preliminary Findings." *American Journal of Orthopsychiatry* 33 (1963): 813–22.

24. John, V., and Goldstein, L. "The Social Context of Language Acquisition." *Merrill-Palmer Quarterly* 10 (1964): 265–75.

25. Hess, R. D., and Shipman, V. "Early Experience and the Socialization of Cognitive Modes in Children." *Child Development* 36 (1965): 869–86.

26. Labov, W. "The Logic of Nonstandard English." In *Language and Poverty: Persepctives on a Theme,* edited by F. Williams. Chicago: Markham Publishing Company, 1970.

27. _____. *The Social Stratification of English in New York City.* Washington, D.C.: Center for Applied Linguistics, 1966.

28. _____. "Some Sources of Reading Problems for Negro Speakers of Nonstandard English." In *Teaching Black Children to Read,* edited by J. C. Baratz and R. W. Shuy. Washington, D.C.: Center for Applied Linguistics, 1969.

29. _____. "Stages in the Acquisition of Standard English." In *Social Dialects and Language Learning,* edited by R. W. Shuy. Champaign, Illinois: National Council of Teachers of English, 1964.

30. Lacivita, A. F.; Kean, J. M.,; and Yamamoto, K. "Socioeconomic Status of Children and Acquisition of Grammar." *Journal of Educational Research* 60 (1966): 71–74.

31. Lado, R. *Linguistics across Cultures.* Ann Arbor: University of Michigan Press, 1968.

32. Lenneberg, E. *Biological Foundations of Language.* New York: John Wiley & Sons, Inc., 1967, Chapter 4.

33. Loban, W. *Problems in Oral English: Kindergarten through Grade Nine.* Champaign, Illinois: National Council of Teachers of English, Research Report #5, 1966.

34. Modiano, N. "A Comparative Study to Two Approaches to the Teaching of Reading in the National Language." New York: New York University School of Education, 1966.

35. Shriner, T. H., and Miner, L. "Morphological Structures in the Language of Disadvantaged Children." *Journal of Speech and Hearing Research* 11 (1968): 604–10.

36. Shuy, R. W. Untitled paper read at Linguistic Society meeting, February 1971, at University of Minnesota, Minneapolis, Minnesota.

37. Shuy, R. W.; Wolfram, W. A.; and Riley, W. K. *Linguistic Correlates of Social Stratification in Detroit Speech.* Final Report, Cooperative Research Project 6-1347. Washington, D.C.: U.S. Office of Education, Part IV, pp. 1–10.

38. Stewart, W. A. "Toward a History of American Negro Dialect." In *Language and Poverty: Perspectives on a Theme,* edited by F. Williams. Chicago: Markham Publishing Company, 1970.

39. Yoder, D. E. "Some Viewpoints of the Speech, Hearing, and Language Clinician." In *Language and Poverty: Perspectives on a Theme,* edited by F. Williams. Chicago: Markham Publishing Company, 1970.

CHAPTER 4

Implications for Early
Childhood Education

Although preschool language programs too often suggest the language-deficit attitude toward poor, minority-group children, the language program described in this chapter is *not* designed to fill in gaps. In every respect our contact with language learning children will respect their level of language, their dialect, their preference for their mother's language; it will help to expand their language level while promoting a natural, informal atmosphere. Toward this end, a statement of basic assumptions for a language program based on the conclusions of the first three chapters is included in this chapter, as are specific techniques for teachers to use in assessing their students' language. Finally, appropriate instruction in syntax, phonology, and language meaning is described in general terms.

The instructional procedures recommended in this book will be similar regardless of whether we are talking about a language program for youngsters of age three or four or planning reading instruction for children of six or seven. In all cases, informal contacts with children are preferred to regimented instruction, but this does not mean that structured lessons for groups of children never occur in this program. Rather, the intent is to suit the instructional technique to the content and to individual student need.

We tend to think of school experience of young children through the age of five as being quite different from that of primary-aged children. Goals, procedures, and individual expectations change drastically when we send our children to first grade. Both the curriculum and the social expectations for first grade are the result of the historical precedent of compulsory first-grade attendance rather than of specific differences in child development. But in these days, when more and more children attend school before the age of five or six, we must begin to analyze our educational goals in terms of our knowledge of child development and of variations in learning interest and style; therefore, we will try to avoid creating stereotyped expectations of language and reading programs in terms of children's ages. Language instruction, preparation for reading, and the beginning reading programs outlined in this book are not determined by children's chronological age alone but also by their interests, abilities, and needs.

In this chapter, we will draw on the information of the first three chapters to outline implications to be included in the language program for maximizing growth in syntax, phonology, and language meaning. Although many of the comments made here about growth of *syntax* and *phonology* refer to children in the lower age range, the program for development of *language meaning* ought to be part of every classroom regardless of the age and developmental level of the children.

BASIC ASSUMPTIONS FOR A LANGUAGE DEVELOPMENT PROGRAM

The position that language as it is being acquired provides children with sophisticated learning strategies for application in general cognitive development is accepted as the central premise of our program. This means that by encouraging the full development of language, we will be partially encouraging the development of intellectual ability. This program reflects the view that a classroom program should be designed to maximize language abilities in order to prepare children for a verbal, literate society and to help them to grow in the cognitive realm. Since acquisition of syntax and phonology are developmental learning processes which are caused by children's innate ability to learn language, the language program should enhance these processes and, therefore, should be informal. More specifically, we recognize that adults cannot teach basic syntactic and phonological rules directly; nonetheless, teachers can plan the language situation so that children clearly perceive mature structures and sounds when they are ready to form the relevant rules themselves. Teachers using this program will take advantage of spontaneous activities that occur in classrooms and will interact with children to provide language data in a natural manner. Since teachers need to know where children are in terms of their individual syntactic and phonological development in order to know what kind of language data is most appropriate for their growth, teacher assessment of the children's development is an important part of the instructional sequence recommended here.

A second major premise in developing the language program is that an understanding of adult meanings of objects, events, descriptive terms, and actions is essential for vocabulary development. Further, adults must help children to acquire attributes of concepts so that their in-depth understanding of words expands. The adult function is to help children focus on the relevant features of words they use. There are, then, two parts to instruction in language meaning. One is to encourage vocabulary growth in terms of quantity, while the other provides opportunities for children to further their understanding of word meaning. All components of the language program are based on teacher assessment and take place in child-structured situations as well as in informal, planned lessons determined by teacher judgment and student need.

TEACHER ASSESSMENT AND PLANNING

When a language program is activated in a classroom, information about students' present levels of attainment is necessary for the teacher to plan instruction which meets the needs of individual children. Those children who have acquired basic structures should be encouraged to engage in prereading and, later, if their interest remains high, in beginning reading experiences. Children whose language development is progressing normally should be identified and their individual needs met so that the program helps them to increase their language knowledge. Those children whose language acquisition is slow but in the regular sequence will require recognition and attention so that full development is ensured before they are required to engage in reading and other complex learning activities. In addition, teacher assessment ought to locate those nonverbal children who need to be referred to specialists for further diagnosis, which will reveal whether they have cognitive handicaps, emotional disabilities, or specific language dysfunctions, followed by specific training. It should be emphasized that the assessment procedures suggested here for classroom teachers are not sufficient for making a specialized diagnosis of this sort.

Once assessment of language abilities has been made, teachers can use the information obtained to plan for group and individual needs. For example, the teacher should plan the type of atmosphere that is appropriate for a given type of learning. Assessment and intelligent planning must precede instruction with children. In teaching the syntactic or phonological components of language, the teacher's contact with children should be extremely informal, for she is most concerned with providing the data the children need to form their own rule systems. Instruction occurs in natural settings and continues until the structure in question appears in the child's speech. When the instruction is in the area of language meaning, the contact with children may vary. The words selected may be determined by classroom activities, but the setting for the instruction should be small, short, group lessons. Dialogue is important here, but adult naming of words and adult questioning to focus on word features is even more important. Specific assessment checklists are included in the next sections to indicate the content of the syntactic and phonological aspects of the language program. Assessment and instructional procedures for the language meaning component of the program will be discussed last.

Syntactic Development

There are three assessment procedures recommended here for gauging children's syntactic development. The first is use of a checklist; the second, use of a sentence repetition exercise; and the third, use of a published test.

When the syntactic structures listed in the checklist are first heard in a child's speech, the teacher makes a check in the first blank and marks the date. By writing in the age when the structure is observed for the first time, the teacher can use the age designations to obtain a summary of development (see Chart 3).

In using the checklist, teachers must recognize that many normally developing children do not achieve these structures by the age cited, since there are normal variations in language acquisition. Thus, it is more important to use the checklist to measure *the sequence of growth* than to use it to make normative judgments.

It is also important to note that speakers of a nonstandard dialect may not necessarily acquire the same forms as those cited in studies of language acquisition. Adjustments for assessing the acquisition of Black English-speaking children are indicated in the checklist by italic type. When an omission or variation noted in syntactic development is traceable to dialect, teachers should not consider this

CHART 3

Checklist for Assessing Syntactic Maturity

Name _____	Structure Observed	Date	Age

Ages 3.0–3.6 (Approximate)

Subject-verb-object-sentences _____ _____ _____

Subject-intransitive verb _____ _____ _____

Use of copula — *"Be" used in habitual action; absent in momentary action*[*] _____ _____ _____

Past tense when appropriate (overgeneralizations expected)—*Absent in many phonological settings* _____ _____ _____

-Ing on verbs when appropriate _____ _____ _____

Negative word inserted in the middle of sentences _____ _____ _____

Wh-word in questions _____ _____ _____

Ages 3.6–4.0 (Approximate)

Plural inflection—*Final phoneme missing in some settings* _____ _____ _____

Possession—*Possessive "s" often lost; possessive pronoun not realized* _____ _____ _____

Subject-verb agreement in present, *"he do," "he have," acceptable; "s" often lost* _____ _____ _____

Use of AUX forms such as *"do," "has," "been"* _____ _____ _____

Negatives attached to *"do"* _____ _____ _____

In yes/no questions, subject and AUX inverted _____ _____ _____

Ages 4.0–6.0 (Approximate)

Pronoun used appropriately with a few exceptions, such as possessive pronouns—*possessive pronoun endings may be lost; subject plus pronoun (John he sang) occasionally inserted* _____ _____ _____

[*] Italics indicate some adaptations for Black English-speaking children.

CHART 3 *(Continued)*

	Structure Observed	Date	Age
Adjectives used to qualify nouns	___	___	___
Infinitives used where appropriate	___	___	___
Future tense used—*in contraction future "will" lost*	___	___	___
Prepositional phrases used	___	___	___
Wh-word question subject, AUX inversion used— *does not occur with many Black English-speaking children*	___	___	___
Simple sentences conjoined with "and" and "but"	___	___	___
Relative clauses used	___	___	___

variation an area for instruction. Dialect change is not recommended in this program for young children.

Children who are learning to speak English as a second language will not follow the sequence of development outlined here; nor will they acquire the structures at the time indicated. Unfortunately, we know very little about the syntactic acquisition of English as a second language by young, foreign-speaking children. The teacher should bear these factors in mind as she uses the checklist to assess her students' syntactic achievement.

The checklist includes only a summary account of the syntactic forms which children learn between the ages of three and six. However, the syntactic structures included in the checklist are important ones which, if present, probably indicate that other related structures are also present. For example, if relative clauses are apparent in the speech of a five year old, it is probably true that he also can use other simple embedded sentences. The content of the instructional program in syntactic development will be similar to the material of the checklist. In other words, the checklist should be used to determine needs, of course, and then to plan instruction based on the outlined structures on the checklist.

The alternative procedure for assessing syntactic maturity is using the sentence repetition test. A number of studies have shown that when repeating sentences which are long enough that they must be processed as language rather than as separate items, children repeat the stimulus sentence in the direction of their syntactic maturity level. That is, in repeating a relatively long sentence, a child will interpret it in terms of his grammatical knowledge and use his own structures in encoding.

The sentence repetition test is given individually in a quiet corner of a room by asking the child to repeat a sentence immediately after the teacher's reading of it. The teacher can mark the answers directly on the test, but when she wants to make more careful assessment than is possible with the test, she will want to tape the recorded responses for later scoring. The sentences in the repetition test are in Standard English, and dialect variation should be noted when it occurs. Interpretation should be carefully made so that dialect variation is not interpreted as immaturity. I would suggest that the checklist be the first choice for assessment since it is a more direct test of children's language; however, for children who are reluctant verbalizers, the sentence repetition test is recommended.

A third measure of syntactic maturity can be made with the *Northwestern Syntax Screening Test* by L. Lee *(3)*. The first section tests receptive understanding of major syntactic structures; in the second part, both understanding and repetition abilities are examined. The test is individually administered and takes up to fifteen minutes. The tasks it presents may be difficult for some children younger than five, and in interpreting the results, it is well to remember that the percentiles were established on the basis of scores by upper- and middle-income children.

Chapter 5 specifies sample instructional techniques to be used for the syntactic aspects of the program. However, by combining the content of the checklist and repetition test with the assumption that children acquire syntactic structures in interaction with adult speakers, it will become obvious that instruction will be through dialogue. Adults will expand, prompt, and comment upon what children are saying to provide the children with the language data needed in order to build their syntactic rule system.

Phonological Growth

The qualifications stated at the beginning of the preceding section for the use of the checklist for assessing syntactic maturity also

CHART 4

Sentence Repetition Test

Name _____ Age _____ Date _____

Sentence	Critical Feature	Repeated**	Partial	Not Repeated*
1. The old man painted a big picture.	Man-Paint-Picture	_____	_____	_____
2. The silly cat runs away very fast.	Cat-Run(s)	_____	_____	_____
3. The big boy is a very mean boy.	Is	_____	_____	_____
4. My mommy told me a funny story.	Told (Telled)	_____	_____	_____
5. The little girl is brushing her teeth.	(Is) Brushing	_____	_____	_____
6. We do not want to go home now.	Placement of *Not*	_____	_____	_____
7. Billy said, "Where is my book?"	Where	_____	_____	_____
8. All of the boys and all of the girls are sad.	Plural on *Boys* and *Girls*	_____	_____	_____
9. It's not your book; it's Sally's book.	Your-Sally's	_____	_____	_____

CHART 4 *(Continued)*

	Sentence	Critical Feature	Repeated**	Partial	Not Repeated*
10.	Susan sings. The girls dance.	Sings-Dance	_____	_____	_____
11.	The man *has been* calling us.	Has-Been	_____	_____	_____
12.	That dirty dog does not want to have a bath.	Does-Not (Doesn't)	_____	_____	_____
13.	The lady asked "Do animals talk?"	Inversion of *Do* and *Animals*	_____	_____	_____
14.	I can do it. You can do it. He can do it.	I, You, It, He	_____	_____	_____
15.	The boy shouted at the tired, thin, old man.	Tired, Thin, Old	_____	_____	_____
16.	The girls said they liked to sing songs and to read books.***	To Sing, To Read	_____	_____	_____
17.	After lunch, we are going to have a nap.	Are Going To (We'll)	_____	_____	_____
18.	The children went to the circus, and they				

CHART 4 *(Continued)*

Sentence	Critical Feature	Repeated**	Partial	Not Repeated*
climbed over the seats.***	To, Over	_____	_____	_____
19. The children asked, "Where are you going?"	Inversion of *Are* and *You*	_____	_____	_____
20. The children ate all their meat and they ate their apples, but they didn't drink the milk.***	And, And, But	_____	_____	_____
21. The book that tells about animals in the zoo is lost.	The Relative Clause	_____	_____	_____

*The structures in the middle column are the ones being examined. Pay attention only to them.

**If the critical feature is repeated exactly mark the first blank. If it is repeated but with a change, write the change in the second blank. If the child shows no sign of repeating the structure, check the third blank.

***The structures being tested in items 16, 18, and 20 are best analyzed in spontaneous speech.

apply to use of the checklist presented in this section. It is especially important that teachers not expect the appearance of phonemes for Black English speakers to be the same as those for Standard English speakers. Specific adaptations are again indicated by italic type in the checklist. In addition, it is noted that Spanish-speaking children will have particular difficulty with the following English phonemes: /ð/, /θ/, /z/, /ž/, /š/, /j/. Again, the checklist provides both the means for assessment of growth and the content material for instruction in this component of the language program.

CHART 5

Checklist for Assessing Phonemic Acquisition

Name _____

	Phoneme Observed	Date	Age

Three and Four Year Olds

/n/				
/t/	— Often lost in final position*			
/g/				
/m/				
/b/	— May be lost in final position			
/d/	— May be lost in final position			
/w/				
/h/				
/p/	— May be lost in final position			
/k/	— In /ks/ for x only /k/ is realized			
/f/	— May alternate with /v/			
/ŋ/				

Five and Six Year Olds

/v/	— May alternate with /f/			
/j/				
/θ/	— Occasionally changed to /f/			
/š/**	— In consonant clusters, next phoneme altered; often lost in final position			
/l/**	— Often lost or reduced in medial or final position			
/r/**	— Often lost in medial or final position			
/s/**				
/z/**				
/ž/**				
/č/**				
/ɟ/**	— Occasionally changed to /d/			
/hw/**				

*Italic type indicates adaptations to be made for some Black English-speaking children.
**These phonemes may not develop until after age six.

It is readily apparent that there are no vowel phonemes on the checklist for assessing phonemic acquisition. There are two reasons for the deliberate exclusion of vowels. First, vowel sounds are even more variable than consonants and are very sensitive to the influence of regional and social dialects. Consequently, setting age expectations for acquisition of vowels simply promotes confusion and misinterpretation. Second, little is known about the sequence of acquisition of vowels after the very early stages at the beginning of the second year of life. Nonetheless, we should expect that most children will use the vowel phonemes of their dialect by the time they are six. The *Goldman-Fristoe Test of Articulation (2)* is a good, quick, individualized test of articulation ability.

Finally, continual assessment of slowly developing children is necessary in order to monitor the pattern of growth. Children who continue to be very slow in developing or who have such severe articulation problems that communication is difficult should be referred for special directed training. As will be discussed in Chapter 7, the ability to hear phonemic differences is more important in learning to read than is the actual oral use of phonemes; therefore, special strategies for increasing discrimination of phonemes will also be necessary in the prereading program.

Once assessment has been completed, instruction will begin. Instruction in phonological development, for the most part, will be very informal and accomplished in group-play settings. If children appear to be developing the normal sequence of sounds, even if their development is slow, no special articulation training is required. These children, like the great majority of children, need only to hear adult pronunciation to acquire phonemes. In many cases, however, the teacher must take special care to pronounce clearly words containing a phoneme being acquired to ensure that children receive the data they need for acquisition. Until children are ready to hear the difference between their pronunciation and that of adults, they probably will not learn the sound; therefore, repetition and contrast of sounds in dialogue and in group games are the instructional techniques used in this part of the language program. These techniques are discussed more specifically in Chapter 5.

Language Meaning

Since there is no ordered, developmental sequence for acquiring words and their meanings, assessment of meaning cannot be accomplished with checklists of growth points. While other techniques will produce evidence of general ability in this area, they will not assess the particular size and quality of children's vocabularies. Since word meaning continues to develop throughout the school years and planned instruction in language meaning should occur at all levels, this section should have relevance to the teacher no matter what the age and attainment of her students.

In this section, we refer to two levels of instruction to increase language meaning. The first level concerns expansion of the size of the vocabulary; the second considers the increase of in-depth understanding of major concepts. These levels often may overlap in real instruction: for example, when a teacher introduces a "new" word and encourages children to identify essential attributes, she may be helping some children who have already learned the word in part to acquire a more stable concept. Although there is overlap in practice, the two levels are discussed separately here in order to give proper emphasis to the critical characteristics of each. Reference is made to individual words, although in teaching, the teacher will deal with words that are embedded in statements. These words will have full meaning when used with full context.

At the level of vocabulary extension, a variety of assessment techniques are available. Teachers can rely on standard measures of vocabulary, such as the *Peabody Picture Vocabulary Test (1)*, which measures passive understanding of words and phrases. Norms are set for all ages so that teachers can compare an individual's vocabulary with that of his classmates and of larger groups of children of his age. This test has the great advantage of not requiring the oral use of language.

Informal assessment also could be used in evaluating vocabulary expansion. Teachers, in talking with children as they play, can ask for names of objects and descriptions of situations in order to assess vocabulary facility. Children can retell a story, thereby demonstrating knowledge of vocabulary items used in the story. Teachers can also set up situations which assess understanding of certain kinds of words which cannot be pictured. For example, if the teacher puts a pencil on a box and asks, "Is the pencil in the box or on the box?" she can discover the child's understanding of the prepositions in the sentence used; with similar procedures, she can assess the child's understanding of other prepositions. Sometimes, game situations illustrate vocabulary understanding without the use of oral language. The box and pencil can be used as the teacher directs the child to follow directions stressing prepositions. Games which require that children find objects or pictures displayed in an array of other objects or pictures also display the children's passive understanding.

Both oral use and passive understanding should be used in assessment so that noncommunicative children have the opportunity to indicate knowledge. Sensitive teachers use much patience and effort to assure the children's security in the testing situation before they reach conclusions about reticent children's language knowledge. Finally, assessment should be continual to insure a dynamic vocabulary program.

Planned vocabulary lessons should be frequent in all classrooms. These "lessons" can be planned for an individual student or for large or small groups. They can last from five to twenty minutes, depending on the age and attention span of the students and can occur in conjunction with spontaneous play or in a formal lesson; the structure of the lesson should be determined by the age, learning style, and success of previous lessons. The lessons can involve as few as two words or a review of ten. All of these alternatives must be considered by the teacher; his choices of which to use should be based on assessment of needs, understanding of learning styles, and, most importantly, on objective evaluation of previous lessons. For example, shy, reticent children may learn best while engaged in play, while children whose vocabulary is meager and whose attention wanders easily may learn best in an individual directed lesson which lasts for four minutes each day.

There are elements which should be included in every lesson regardless of the instructional situation used. The words to be introduced should have some relevance to the class program. For example, words about farming should precede and follow a class trip to the farm. Furthermore, when the words are presented, children must be provided with concrete experiences which are the media of word learning. The experiences obviously are determined by the kind of word being introduced. If possible, objects should be used in the experience, although clear pictures can be substituted. With words which display feelings and movement, understanding can be shown by action. The concrete experiences should elicit sense reactions on the part of the students; they should be able to touch, see, hear, and even smell the referent as they learn the word name. After the teacher identifies the word, the children should be encouraged to comment briefly in their own words on the essential features of the word referent. Finally, the new words should be reviewed in a variety of meaningful situations after initial presentation.

Although the words to be taught will be determined on the basis of the assessment of individuals and groups of children and on the basis of the activities in the classroom, research in vocabulary growth and experience with young children indicate that terms from the following word groups provide a good place for the teacher to start:

relational and opposing terms (*on-off, small-big, beginning-end, more-less, same-different, affirmation* and *negation,* etc.)
animals
people
family relationships
colors
shapes
prepositions
containers
machinery
clothes
weather
foods
tools
household implements
furniture
body movements
feelings
toys
liquids
plants
temperature

The other level of language meaning which should be an important part of the language program for children of all ages is the in-depth meaning of concepts. In Chapter 1, the phrase *horizontal vocabulary expansion* was used to describe the child's gradual attainment of word atrributes as understanding grows from early perception of a word to mature conceptual level. In this area, adults help children focus on the essential features of words. Actually, parents and teachers do this unconsciously in dialogue with children, but our language program is intended to make this important part of language growth explicit. In order to attain mature concepts of words, children need to learn how to distinguish a word from other, similar words. They not only must identify objects by name but also must have an idea of the word cluster, its common features, and the differentiating attributes of each item. This part of the language meaning program is important in helping children develop categorical thinking.

Assessment in this area is extremely difficult. To accomplish it, teachers must become good listeners. Evidence of confusion between like terms, responses to specific questions, and children's comments on the features of words introduced and reviewed become the material for assessment. Continual reevaluation of children's understanding is also necessary. And because of our knowledge of children's cognitive development, it is important to bear in mind that some kinds of understanding cannot be achieved during the early childhood years. For example, certain relational terms cannot be understood in adult terms. The word *heavy* is not usually understood as a relational term by young children. Such sophisticated terms as *democracy* and *justice* illustrate that teachers must use judgment in determining the limits to expect as children learn the full meaning of words. Cognitive ability provides the boundaries for growth in conceptual attainment.

Instruction in this area requires a good deal of creative questioning on the part of the teacher. Of course, she can simply explain the common and distinguishing features of words to children, but didactic teaching should not be an important part of our language program. In fact, didactic teaching will not serve our purpose of *helping* children build their own categories and specific concepts. Instead, this kind of help is provided by focusing the children's attention on relevant aspects. Once children have acquired the ability to name a number of terms in a group of words (let us say the words from the group *clothes*), the teacher can place pictures of the known words before a small group and ask questions which will lead them to identify in their own words what is similar about the group and what is singular about each item. Essentially, this procedure is the basic instructional approach to be used with most groups of words. Chapter 5 contains a more specific discussion of the content and instructional procedures of the meaning component of the language program.

REFERENCES

1. Dunn, L. M. *Peabody Picture Vocabulary Test.* Circle Pines, Minnesota: American Guidance Service, 1965.

2. Goldman, R., and Fristoe, M. *The Goldman-Fristoe Test of Articulation.* Circle Pines, Minnesota: American Guidance Service, 1969.

3. Lee, L. *Northwestern Syntax Screening Test.* Evanston, Illinois: Northwestern University, 1969.

CHAPTER 5

Language Instruction
for Young Children

We turn now to specific instructional considerations which grow out of the implications reviewed in Chapter 4. However, before we turn to the instructional recommendations, it is necessary to take one more detour. Many language programs have been designed for young children and some research is available on the effect of language-oriented preschool programs. A brief look at the results of this research will precede the specific recommendations of teaching techniques.

POPULAR LANGUAGE PROGRAMS

Although it is impossible to do justice to all of the research on preschool programs in a book of this length, a few good reviews are cited here. For example, specific language programs have been described by Parker, et al. *(10)*, *(11)*. Other good general references appear in Hess and Bear *(9)*, while Cazden *(3)* also has written an excellent analysis of evaluation of language development.

In this section of the chapter, two highly visible language programs are reviewed. These programs, which are commercially available, are quite different from each other and represent different trends in American education. Both programs have resulted in positive language growth for prekindergarten and for kindergarten children.

Before the 1960s, most preschool programs were morning nursery schools for the children of the middle classes which emphasized socially oriented goals and some academic study as presented in unit work. The only other common programs were child-care centers which had surrogate mothering as their main goal. During the 60s, more interest in academic preschool education for all children became evident, and the federal government supported a number of experimental preschool programs designed to serve disadvantaged children.

In 1966, Bereiter and Engelmann *(2)* published a long account of an instructional program they had designed and used successfully with disadvantaged preschool children in Illinois. The Bereiter-Engelmann program received considerable attention from educators and laymen because it represented a radical departure from traditional preschool curriculums in terms of both its unique instructional approach and the controversial theory on which this approach was based.

There are two factors in the Bereiter-Engelmann program which demand differential attention. One is the innovative curriculum. Based on the assumption that disadvantaged children lack information and skill, particularly the verbal skill needed for academic work, the curriculum was built to provide compensation for these deficiencies. Thus, rather than measuring general growth in language and cognition by means of the normative tests, as was done in many other research-oriented preschool programs, the authors of this program decided to measure pupil growth by testing acquisition of specified academic skills on criterion-based tests. The curriculum focused on language, arithmetic, and reading of fifteen four-year-old children from "very deprived" families who participated in the project for two years. In the area of language, a major concern was the development of grammatical sentence patterns and use of "precise" pronunciation (Standard English) as a means to that end. The curriculum initially stressed the acquisition of the following minimum language essentials *(1)*: affirmative and negative statements, ability to use polar sets, correct use of prepositions, ability to classify simple sets, and use of simple *if-then* sentences. As each curricular goal was met, the subjects were trained in successively more complex tasks. Thus, the children were first required to repeat statements as they heard them. They then responded to *yes-no* questions and learned to indicate location. Finally, they mastered the production of sentences and simple deductions.

The other unusual factor in this program was the direct instructional approach. Such direct, systematic instruction created a "highly task-oriented, no-nonsense manner (where) full participation of all children in the learning tasks is treated as a requirement to which children must conform."[1] Attention to the task, effort, and mastery on the part of the pupils was considered critical. During the lessons, children were immediately rewarded for making correct responses. If they did not respond correctly, they were told so and, if necessary, even removed from the lesson. Children were rewarded for trying, however. Although this approach is in partial conflict with our discussion, it did prove successful.

At the end of one year, the children had improved greatly on the subtest of the Illinois Test of Psycholinguistic Ability which examined production of grammatical inflections, an ability stressed in instruction. Although little additional growth occurred in that area during the second year, by the end of the second year, the group was nearly average (in comparison to national norms) in making verbal analogies. Gains were indicated by scores on other tests as well. Furthermore, most of the children achieved the stated objectives.

It should be noted in evaluating these gains that the fifteen children had received two hours of instruction five days a week from four teachers to achieve these gains. In other studies where this curriculum has been used, the results have not been as positive. For example, Day *(4)* found no difference in the gains made by children using this curriculum and those using a traditional unit approach. Where three different prekindergarten programs were compared by DiLorenzo, Salter, and Brady *(5)*, both the Bereiter-Engelmann program and a program stressing reading readiness promoted growth for disadvantaged children.

The Distar Language Program *(7)* is the progeny of the Bereiter and Engelmann program. Major aspects of the curriculum and teaching techniques described above also applied to Distar. In Distar language, teachers are advised to use both verbal and physical reinforcement, to move quickly, and to demand attention of all members of the group. Responses are sought both in unison and by the individual.

In assessing the overall value of the Bereiter-Engelmann approach to language development, we must consider the curricular and instructional characteristics separately. While the curriculum's basic assumption that a language deficit exists is in conflict with the view advocated in this book, the idea of specifying language goals and measuring growth in terms of achievement of objectives is con-

---

[1]C. E. Bereiter, "Academic Instruction and Preschool Children," in *Language Programs for the Disadvantaged,* ed. R. Corbin and M. Crosby (Champaign, Illinois: National Council of Teachers of English, 1965).

sistent with the diagnostic approach recommended here. Furthermore, aspects of the instructional procedures appear to be alien to the language learning strategies of young children. For example, heavy reliance on repetition of structures that are not part of children's dialects may be questioned. On the other hand, the techniques used in Distar for getting and maintaining attention and the clear verbal feedback system employed may be excellent techniques to draw out nonparticipating children.

Another highly visible language development program is the commercially available *Peabody Language Development Kits (6)*. There are four kits: *P* for prekindergarten level, *K* for kindergarten, *1* for first grade, and *2* for second. As with Distar Language, the teacher using these kits is given explicit directions and structure for teaching groups of children. Pictures of objects and people, plus motivating games, songs, etc., are provided in a program which emphasizes receptive, expressive, and conceptual aspects of language. In sharp contrast with the Distar Program, these kits attempt to train for global language goals; for example, at level *P*, the stress is on developing sentence structures containing major grammatical constructs. Most studies assessing the effect of the kits show that they are effective in stimulating oral language development *(10)*, *(6)*. Furthermore, they have been found to produce effective results when used by paraprofessionals.

The major difference between the Peabody Kits and Distar is that spontaneous responses are encouraged. The Peabody program recommends that a gamelike spirit be promoted rather than a work-oriented atmosphere. Furthermore, a wide range of language skills and abilities is involved and organized through twenty-three kinds of activities. Each group lesson involves two or three of the following different activities *(6)*:

1. Activity time
2. Brainstorming time
3. Classification time
4. Conversation time
5. Critical-thinking time
6. Describing time
7. Dramatizing time
8. Following directions time
9. Guessing time
10. Identification time
11. Imagination time

12. Listening time
13. Looking time
14. Memory time
15. Pantomine time
16. Patterning time
17. Relationships time
18. Rhyming time
19. Speech development time
20. Speed-up time
21. Story time
22. Touching time
23. Vocabulary-building time

Many teachers who use the Peabody kits like to alter the lessons somewhat to reflect the needs of their pupils. For example, one day a teacher might do two of the recommended activities but also substitute another that seems appropriate for her students. Some teachers also specify objectives to be gained from the activities and provide informal assessments of achievement gains with each lesson. In addition, many teachers group children by their language needs and use the kits with smaller groups so that some individual attention is possible. Because the Peabody kits encourage spontaneous language and an open atmosphere for learning, their approach is not unlike the recommendations of this book. Indeed, the teacher who has a kit and wants to use it in conjunction with suggestions made here will find that such adjustments are possible.

In summary, whatever program a teacher uses, it is important to note one factor: All studies examining the educational value of preschool language programs have shown that successful, instruction in language is consistent, regular, and planned. In most cases when such a program was initiated and compared with a nonlanguage-oriented curriculum, the language development of participating preschool children was enhanced. Apparently, then, provision of regular language instruction is helpful.

RECOMMENDATIONS FOR INSTRUCTION

Each of the three components of language (syntactic, phonological, and semantic) is treated separately in this section. Dialogues are used to illustrate teaching techniques and to maximize the effectiveness of the presentation of overall content goals and delivery methods. Activities to supplement the dialogues also are included. In contrast to the two programs described above, this section presents only a few teaching suggestions, and the classroom language program is dependent on teacher creativity, knowledge, and organizing ability. Because the material in this chapter only brushes the surface of a complete language program, the assumption is that teachers can and should adapt a program to their class needs.

Syntactic Development

Program goals: The school should set as a primary goal the creation of an environment conducive for optimum syntactic development. Previous discussion has suggested that the optimum environment is one in which growth in syntax occurs because children have ample opportunity to compare their language structures with mature structures. Ample opportunity for comparison requires plentiful dialogue between child and adult. When adults *expand* children's immature forms to the mature structures in meaningful ways, when adults *comment* directly on children's remarks, and when adults *prompt* children to identify specific parts of their ideas, dialogue efficiency appears to be increased. Dialogue between child and child should be encouraged in order to offer opportunity to practice and try out new structures. Supplementary games may reinforce acquisition of new structures once they have appeared.

Continual assessment of syntactic development must be a major goal of a language program. Early assessment using either the checklist for the verbally active child or the sentence repetition test for the reluctant speaker is only the initial step in measurement. Teachers should avoid blanket expectations that all children will achieve certain levels in specified time periods.

Program content: The outlines of major syntactic structures expected during the preschool period are outlined on the checklist for assessing syntactic maturity in Chapter 4. Each structure included in the checklist appears as a topic in Chart 6.

Instructional techniques: Dialogue is an essential instructional tool in Chart 6. The first structure demonstrates use of expansions, commenting, and prompts as they might occur spontaneously when adults engage in talk with children. For each other structure, suggested activities are presented which will serve as reinforcement of structures being acquired.

CHART 6

Illustrative Instructional Activities to Enhance Syntactic Development

I. Period of Acquisition of Basic Structures (Generally Three and Four Year Olds)

Topic

Subject-Verb-Object Sentences

Sample Dialogues

Interaction at this point will be spontaneous. The following examples are intended to illustrate types of adult responses which are helpful to the child's growing syntactic knowledge.

A. *Expansion.* In these responses, adults repeat the child's structure in mature form.

Child: "Look, Teacher. *Smash snake.*" (Another child has just smashed the speaker's plasticene snake.)

Teacher: "Oh, too bad. *Johnny smashed the snake.*" (Teacher emphasizes the expansion of the child's structure.)
"Billy, make a new one, and maybe Johnny will help.

Child: *"Hurt finger."*

Teacher: "Oh, I'm sorry. You hurt your finger. Let's fix it.

B. *Prompts.* Adults prompt for words and then repeat the words in mature sentence structure.

Child: "Look, snake." (He points to a plasticene snake before him.)

Teacher: "Oh, you made a....?"

Child: "Snake."

Teacher: "You made a nice Snake."

Child: "Want drink."

Teacher: (Looking around): "Who wants a drink?"

Child: "Me."

Teacher: "Oh, Billy wants a drink."

Child: "Gimme." (Points to toy.)

Teacher: "What toy do you want, Billy?"

Child: "Truck."

Teacher: "OK, Billy, you want a truck."

C. Comments.   With such remarks adults simply engage in dialogue with the child by continuing the child's remark.

CHART 6 *(Continued)*

Child (making a plasticene snake):	"Me smash snake."
Teacher:	"What? You are going to smash that nice snake?"
Child:	"More juice."
Teacher:	"I'm sorry. We don't have any more juice. Do you want some milk?"

Activities

A. The children and teacher say favorite nursery rhymes, such as "I Love Little Pussy" and "Simple Simon Met a Pieman," over and over again.

B. A sentence completion game, such as the one which follows, helps to emphasize this sentence structure. First, the teacher says, "I like_____." He then asks for suggestions with which to fill in the blank. The children then all repeat the sentence. Other suggestions might be: "The dog ate his _____" and "This is a big_____."

C. A rhythm game in dialogue form can provide practice in forming subject-verb-object sentences.

Teacher:	"Who can say, 'You are nice'?"
John:	"I can say, 'You are nice.' "
Teacher:	"John can say, 'You are nice.' Who can say, 'I like you?' "
Amy:	"I can say, 'I like you.' "

Topic

Subject-Verb Sentences

The dialogue forms illustrated above (expansion, prompting, and commenting) are the most important instructional activities for all syntactic structures in this chart.

Activities

A. The teacher shows pictures of people engaged in recognizable actions. He then discusses the pictures with the children.

Teacher (showing a picture of a boy crying):	"What is the boy doing?"
Child:	"Boy cry."
Teacher (showing a new picture):	"The lady?"
Child:	"The lady dances."

B. Use of Gotkin's, *Language Lotto Set, Actions and More Actions* (8).

90

CHART 6 *(Continued)*

Topic

-Ing on Verbs when Appropriate

Activities

A. As a child performs an action in the center of the circle, the others say, "Billy is sweeping;" Donny is crying;" etc.

B. Descriptions of actions or pictured events are used to elicit *-ing* forms.

Topic

Past Tense when Appropriate

Activities

A. Nursery rhymes, such as "As I Was Going to St. Ives" and "Old Mother Hubbard Went to the Cupboard," are said in unison.

B. A child performs an action before the group and sits down. A dialogue follows:

Teacher: "Amy ran. What did Amy do?"
Children: "Amy ran."

This procedure of action followed by dialogue continues until all of the children have had an opportunity to do an action.

C. At the close of the day, the teacher and children should review all of their activities in sequence.

Topic

Use of Copula

Activity

A. *Finger play.* For example, "Here is the church. Here is the steeple. Open it up and see all the people."

Topic

Negative Word in the Middle of a Sentence

Activities

A. Beginning development of the concepts *same* and *different* emerge when two identical groupings of objects or pictures are placed on the table and the following dialogue results:

CHART 6 *(Continued)*

Teacher:	"This pile of blocks is the same as this one."
Teacher (adding blocks to one pile):	"Are they the same now?"
Children:	"No."
Teacher:	"Right. They are not the same. Say that."
Children:	"They are not the same."

B. "In the foolishness game," the teacher names a well-known object incorrectly. The child responds, "You're silly. That's not a _____. It's a _____ ." The teacher then encourages the child to be the "silly one."

Topic

Wh-word Questions

Activities

A. Songs, nursery rhymes

    1. Songs, nursery rhymes.
    2. In the "question-answer game," each child asks where an object is. The game continues from child to child.

II. Period of Acquisition of Inflections and AUX

Topic

Plural Inflection

Activities

A. In a game activity with pictures of various common objects, the teacher says, "Here is a dog." He then shows a picture of one dog. He then says, "Now here is a picture of two of them. There are two what?"

Topic

Possession

Activity

A. In a game of possession, the following dialogue occurs:

Teacher:	"This is my shoe. It is mine."
Child:	"This is my dress. It is mine."
Teacher:	"This is your dress, It is yours."

CHART 6 *(Continued)*

Topic

Subject-Verb Agreement

Activity

A. Any group of pictures of like animals or people involved in action can be
be used. The following dialogue occurs.

> *Teacher:* "Look. The ladies dance. What about the clown?"
> *Children:* "The clown is laughing."
> *Teacher:* "Right. The clown laughs."

The conversation continues in this way until the children respond with the
present tense. If they do not inflect as adults do, the teacher expands their
comments without being negative.

Topic

Use of AUX Forms

Activity

A. Nursery rhymes, such as "Baa, Baa, Black Sheep," "Seesaw, Margery Daw,"
and "Jack Shall Have a New Master," are helpful instructional aids in
teaching the use of AUX forms.

Topic

Negatives Attached to *Do*

Activities

A. Negative games are played in unison by the children. For example, they
might say:

> "Look at the horse. He doesn't fly.
> Look at the cow. She doesn't bark.
> Look at the cat. He doesn't_____."

B. In the "I don't" game, the teacher asks the children to answer this question:
"I don't want to_____." One child answers, and all the children continue
with a statement like, "Johnny doesn't want to_____."

Topic

Subject-AUX Inversion in Yes/No Questions

CHART 6 *(Continued)*

Activity

A. Individual children ask for something to play with. The teacher and the other children repeat the question in unison and the child who asked the question gets a toy. This game continues until all of the children have toys.

Child:	"I want the Leggo."
Teacher (expanding):	"John asks, 'Can I have Leggo?' "
Children (in unison):	"Can John have Leggo?"
Teacher:	"John can have Leggo."

III. Final Preschool Period

Topic

Pronouns Used Appropriately

Activities

A. In a rhythm game, the following dialogue might occur.

Teacher:	"Listen...I am a teacher. Now you say, 'You are a teacher.' "
Children:	"You are a teacher."
Teacher:	"Now one of you say what you are."
Child:	"I am a boy."
Children:	"He is a boy."

B. Possessive games are also good tools in teaching children to use pronouns appropriately.

Topic

Use of Adjectives

Activities

A. The children expand simple sentences by using pictures and objects.

Teacher:	"What do you see here?"
Child:	"A dog."
Teacher:	"Yes. What does he look like?"
Child:	"He's a big dog."
Teacher:	"What else?"

B. On a particularly cold, snowy, rainy, or beautiful day, the teacher asks the children to tell what kind of day it is by using "weather words."

CHART 6 *(Continued)*

C. Unknown objects with distinctive tactile qualities are placed unseen by the children in a cardboard "magic box." Each child in a small group feels one object and says words which tell how the unseen object feels. The teacher reinforces good descriptive terms.

Topic

Future Tense

Activities

A. Children can play a game of "wishing" by saying, "When I grow up, I will be a_____" or "On Saturday, I will_____."

B. In projecting from picture stories, the teacher selects pictures which portray events and asks the children to say what will happen. He then expands their comments to include the future tense.

Topic

Prepositional Phrases

Activities

A. To play "object games," the teacher or a child places an object *in, on,* or *between* books on a table. Each child identifies an object and describes its location. The teacher expands where necessary and stresses the correct use of prepositions.

B. In playing a rhythm game, the teacher asks, "Where is the_____?" The children reply in unison, "It's on the_____."

C. Gotkin's *Language Lotto* set for prepositions can be used.

Topic

Wh-Word-Question-Subject-AUX Inversion

Activities

A. In playing a "who-what-where" game, the teacher shows the children that they are to ask *who* and *where* questions in the following situations:

Teacher: "I put the book somewhere."
Children: "Where did you put the book?"

Teacher: "I am thinking of a boy."
Children: "Who is the boy?"

CHART 6 *(Continued)*

B. Before a resource person visits, the teacher and children can develop interviewing skills by planning *who, what,* and *where* questions to ask.

Topic

Simple Sentence Conjunctions

Activities

A. Picture descriptions can help to develop the conjunction *and.* The teacher shows pictures to the children with more than one person or animal. The following dialogue occurs.

Teacher: "What's happening here?"
Child: "The boy is sitting down. The other boy is walking."

The teacher continues the dialogue in this fashion and expands by repeating the single sentences as a conjoined sentence.

B. Picture descriptions also help to develop use of the conjunction *but.* The same system is used here except the teacher starts off by saying, "The little boy is sitting but_____." He then asks who can continue with other pictures using *but.*

Topic

Relative Clause

Activities

A. Singing the song "This Is the House That Jack Built" is a good instructional device.

B. The teacher encourages sentence repetition by showing the children a picture and saying, "Here is a dog who is chasing a cat." The children repeat the sentence in unison.

In summary, a program which enhances syntactic growth will emphasize dialogue. Supplementary activities only reinforce structures acquired or being acquired. These activities and others can be written on cards and filed for easy reference.

Phonological Development

Program goals: The prekindergarten and kindergarten classrooms should provide children with opportunities to acquire the phonemes of the English language. Dialect variation and bilingual influences will affect the phonemes acquired and the ease of acquisition. Although in Chapter 3 it was stated that it may not be best to teach Black English-speaking children Standard English until they have learned to read with some ease, this statement should not be interpreted as if there should be no attention to phonological development during the preschool years. Instead, teachers should be sure that they are not producing language conflicts by expecting dialect speakers or Spanish-speaking children to produce sounds which are not common to their speech communities. Adults should be sure to provide clear models of major speech sounds. In addition, *expansion* should be used when children's articulation indicates specific substitutions of sounds. Sound games can also supplement the acquisition process but should not be thought of as the major means for learning phonemes. An important goal of the program is to assess children's phonological development, to monitor development of normal children, and to detect those with severe articulation problems.

Program content: Attention is focused on acquisition of consonant phonemes, although some work with rhyming words will involve vowel phonemes as well. This approach will gradually evolve into the prereading auditory discrimination instruction described in Chapter 7. See Chart 7 for this program.

Instructional techniques: As has already been indicated, the learning of language phonemes is normally accomplished inductively by the child. But since adults serve as models so that children can compare their sounds with those of mature speakers, careful modeling is an important part of the learning environment schools will want to produce. Since children will not acquire sounds they do not perceive, auditory perception will be needed for children who are not acquiring phonemes in the normal sequence and at the expected rate. As in the previous section of this chapter, the techniques suggested here are only the bare beginning of a total program. Teachers are encouraged to unleash their creative energy and to include additional techniques, such as those used in the Peabody Kits and other complete language curricula.

The program to promote phonological development will stress clear modeling of important consonant phonemes and phonemic patterns with vowel-plus-consonant combinations. Monitoring of growth continues and supplementary activities which promote active involvement in the sound "games" are introduced when the assessment procedures indicate readiness.

CHART 7

Illustrative Instructional Activities to Enhance Acquisition of Phonemes

I. New Sounds for Three and Four Year Olds: /n/, /t/, /g/, /m/, /b/, /d/, /w/, /h/, /p/, /k/, /f/, /l/

    A. *Expansion*

       1. *Child:*   "Give my my *doy*" (*toy*).
           Teacher: "Oh, you want your *toy?*" (Stress on initial phoneme)

    B. *Alliteration Fun*

       The teacher uses words that begin with the same initial phoneme in silly sentences just for fun; he does not expect the children to identify or to supply examples at first.

       The nasty neighbor took a nap.
       Find the funny fox, Fred.
       Peggy took a pill for her pain.
       The dizzy dog dragged a door to his den.
       Can the cook cook a cake?
       William wants to wear a winter coat.
       Go away, gorgeous goat.
       Make the mailman mail a message.
       Tilly, the tall tiger, took a test.
       Blow, blow the bubbles out of the box.
       How can the horse be hurt?

    C. *Unison Rhymes and Songs*

       Songs and rhymes can be chosen which include the phonemes which the children need to repeat.

    D. *Rhyming Words: From Reading of Books*

       Nursery rhymes should be read to the children regularly before the daily storytime. The children should be allowed to chime in when they are ready. The teacher can encourage this by hesitating just before a rhyming word at the end of a line is reached. Dr. Suess books are especially fun for this exercise as they have a great many rhyming words children love. (As is true with alliteration games, the teacher should not expect the children to supply examples or to identify rhymes unless they have had many prior listening experiences.)

    E. *Rhyming Words: In Oral Language*

       For fun, the teacher can produce rhyming words and ask the children to repeat them again with him. Sometimes, I just say words with particular emotional emphasis. For example, with a frightening face, one can say slowly: "Squishy, squashy, wishy, washy." Or, with a staccato rhythm,

CHART 7 *(Continued)*

one can say: "Stop, mop, flop." Or, with emphatic strength: "Make, cake, bake, stake." After doing this for a time, the teacher should hesitate for a moment at the end to see if the children respond with another example.

II. New Sounds for Five and Six Year Olds: /v/, /r/, /j/, /θ /, /δ/, /s/, /š/, /z/, /ž/, /ð /, /c/, /hw/.

    A. (This part of the program begins with the same content as that listed above, but now the children are also expected to supply examples and to identify the repeated sounds.) The teacher demonstrates the exercise in the following way: He has presented four words beginning with /t/, let us say, and then shows a chart with four pictured objects, one of which begins with /t/. He waits expectantly for the children to identify the pictured word that also begins with /t/. If no one does, he prompts. He continues this way until the children respond on their own without prompting.

    B. *Cut-out pictures* can be pasted on large charts which show objects which begin with the same consonant. The consonant grapheme is not identified until the children can supply easily an oral example or can find one in a small group. The children must have plenty of listening experience before they will be ready to identify words which *begin with the same sound.* Furthermore, they will need considerable experience in visual discrimination (discussed in the next section of this book) and ability to name letters before this skill is achieved.

    C. *Rhyming sequences* can be expanded until the children can supply examples.

    D. *Expansion* of sounds, particularly when substitutions are observed, can be continued. *Note should be made of the substitutions the children make* for ongoing assessment of development.

    E. *Alliteration Fun*

    The new sounds include some difficult ones which may not be evidenced in speech until later in the children's development. However, they should be presented often in situations where they are clear for discrimination. The following sentences stress alliteration where these sounds are emphasized:

    Vera was vexed with her velvet vest.
    Ronny, the real robot, ran the race.
    Just jingle the gems and the jewel thief will jack them away.
    There they go into the thick jungle.
    Little Lilly, the lost lamb, limped home at last.
    Sam, the silly seal, swam off with the cereal.

CHART 7 *(Continued)*

The short boy shined shoes in his shack.
Zelda, the zany giraffe, zipped past the zoo.
The churchmouse chewed on the checkered rug.
Where did the whale leave the wheel?

F. *Auditory Discrimination*

Once the children are familiar enough with the easier consonants and are able to supply words beginning with these more difficult consonants, they can begin preliminary auditory discrimination exercises. However, it is important that the first groups of words used illustrate only gross differences in the phonemes. A picture can be shown (for example, a picture of a *bee*) and then the teacher can say some other words. When he says the word which shows the named picture, the children raise their hands. An aide can be checking the children as they respond. The following words might be used on pictures: *bee, see, bee, fee; man, fan, nan, man; pad, pad, fad, jad.* Gradually, the teacher will come to want to include phonemic contrasts which are not so diverse. For example: *pail,* sail, whale, pail, bale; *shoe,* Sue, shoe, zoo; *back,* tack, jack, back, *run,* run, won, fun.

G. *Rhyming Fun*

When children have been observed to use many of the phonemes discussed above and have been able to discriminate initial sounds, the teacher can expect them to be able to participate in rhyming exercises. At this point, the teacher asks, "Who can hear the word that doesn't belong?" He then says words like those which follow:

> call, ball, tall, tree
> cat, bat, hat, horse
> boat, coat, goat, bear

When the children become familiar with the game, it can be expanded to include the following:

> hook, come, book, cook
> bear, page, chair, pear
> leg, house, louse, mouse
> luck, duck, now, truck
> pen, cake, rake, make
> clip, clock, lock, block
> train, tape, rain, chain

H. *More Rhyming*

Children ought to enjoy providing examples for nonsense rhymes. To encourage such rhymes, the teacher says: *"Fish, swish, dish.* We all know these words. Say them with me....Now everyone listen to these silly words: *mish, quish, lish.* Who can think of some more? *Mish, quish, lish....*Or *king, swing, ring...ding, fing ting...."*

Development of Language Meaning

Program goals: The most obvious need of the language-learning preschool child is the expansion of language in both the listening and speaking vocabularies. In the previous chapters, we have emphasized the importance of meaning expansion in the language program. Thus, planned instruction in vocabulary expansion ought to be extensive. It is also important that children obtain in-depth understanding of crucial concepts. Again, sample instructional procedures designed to achieve this goal are described in Chart 8.

In order to motivate interest in words, the teacher must be aware enough of individual progress which reinforces individual children's use of unusual and new words. Assessment procedures will include follow-up questioning of new concepts and of review words from earlier lessons. When children understand the terms, the teacher has important information with which to plan the reteaching efforts.

Program content: The items chosen for vocabulary *extension* will be determined partially by the activities of the classroom. Thus, field trips, visitors, classroom and home objects will serve as sources for words which will *extend* vocabulary. These and some basic concepts are studied and grouped to provide for *expansion of meaning.* Throughout this instruction in language, teachers will want to use new words in complete sentences because individual word meaning is strongly influenced by grammatical context.

Instructional techniques: In Chapter 1, the relationship between language and thought was explored. No matter what theory is used as a source, it is evident that conceptual understanding involves much more than unconscious absorption of data in the environment, although a rich environment is, of course, necessary for full cognitive growth. The point is that a rich environment alone is probably not sufficient for full cognitive growth. *Interactive involvement* with objects and materials of many sorts, with people, with actions, and even with pictures, contributes to cognitive development. The language aspect of this process involves the naming of objects, actions, events, etc., but it also involves the critical elements of description, classification of events, explanation, and communication. The instructional techniques used to promote conceptual understanding through language should be as varied as is possible. The physical environment provides one aspect of the instruction in terms of its richness, and the teacher provides opportunities to make understanding explicit by interaction with children as they spontaneously involve themselves in the objects and with the people around them.

The instructional procedures recommended in the next pages involve many levels of activity. First, the adults in the classroom will function as *namers,* thus providing children with the labels necessary to build their language and conceptions. Second, the teacher will plan classroom events which require additional labels. Third, teachers will plan activities which will encourage children to examine and extend their ability to classify objects. Descriptions and explanations will be offered by children. Prompting and probing by the teacher lead children toward desired conceptual understandings. It should be noted that different children in a classroom will be learning at different levels at one time. Additions to the activities presented is encouraged. Many of the activities described are familiar ones in preschool classrooms; the reader should note variations in *instructional method* described, since these variations from the common procedures are meant to emphasize meaning.

In summary, the instructional recommendations made in this chapter must be recognized as being only the bare beginnings of a preschool language program. Each teacher will expand these activities far beyond these suggestions if she inaugurates a real language program for her children. Further, it should be noted again that these activities are supportive of other language programs; they do not supplant any program now in use. Where no program in language development is available, the teacher can start from the suggestions given here. Whatever the classroom situation, the teacher will want to make some initial assessment of children's language facility in these three areas. The results of this assessment will indicate, particularly in the areas of syntax and phonology, the direction that instruction should take. Therefore, whether a complete program is available or the recommendations contained in this book will be the basis for instruction, the teacher must make rational decisions based on her children's needs and her understanding of language learning. In the area of language meaning, it is particularly critical that teachers plan for regular instruction for *all* children. Attention to new words, activities to promote groupings of concepts, and activities to help specify concepts and generalizations are critical to all later verbal learning the children encounter. This aspect of the language program should continue through the elementary years and should parallel with instruction in reading. In fact, although the two parts of this book separate language from reading, the two are not distinct in learning strategies, in instructional needs, or in chronological order. We turn now to discussion of reading but with the understanding that reading is a part of children's total language development.

CHART 8

Illustrative Instructional Activities in the Semantic Sphere

Acquisition of New Words

A. *Words are introduced as a result of Unit Study.* For example, as a result of a unit on the *circus*, the following words might be introduced: clown, all animals, ring, ringmaster, acrobat, parade. A unit on *farms* might introduce the following: farm animals, farmer, pasture, barn, garden, field, plant, bush, tree, vegetables, hay, grass, dairy, milk, milker, milking machine, bailer, truck, wagon, mowing machine, tractor. A unit on *cities* might introduce: apartment building, house, apartment, elevator, escalator, skyscraper, warehouse, store, library, school, park, playground, street, sidewalk, highway, superhighway, policeman, cop, fireman, nurse, conductor, bus, car, train, subway, helicopter.

This list obviously could go on forever. Some words can be introduced before a field trip. The teacher might do so in this manner: "I have pictures of some of the animals we will see at the zoo. Do you know the names of any of them?" (Only a few words are introduced at this time.) The teacher names the rest and then continues: "OK. Here is a way to remember. Ronny, pick up the smallest animal. What is it? Dick, pick up the next smallest. What is it?" The teacher continues and then arranges the picture in a different way, stressing the names of the animals each time. Since it is important for new words to be repeated in meaningful contexts, new and old terms used in a unit or in preparation for a field trip should be used in other activities.

B. *Common Clothing, Household Objects, Classroom Objects* should be named and practiced until all of the children can name these available objects. The teacher will want to vary the practice and the original naming lessons rather than engage in repetitive naming. He can do so in the following manner: "These are old words to us. See how fast you can name these objects. Remember, don't call out the name until I point to you." Or the teacher might say: "Each person in this circle will name an object placed in the middle. The next person cannot name the one the first person named. He has to find another one to name. See, if I point to *shoe* and say 'shoe,' she must say something else. Carol will name a *different* thing."

C. *Actions are sources for important words.* The teacher pretends to cry and then asks the children what he is doing. Other less obvious actions can be role-played and then named. (Thus, young children learn to abstract their language as they first act and then describe.)

D. *Descriptive terms are also important to incorporate into the language program.* The teacher, in talks with individuals and small groups of children, describes the toys and objects they are using. Later, he asks the children, when they review the day (and have further opportunity to abstract), what they played with, what it felt like, how hard it was, its color, its size, etc.

CHART 8 *(Continued)*

In another exercise, the children each touch an unusual object, such as an acorn squash. The teacher then asks:

"Is it soft or hard?"

"Is it smelly or not?"

"Is it smooth or rough?"

Thus, the teacher is providing descriptive terms. Later, he will want to ask more open questions so that the children can use their own repertoire of descriptive words.

E. *Magic Box, Tactile Terms.* The teacher places two objects with decisive characteristics in a Magic Box. The children feel one object and then the other and describe the difference. Characteristics, such as hot/cold, smooth/ rough, hard/soft, dry/moist, thin/fat, sharp/round, should be controlled so that only one distinctive characteristic is available at first. Some objects which contain only one distinctive feature are a warm moist sponge and a cold moist sponge, a rock and a sponge, a rock and a smooth sponge ball, a dry sponge and a moist sponge, a thin rock and a thick rock (or any other object with this feature distinction), a sharp-edged rock and a round rock. At first, the teacher will ask questions about the distinctive feature: "Is the object *hot* or *cold* (*smooth* or *rough*, etc.)?" Once these terms have been introduced, teacher naming of the descriptive feature should be reduced. When the children have learned to handle these singular distinctions, the teacher can place objects with more than one feature that is different in the Magic Box. For example, the following objects might be used: a warm moist sponge and a dry sponge, a rock and a moist round smooth sponge ball.

F. *Smell Box.* As an alternative to the Magic Box which helps to explore the sense of smell and associative descriptive terms is a "Smell Box" which the teacher can make.

G. *Relational Terms.* The crucial concepts which indicate differences on one dimension, such as on/off, small/big, beginning/end, more/less, same/ different, etc., should be used and emphasized in dialogue whenever possible during play. Specific attention to these terms comes at meaning levels beyond the naming level.

II. Classification: In-Depth Understanding of Words

At this level of meaning, expansion, all children are not expected to supply generic terms for the objects they name or even explanations for their groupings, although the teacher will use the category name often as the children develop a sense of the category membership. The major activity at this point is to build categorical *membership*.

CHART 8 *(Continued)*

A. *Weather Chart: Classification of Clothes.* (Commercially prepared flannel boards.) The teacher explains the problem to the students in the following way: "We're going to talk about what kind of things this boy would wear. We have to plan what's best to wear on different days. We'll put up lots of different things to wear and then decide." The teacher then holds up a cut-out *jacket.* "Is this something the boy might wear?" Then he holds up a cut-out kitchen pot. "Is this something the boy might wear?" He continues until he has a *few* pieces of clothing. Then, he proceeds to show a picture of a snowy day and the children choose the appropriate clothing for the boy to wear on such a day. Thus, the teacher has promoted both the broad classification — clothing — and also the development of the subgroup — warm clothing. Later, lessons will be designed to expand the large set of clothing items and other subsets of clothing for different weather conditions.

B. *Food Game.* Toy foods and nonfood objects are placed on a table with a small group of children. The problem is described: "You are planning a tea party for your friends. Let's get all the possible things you *might* want to have for them to eat or drink and then you can decide exactly which ones you will use." The same procedure which was used in introducing the weather chart will be used with the same objective in mind, the development of the general category as well as subgroups. (Plastic foods are quite inexpensive and can be found in plastic centerpieces in dime stores.)

C. *Clean-Up Time.* To set up the problem one should note that every classroom has an organization of materials problem; at least this is true in every classroom where there is lots of activity. Over many days, the teacher can collect unused pieces of string, yarn from art projects, small pieces of paper, plastic pieces from games, etc. in a large box. He then asks the children, in small groups, to sort the material so that it can be put away neatly. He places a collection of these materials in front of pairs or groups of children for them to sort. The children can then name each group if they are ready.

D. *Family Game.* The problem set-up might be expressed in the following way: "You have all been telling us about your mothers, your sisters and brothers, your cousins. Let's play a game so that we can get all of those people straight." The teacher has a set of pictures of people of different ages arranged on the edge of the chalkboard. "Now to begin with, this is the family of *Ben* so we'll put the picture of Ben on the chart (pocket chart)." He continues with the immediate family, noting that in some families, there is no father and that not all children have brothers and sisters. Drawing on the children's experiences, the teacher spends one brief discussion on the immediate family. Another time, he proceeds to the previous generations. The pictures of the people should be grouped finally on the pocket chart.

E. *Relational Terms.* The basic idea that children need in order to deal with

CHART 8 *(Continued)*

these important concepts is that relational terms are used to show *differences* in the same situation. For example, *more* and *fewer* both refer to quantity. "Here are some blocks in this box," the teacher says. "Look, I'm putting some blocks in this other box, too. Both have some blocks, but one box has *more* blocks than the other." This procedure should be done with questions, of course. Once the children have had experiences with the concept *more*, the idea of *fewer* is begun, first with naming and then with questioning. *Same/difference* should be referred to often in discourse. Similar pictures are displayed and the children assert that they are the *same*. The teacher then marks one and asks if they are the same. He uses the word different at first as an equivalent term for *not the same*.

Beginning/end should be used in reference to stories, time sequence at home (breakfast, lunch, supper) and, later, with the sounds in words. Many other relational words will be introduced as well.

F. *Prepositions*

Naming of prepositions occurs all the time. Explicit instruction is also advised. For example, books, boxes, and small objects can be placed strategically to meet certain prepositional use. Questions and games offer practice with these critical words. Gotkin's *Language Lotto Set, Prepositions (8)* can also be used.

III. *Use of Generic Terms: Generalizations Achieved*

At this level, children are expected to acquire generic terms and to be able to explain their grouping of objects. The main objective is for children to learn the common features that concepts in a category share. For example, children at this level will be able to use *animal* as the general term for the members of that set which they can name. In addition, they should be able to explain what all animals have that people, for example, do not have. To be successful in the following activities, children need to have developed in ways other than "verbally." These activities require cognitive skill usually found at the end of the preschool period and at the beginning of the primary grades. These activities ought to promote both cognitive and language development.

A. When words are introduced from the unit study, they should be presented so that critical features are emphasized. For example, with the unit *circus,* the people who work in the circus can be grouped — acrobats, trapeze artists, clowns, animal trainers. Another day, the teacher can remind the children of these words and they might choose pictures of each worker. Then, he might ask them to think up a name for these workers. The name can be discussed until the children use a word which refers to just these people and no others.

106

CHART 8 *(Continued)*

B. *Attention to Concept Attributes. Man* and *woman* — or any similar pair — can serve as the topic for this work. What is different between these two? What is alike? The children, in answering these questions, identify the critical attributes which separate the two and then identify the shared attributes.

C. *Common Object Groupings.* The teacher hides a number of pots and pans about the room and puts one pot on a central table. "Who can find another thing which is like this thing on the center table?" he asks. The objects are collected, named, and shared features identified.

D. *Classification by Obvious Attribute.* Two children are allowed to decide together how to group red and blue blocks. They are asked why they grouped the blocks as they did. They are then given some smaller red and blue blocks to be grouped with the others. (They might continue the two color groups or they might form subgroups of large and small red blocks and large and small blue blocks.) Again, the children are questioned simply. If they are skillful, the teacher might ask them if they can think of another way of grouping the objects besides the way they used.

E. *Communication of Classification.* Children who can group objects by maintaining a single attribute and who can alter the grouping when another feature is added can try to communicate a similar problem to another child. One child sits on either side of a table which has an opaque mask between them. Each child is told that they both have the same familiar objects — red and blue blocks, for example. One child is designated as the *teller* and the other as the *doer.* The teller is asked to group his objects and then to tell the doer how to do the same. Both children are then allowed to see the results of their work. Once they can communicate a familiar problem, the teacher can try a very simple, but unfamiliar one.

F. *Ten Questions (For Sophisticated Children).* The teacher explains that he is thinking of an object in the room. He gives a couple of broad hints at first and then directs the children to ask him questions. He explains that he will only answer "yes" and "no." (At first, practice is necessary to show the children what the teacher means.) When the children use up their ten questions, they lose the game. The teacher should explain after one trial that some questions are better than others, for if the children begin right by asking about specifics, they will use up their questions too quickly. The children will soon get the idea of questioning for groupings.

G. *Categorizing Books.* The teacher explains that a book that the class has just read is a story from the author's imagination; it didn't really happen. Can the children think of other such stories? Are there stories that tell things that really did happen? Are there stories that tell how to do something? Covers of books can be used to help the children recall books which have been read.

REFERENCES

1. Bereiter, C. E. "Academic Instruction and Preschool Children." In *Language Programs for the Disadvantaged,* edited by R. Corbin and M. Crosby. Champaign, Illinois: National Council of Teachers of English, 1965.

2. Bereiter, C. E., and Engelmann, S. *Teaching Disadvantaged Children in the Preschool.* Englewood Cliffs, New Jersey: Prentice-Hall, Inc., 1966.

3. Cazden, C. B. "Preschool Education: Early Language Development." In *Handbook on Formative and Summative Evaluation of Student Learning,* edited by B. S. Bloom; J. T. Hastings; and G. F. Madaus. New York: McGraw-Hill Book Company, 1971.

4. Day, D. E. "The Effects of Different Language Instruction on the Use of Attributes by Prekindergarten Disadvantaged Children." Paper presented at the meeting of the American Educational Research Association, February 1968, in Chicago.

5. Dilorenzo, L. T.; Salter, R. T.; and Brady, J. J. "Prekindergarten Programs for the Disadvantaged: A Third Year Report on an Evaluation Study." Albany: University of the State of New York, State Education Department, 1968.

6. Dunn, L. M., and Smith, J. O. *Peabody Language Development Kits.* Circle Pines, Minnesota: American Guidance Service, Inc., 1965.

7. Engelmann, S.; Osborn, J.; and Engelmann, T. *DISTAR Language, Preschool-Grade 2.* Chicago: Science Research Associates, Inc., 1965.

8. Gotkin, L. G. *Language Lotto* New York: Appleton-Centry-Crofts, 1966.

9. Hess, R. D., and Bear, R. M. *Early Education: Current Theory, Research, and Action.* Chicago: Aldine Publishing Co., 1968.

10. Parker, R. K.; Ambron, S.; Danielson, G. I.; Halbrook, M. C.; and Levine, J. A. *An Overview of Cognitive and Language Programs for Three-, Four-, and Five-year-Old Children.* Atlanta, Georgia: Southeastern Education Laboratory, 1970.

11. Parker, R. K., editor. *The Preschool in Action: Exploring Early Childhood Programs,* Boston: Allyn & Bacon, Inc., 1972.

PART II

Preparation for Reading and Beginning Reading

CHAPTER 6

Language and
Beginning Reading

Our main concern in this section is the preparation for and acquisition of reading. In addition, discussion of a number of relevant subtopics is needed to give an overview of beginning reading. One important subtopic is language. The role of language in reading is the major theme of the present chapter. Recent growth of interest in the role of language in reading has provided new theoretical understandings of reading not available a decade ago. This chapter presents a brief review of the reading process and the influence of language on reading. After this introduction to reading behavior, we turn, in Chapter 7, to reading readiness—preparation for reading. In this chapter, findings from research are applied to instructional matters. The question of early readers and programs promoting early reading is the topic of Chapter 8. Specific instructional suggestions for the teachers of beginning readers are presented in Chapter 9.

The questions to be answered in this chapter are: What understandings will help teachers of beginning readers to maximize young children's potential for reading acquisition? Are there natural language abilities in young children which will help them in reading acquisition? In what ways does language influence successful acquisition of reading? Does divergent dialect cause reading difficulty?

111

THE READING PROCESS

The following discussion of the *reading process* is intended to provide a conceptual framework with which to make judgments regarding the instructional needs and approaches to be used in helping beginners learn to read.

Reading process is a term used often in recent work in the field of reading. It is used to describe what people *do* as they read. To illustrate it, writers have developed reading models of what might be happening from initial perception of written symbols to the point where a meaningful message is understood. You will appreciate that, because few of the behaviors involved in reading are observable, there is great difficulty in uncovering what people do as they process written material. We can observe eye movements, of course, but we cannot observe the mental equipment used in translating the written symbols to meaning. There are data, however, which support recent formulations of the reading process, but before we turn to the description of the reading process and these data, we need to understand why it is necessary to discuss theoretical aspects of reading behavior when there is already available a wealth of information about instruction in reading.

Goodman's *(13)*, Smith's *(26)*, and other educators' thesis is that teachers of reading ought to understand the process of reading so that instruction is not simply a mindless application of instructional programs. The teacher of young children who are getting ready to read must understand what tasks are used in reading if he is to help children acquire reading ability. Knowledge of reading is as important to the teacher as is skill in following a series of outlined skills. However, Jenkinson *(17)* has pointed out that educators concerned with reading have been more preoccupied with reading *instruction* than with the total *process* of reading. As a result, there has been some misunderstanding of reading.

Reading has been researched more than any other field of education. The bulk of the research has studied topics such as the correct age to begin reading, testing of reading readiness and reading achievement, vocabulary counts, vocabulary control in textbooks, benefits accrued from phonics, differences in various phonic and linguistic programs, classroom organization for reading, material difficulty, and other related topics. Some of the work has been extremely important, of course, although there has not been enough corollary study of the reading act. As early as 1908, Huey *(16)* summarized research in this area. His interest in the visual aspects of reading still continues today *(8)*. Research on how comprehension occurs began as early as 1917 with Thorndike *(31)* and is also still under discussion today *(22)*. But it has been only in the last decade or so that these different streams of interest have been united in attempts to build models of reading. In addition, educators have now been joined in this pursuit by linguists and psychologists. As a result, the contemporary models reflect insights from generative grammar and from study of information processing.

Among the misunderstandings resulting from the preoccupation of the last few decades with reading instruction is the belief of some educators that reading is the summation of discrete skills which are acquired in a step-by-step fashion. Of course, any skills which can help children acquire accomplished reading behavior should be taught; the difficulty has come from an *overemphasis* on skills *(13)*. Another difficulty has occurred because concern with instructional matters has perpetuated the "debate" over whether reading is mainly word identification *(9)* or comprehension *(5)*. Actual reading involves both, but the definition of reading used in this book stresses comprehension. Of course, beginning readers are more concerned with methods for identifying words in order to attain comprehension than are skilled readers, but for both groups the goal is the same— comprehension. Therefore, while *instruction* varies considerably depending on the level of the reader, the result—understanding of a written message—will be the same whatever the level of attainment.

We will examine the reading behavior of skilled readers first and then turn to that of beginning readers. In this way, we can uncover the kinds of learning needed at the start of reading so that instruction will complement the reading process.

Skilled Readers

Before we turn to technical matters, I must ask you to engage in a little introspection with me. Recall your reaction to a novel you recently read and enjoyed. Were you lost in the material once you "got into it"? Do you remember being annoyed when practical matters called you away from your book? Were you reading so fast that you finished in very little time? Most of you probably will respond "yes" to these questions; however, a few adult readers do not read swiftly. Slow word-by-word readers are subvocalizing, unskilled readers. (By the way, some children as young as seven can be considered skilled in the sense we use here.) Skilled readers who are reading easy material clearly do not read every word. These readers bring a great deal of information to their reading. Some of the information comes from within themselves and some from their experiences with the world; much information comes from the building up of knowledge from the material being read—the plot movement, the characters, the setting, the mood, and style. As a result of outside knowledge, language ability, and familiarity with the material, readers build up expectations for the material which reduces the need to read every word. These expectations are treated like predictions to be tested. Readers swiftly sample the written material and use as little data as possible to verify predictions. Skilled reading behavior has been called a *psycholinguistic guessing game* by Goodman *(12)*. It involves a steady reduction of uncertainty *(26)* as the reader actively communicates with the author. In communicating through reading, according to Hochberg and Brooks *(15)*, the reader is not just *absorbing* the information present; he is also *supplying* information from a variety of sources.

Carroll *(4)* has described two levels of activity in skilled reading. The first level is perception of written symbols. For skilled readers, perception is immediate; most of us do not use spelling and phonic generalizations or analyze closely any of the words except unfamiliar or proper nouns in easy material. Even with uncommon long words, readers need attend only to the beginning and ending letters to recognize the word. The second level of reading is immediate grasp of the meaningful message contained in the material. Skilled readers use expectation and prediction, understanding of grammatical structure, semantic familiarity with language, knowledge of the world, and personal reaction to grasp the author's meaning. Goodman *(10)* uses the diagram to illustrate the behavior of the skilled reader.

The written symbols are instantly translated into meaning. What is important is that skilled readers communicate actively with the writer by matching their predictions with enough features to verify them in terms of their knowledge *(15)*, *(3)*. As Ruddell *(21)* has pointed out, a high interest level is essential to achieve this behavior.

Smith, Goodman, and Meredith *(25)* have stated that there are a number of cues available to skilled readers as they select needed data from a passage. These cues are either grammatical (syntactic) or semantic. The following exercise has been designed to explicate the cues used by skilled readers. [The idea is an expansion from the work of Smith, Goodman, and Meredith, *(25)*.] Try to figure out what *kinds of words* (verb, noun, pronoun, adverb, etc.) might fit into the blanks in the sentences of a connected story below.

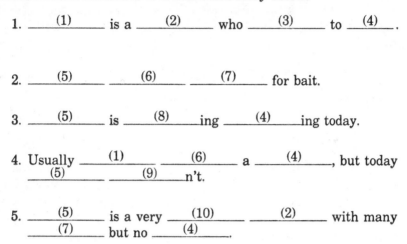

1. ___(1)___ is a ___(2)___ who ___(3)___ to ___(4)___.

2. ___(5)___ ___(6)___ ___(7)___ for bait.

3. ___(5)___ is ___(8)___ing ___(4)___ing today.

4. Usually ___(1)___ ___(6)___ a ___(4)___, but today ___(5)___ ___(9)___n't.

5. ___(5)___ is a very ___(10)___ ___(2)___ with many ___(7)___ but no ___(4)___.

At first, the preceding story seems to present a difficult problem; however, our knowledge of English syntax will come to our aid. First of all, the periods and commas define the sentences, and the function words indicate general word order. We realize that the answer for blank (1) must be filled with a noun or pronoun. Could any other kind of word fit there? Blank (2) is probably a complementary noun, while blank (3) must be a verb, and blank (4) an infinitive. Notice that blank (4) is repeated in the third, fourth, and fifth sentences. In the third sentence, blank (4) must be a verb to be combined with *-ing*. In the fourth and fifth sentences, blank (4) seems to be in noun position. Since there is the semantic clue *(bait)* provided, is it possible to guess what blank (4) is? Are there any other nouns? Could either of these nouns, blanks (5) and (7), be a pronoun? Which of the remaining blanks are in verb position? The answers to this last question are blanks (6), (8), and (9). Blank (10) lies between an adverbial marker *(very)* and blank (2), which we now know is a noun; blank (10) is probably a modifying word. Although this process obviously is contrived and is not representative of skilled reading behavior, it does show that word order and placement of function words provide cues to meaning. The function words play a very important part in assignment of word class membership in the exercise. For example, the *a's* in the first, fourth, and fifth sentences indicate that a noun must follow. Before the *-ing's* in the third sentence, verbs are expected. After *with many* in the fifth sentence, only a noun is possible. Although most of the information has been provided by syntax, the clue to meaning provided by *bait* also has been helpful.

Speakers of English have little difficulty in pronouncing the following nonsense words, since they follow the phonemic constraits of English.

swit	bogle	gom
sloapy	op	mo
flote	Tangot	skat
plage		

The only cues to meaning are that *Tangot* must be a proper noun and the *sloapy* may be an adjective since it resembles common English adjectives which end with a *y*. When these nonsense words are placed in the original sentences, the grammatical cues already discussed and the information now provided by the inflections in the story provide enough clues to unravel the story meaning.

   (1)   (2)   (3)   (4)
1. Tangot is a plag who goms to swit.

   (5) (6)   (7)
2. Op flotes bogles for bait.

      (8)
3. Op is skatting switting today.

              (9)
4. Usually Tangot flotes a swit, but today op mon't.

      (10)
5. Op is a very unsloapy plag with many bogles but no swit.*

The combination of word order cues, cues from the function words, and the addition of more inflections actually provides more grammatical information than is needed. It has already been established

---

*A hint: *Swit* means fish.

that *gom* is a verb from its position in the first sentence; the final *s* gives the additional data that it is a third person singular verb. While it may have already been apparent that *op* is a pronoun, on examination of *op* in the second, third, fourth, and fifth sentences, it is clear that *op* functions in subject position as does the name *Tangot* and therefore stands for *Tangot*. There are also more than enough clues to support the earlier speculation that *sloapy* is an adjective; word position, word shape, and its new form in combination with the prefix *un* all serve as clues. English is highly redundant in that the same grammatical knowledge comes from a variety of sources. Skilled readers make good use of the redundancy of language in their selection of information to fulfill predictions.

This exercise illustrates the syntactic cues available to readers. These cues reduce uncertainties and provide constraints so that they can be applied *(3)*. Skilled readers expect to receive a meaningful message from the material, and shared syntactic knowledge of the reader and writer provides the boundaries of sentence structure and individual words; semantic clues and knowledge are applied until the expectation of meaning is fulfilled.

The reader may well be asking how this searching and selection process occurs when the eyes appear to move swiftly and smoothly across a line. The visual aspects of reading actually complement skilled reading behavior. The eyes stop or fixate and it is only during fixation that written symbols are perceived. Skilled readers reading easy material only fixate two or three times to a line. Since only part of the total information (the letters of a word or words) is necessary for the brain to translate the symbols into meaning, the eyes somehow select just enough material in these few instantaneous fixations to provide the information needed. Hochberg *(14)* has suggested that peripheral vision supplies the brain with information about where the eyes should fixate next. Between fixations, the eyes move jerkily or with *saccadic* rhythm. Although most reading is in a left-to-right direction, regressions also occur. Sometimes, regressions are caused by lack of comprehension. Smith *(26)* has suggested that skilled readers also regress to pick up needed information. So what seem, on introspection, to be regular, smooth eye movements are actually jerky movements to the right with occasional movement to the left and few fixations. The brain does a great deal more work than the eyes. Instantaneous recognition and understanding, which is characteristic of skilled readers, is not possible for beginning readers. We turn now to beginning reading for clues to the growth of reading behavior and what teachers can do to facilitate that growth.

Beginning Readers

Ruddell *(21)* has raised an important question to be discussed in reference to beginning readers, whether the complex strategies used by skilled readers are possible for young children. Certainly, unpracticed readers cannot uncover quickly those cues available to the mature reader; however, prediction, search for data to confirm guesses, and understanding of the message are characteristic not only of skilled reading behavior but also of the process used in language acquisition. Therefore, it is not unreasonable to expect (but also not proven) that children can make use of the same strategies in order to become skilled readers that they use in the acquisition of language. In fact, the very similarity of process in reading and language may be an important tool for teachers to use to help children make sense of reading.

Before looking at the behavior of beginning readers, it is well to remember that some important concepts about reading *must* be learned before reading begins. First, children need to know what reading is—a meaningful communication between writer and reader. At all times, readers must expect to obtain meaning from the material they are reading. Children should understand that the markings on paper can be transformed into sensible oral language. Second, children need to know what a *word* is. Why should we expect an illiterate youngster to know that *going to* is made up of two words when he usually hears them combined into *gonna* as in "I'm gonna go to the store." (If you do not think you say it this way, turn to a member of your family and announce this intention as you normally would and listen to yourself.) Until children learn that the words used in speaking are used in writing and that the white spaces mark off words, they will not know what a word is. And even then they are in for some surprises when, for example, they learn that *gonna* is really *going to*. Further, as Smith *(26)* has pointed out, before children can read, they must be able to discriminate the essential features of written symbols. In the beginning, discrimination of features is necessary for differentiation of letters. In addition, children profit from discrimination of sounds and application to letters associated with the sounds. (Discrimination of these features is a major topic in Chapter 7.)

If you look at the diagram of skilled reading behavior on p. 114 and imagine that the steps are stretched out, you will begin to get a picture of the behavior of beginning readers. For example, beginning readers do not recognize words immediately, so the first box, graphic code, becomes quite complicated. More importantly, young readers cannot attach meaning to the words they figure out right away. At the beginning, children have to translate the words into oral language so that they can realize the meaning. Smith, Goodman and Meredith *(25)* diagram the process in this manner:

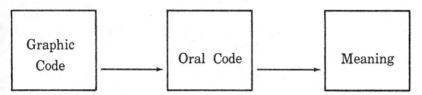

A hypothetical example may help you understand this reading process for less proficient readers. Imagine a youngster haltingly reading word-by-word the sentence, "A . . . long . . . came . . . a great . . . big . . . f . . . fish." After hesitating in this manner, the child repeats, "Oh, along came a great big fish!" The first time through, he is busy using all his memory and word attack skills to figure out the words. Then he reads again so that he hears the words together, and this time the sentence makes sense to him.

There are a number of additions which need to be made to the diagram so that it reflects major strategies possible for children to use in perceiving graphic symbols as words. When a child has sufficient visual memory of a word so that he recognizes it immediately on sight, he obviously does not need other word recognition devices. If a child fails in responding immediately to a word, the following techniques are usually taught and used to a greater or lesser extent.

Some children are trained to respond to the memory of a word's shape, its *configuration;* however, use of word shape cannot be very efficient for very long since many words have the same shape: *day, dog, top, boy,* etc. Another technique used to figure out words is use of some kind of sound/symbol correspondence. Some children are taught to blend sounds supposedly represented by the letters of a word together to make a word in the *synthetic phonics approach.* For example, in figuring out *dog,* a child will be taught to respond: /d /. . ./o/. . ./gə/. (The addition of a vowel phoneme with the consonants /d/ and /g/ is necessary since consonants cannot be sounded alone; this is a point which linguists use in arguing against this instructional approach). He will then "put the sounds together" like this: "d. . .o. . .g" and then say "dog" as he hears the word in his oral code. Other phonics and "linguistic" approaches use substitution of consonants in familiar spelling patterns. There are other combinations of sound/symbol approaches as well. Another technique children use is to find small words within larger ones. This technique is fine for *into (in, to)* but not very productive with *father (fat, her).* Finally, as Weber *(33)* has shown, young children, during even the beginning reading stages, do make use of context to recognize words. Thus, children either recognize the word from visual memory built up with practice, recognize the word because of its shape, sound the word out, use substitution with a familiar word, use contextual meaning, and/or use a combination of techniques. There are probably many other individual techniques children use, but some of these methods, such as memorizing which word on a flash card is the one with the smudge on the corner, may be unproductive.

The box labeled *Graphic Code* in the diagram represents the steps which may occur as beginning readers attempt to recognize words and which are illustrated in Figure 3.

Meaning is the final goal for beginning readers just as it is for skilled readers, although the path to meaning is a much more arduous one.

While it may appear that reading instruction has wormed its way into the discussion in spite of the distinction made earlier between reading process and instruction, actually what has been attempted is analysis of the possible methods available to children. Instructional techniques grow out of the obvious need for children to have strategies for attacking new words. The main point is that children often go through a prolonged series of steps to achieve meaning. If we compare this difficult process to the behavior of skilled readers, we can see that perhaps there is need to reanalyze beginning reading in light of skilled behavior.

Systematic use of syntactic and semantic cues should be emphasized from the start. If written material represents the living language of children, early concentration on the context of language as cue to words may shorten the procedure described in the Graphic Code box. In this way, children's rich store of syntactic knowledge is made explicit as an aid in reading. Further, from the beginning, children will develop the ability to test and to judge the efficacy of their testing. In practice, children will learn to ask *themselves* what word makes sense in a sentence context. They then combine questions about contextual meaning with questions about initial letters and associated sounds. Thus, they ask themselves what makes sense in the sentence that begins with a /t/, /d/, or whatever. As Goodman *(13)* has suggested, early use of the cues which skilled readers use may hasten youngster's development of skilled reading behavior.

A few studies have shown that children do, in fact, use grammatical context, even in the beginning. Goodman *(11)* has shown that children read words in context more accurately than in list form.

FIGURE 3

The Beginning Reader*

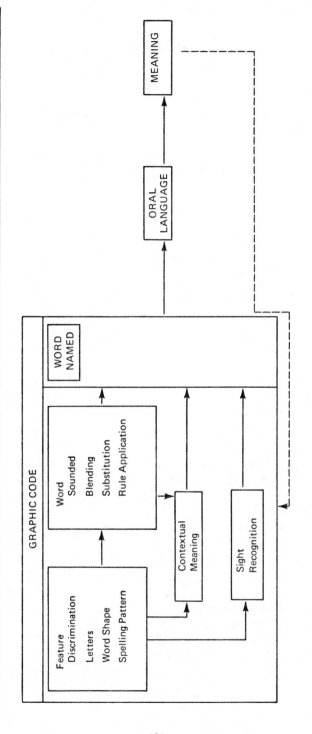

* Inspired by and changed from "Psycholinguistic Nature of the Reading Process," in *The Psycholinguistic Nature of the Reading Process*, ed. K. S. Goodman (Detroit: The Wayne State University Press, 1967), pp. 17 and 19. Copyright © 1967 by The Wayne State University Press. Reformulated by permission of the publisher and the author.

Ruddell's *(20)* study indicated that comprehension was greater for fourth graders if the written material closely resembled the language used in oral communication than if the written language was unlike oral language. Would familar syntax facilitate comprehension for children at the beginning stages of reading? Apparently, use of the language experience method, in which children's dictated stories are the material of instruction for the first stages in reading, has some long-range positive effect on reading *(28)* for white, middle-class children and for black, inner-city children *(23)*.

Weber's study *(33)* demonstrates that grammatical context is a major cue used by first-grade readers. Of all oral errors made by first graders during many months of study, 91 percent were grammatical according to the preceding context. In fact, the children studied *either* used context *or* responded to the graphic code of the word, and they used context far more often. Weber also taped her first-grade subjects' oral reading. She analyzed the spontaneous corrections and found that the better reader corrected only 27 percent of his errors which did not affect the grammaticality of the sentence but corrected 85 percent of the errors which adversely affected the grammaticality of the sentence. By contrast, poorer readers corrected only 58 percent of the errors which changed the sense of the sentence. This was the only discovered difference in the use of context between successful and unsuccessful first-grade readers; the difference indicates that teachers ought to help children to distinguish sentences which make sense from sentences which do not and to distinguish which words are sensible in a given context from those which are not. Weber has stated that first graders overuse context. I would suggest instead that the sensible reading behavior of beginners is healthy. For young children as well as for skilled readers, language is used actively to help readers communicate with writers.

When we compare the visual behavior of skilled with beginning readers, we find expected differences. Beginning readers fixate many more times in a line, sometimes more than once on a single word. Brown *(3)* has pointed out that the fixations do not last longer for young children but that the amount of information perceived is much less. And because of the need for beginning readers to recode material through the oral code, regressions necessary to attain comprehension are quite plentiful. Since habitual eye movements of left to right and the return sweep from the end of one line to the beginning of the next have not been established, children often lose their place in the material. Thus, the visual requirements for beginning readers are generally greater than for skilled readers, since it is necessary to obtain more information to achieve comprehension.

Beginning reading, when viewed in light of skilled reading behavior, appears to be more than a series of discrete skills. Children need to be helped in their development of behaviors which will be of lasting importance throughout their lives. And natural language ability is a force to be generated to this end. Youngsters who are ready to read have a store of sophisticated syntactic knowledge which Weber has shown they use to uncover unknown words; we must improve this use through instructional techniques. Once children understand that reading is a form of communication just as talking is and once they know that oral and written language is made up of *words* which convey meanings, they develop consistent expectations for meaningfulness in reading. Aided by instruction which probes into their knowledge of syntax, children ought to search for a match between their language knowledge and the written language. In this way, context becomes an important and acceptable technique for uncovering unknown words. Since context is one source for the searching behavior of skilled readers, beginning reading instruction should emphasize the syntactic cues adults use. Decoding skills stressing sound/symbol correspondences should be combined with contextual analysis to increase the accuracy of children's testing procedures. With experience, children will begin to realize the specific roles which word order, function words, and inflections play as cues to structure and meaning. Strategies to promote syntactic prediction and verification through meaning should be promoted, practiced, and reinforced. Chapter 9 combines specific suggestions for instruction in use of context with awareness of sound/symbol correspondence.

LANGUAGE INFLUENCES IN READING ACHIEVEMENT

Thus far, the discussion of reading and language has made claims about the *beginning reader* as though all children could be lumped together. But there are widespread differences in children's reading ability even at the beginning. Further, there are group differences in reading achievement, for such achievement is very closely related to socioeconomic status. A pertinent question to be answered is: How much does language variance affect beginning reading achievement? Unfortunately, there are so many variables which influence successful reading that it is basically impossible to answer this question at the present time.

Loban's *(18)* longitudinal study of children's language from kindergarten through the sixth grade examined the relationship between reading achievement and language. The measures of language included vocabulary and syntactic measures. In this study, highest and lowest scoring subjects were placed in high and low groups for analysis on the basis of language. From the end of the third grade through the sixth grade, those subjects who scored high in language also scored high in reading achievement. As additional evidence for the influence of language on reading, Stickland's *(30)* study showed that there was a positive relationship between sixth graders' oral language complexity (syntactic measure) and their reading achievement. Evidence of the relationship between early reading and language is provided by Brittain's *(2)* study which shows strong positive correlations between second graders' ability to use inflection and their scores on general reading achievement tests. In Chomsky's *(6)* study of five- to ten-year-old children's comprehension of certain specific syntactic structures, individual variation was found. Further analysis by Chomsky *(7)* indicated that those subjects who were advanced in syntactic knowledge also had had more reading exposure than those whose syntactic comprehension was slower.

Research indicates what one would suspect—that ability in language tends to influence reading achievement; however, much more work in the area is needed to discover what causes this language influence on reading. We need to know what kinds of variance exist in children's syntactic comprehension at the start of reading. Further, before we assume that it is language alone which is affecting reading ability, more study of the effect of literacy on language development is needed.

The influence of dialect on reading achievement is a better way to focus on the relationship between the language of lower-class black children and their reading achievement than to examine lacks in black children's language as was suggested in Chapter 3. Unfortunately, we are only beginning to find data on this question. However, Baratz *(1)* has found that fifth grade subjects process sentences in an oral sentence repetition imitation test in terms of their own dialect, whether it be Black English or Standard. She has suggested that the data support the idea that reading materials written in Black English are processed more easily by speakers of that dialect than are conventional materials. But since response to oral processing is not guaranteed to be duplicated in reading, her data do not directly support the need for dialect readers. Nevertheless, many sociolinguists share her view that dialect causes sufficient interference to warrant the development of materials written in dialect *(29)*, *(24)*. An excellent study by Melmud *(19)* investigated specific sources of dialect interference in auditory discrimination and in oral and silent reading. When lower-class white and black third-grade children were tested, it was found that Black English did not interfere with reading comprehension; however, there was interference caused by dialect at the level of auditory discrimination and oral production. Confusion at the phonological level due to words which are homonyms in Black English but which are distinguishable in Standard English (see Chapter 3) disappeared when contextual cues were available. Melmud's evidence and additional support from Venezky *(32)* suggest that Black English does not cause reading interference. Melmud and Venezky question the need for dialect readers. Since there are wide variations in Black English, it would be difficult to make a match between every individuals' dialect and materials. In addition, the problems of developing reading materials for all of the people who speak the following dialects make such a project an insurmountable chore: southern mountain, Spanish-American, American Indian, Hawaiian pidgin, and southern rural (black and white speakers). Further, the social implications of dialect-based readers in integrated schools are particularly unhealthy ones. We do not want to see teachers dividing children according to their dialect for reading instruction.

In contrast to the evidence from Melmud's study, earlier discussion in this chapter on beginning reading stressed the importance of children's being able to match their language with that of their reading materials. In order to resolve the apparent contradiction that has arisen, we must look again at language and how it operates. Previous discussion has shown that adults and children alike operate with a system of rules which underlie their production and understanding of language. The language we hear and the language we read is processed through this rule system. The second point to remember is that dialects vary little in basic rules from one another; most dialect variation is fairly superficial. Therefore, while Black English is distinguishable from forms of Standard English, the basic rules used for processing language are similar. Furthermore, television and radio present a general form of Standard English that is undoubtedly understood in varying degrees by all speakers of the language. Even though research suggests that it is not necessary to write materials for speakers of Black English with the specific characteristics of that dialect, if we are to make use of context for maximizing cues of syntax in learning reading, the language used for beginning reading should be childlike. There is evidence that language which represents the rule systems of children is more comprehensible than syntactic patterns that are unlike children's language *(20)*. For the first stages of reading, this means that dictated oral stories from the experiences of children will provide the written materials for reading instruction. This is the essence of the language experience approach *(27)*. Thus, whatever the dialect of the students, the language experience approach will provide sound representative language as well as evidence of the communicability of written language to children as they share their experiences and ideas with others. How this method is to be implemented with young children is described in the last chapter of this book.

In answer to the four questions raised at the start of the chapter, we can see that understanding of the role of language in reading is extremely important. Children's language ability can be put to use to facilitate the learning of reading in a number of ways. First of all, the strategies used in language acquisition appear to be similar to the strategies used by adult readers. Evidence exists that children naturally use syntactic patterns or context to comprehend reading material. Emphasis on prediction and verifying strategies in children's beginning reading behavior will encourage them to develop more efficiency in use of strategies of skilled reading behavior. Further, explicit instruction on how word order, function words, and inflections cue meaning is suggested as an important addition to traditional instruction in sound/symbol correspondence analysis. The specific influence of language abilities on success in reading is not completely known, but it appears that language facility and reading achievement are related. Instruction in vocabulary and oral language development during the preschool and elementary years will undoubtedly be important to reading growth. Some sociolinguists who study Black English and who are aware of the vast difference in reading achievement of inner-city poor black children and middle-class children suggest that dialect readers will alleviate some of this differential. However, specific studies of interference caused by dialect have not found support for the assumptions underlying dialect readers. Finally, since all children need to learn the communicability of the reading process as well as the meaningfulness contained in written messages, they will probably profit from use of the language experience approach at the beginning stage of reading.

REFERENCES

1. Baratz, J. C. "Teaching Reading in an Urban Negro School System." In *Teaching Black Children to Read,* edited by J. C. Baratz and R. Shuy. Washington, D.C.: Center for Applied Linguistics, 1969.

2. Brittain, M. "Inflectional Performance and Early Reading Achievement." *Reading Research Questerly* 6 (1970): 34–48.

3. Brown, R. "Psychology and Reading." In *Basic Studies on Reading,* edited by H. Levin and J. P. Williams. New York: Basic Books, Inc., 1970.

4. Carroll, J. P., "The Nature of the Reading Process." In *Individualizing Reading Instruction: A Reader,* edited by L. A. Harris and C. B. Smith. New York: Holt, Rinehart, & Winston, Inc., 1972.

5. Chall, J. *Learning to Read: The Great Debate.* New York: McGraw-Hill Book Company, 1967.

6. Chomsky, C. *The Acquisition of Syntax in Children from Five to Ten.* Cambridge: The M.I.T. Press, 1970.

7. _____. "Stages in Language Development and Reading Exposure." *Harvard Educational Review* 42 (1972): 1–33.

8. Crovitz, H. F., and Schiffman, H. R. "Visual Field and the Letter Span." *Journal of Experimental Psychology* 69 (1965): 218–23.

9. Fries, C. C. *Linguistics and Reading.* New York: Holt, Rinehart, & Winston, Inc., 1963.

10. Goodman, K. S. "A Communicative Theory of the Reading Curriculum." *Elementary English* 40 (1963): 290–98.

11. _____. "A Linguistic Study of Cues and Miscues in Reading." *Elementary English* 40 (1963): 639–743.

12. _____. "Reading: The Key Is in Children's Language." *The Reading Teacher* 25 (1972): 505–08.

13. _____. "Reading: A Psycholinguistic Guessing Game." *Journal of the Reading Specialist* 7 (1967): 126–35.

14. Hochberg, J. "Components of Literacy: Speculations and Exploratory Research." In *Basic Studies on Reading,* edited by H. Levin and J. P. Williams. New York, Basic Books, Inc., 1970.

15. Hochberg, J., and Brooks, V. "Reading as an Intentional Behavior." In *Individualizing Reading Instruction: A Reader,* edited by L. A. Harris and C. B. Smith. New York: Holt, Rinehart, & Winston, 1972.

16. Huey, E. B. *The Psychology and Pedagogy of Reading (1908).* Cambridge: The M.I.T. Press, 1968.

17. Jenkinson, M. D. "Sources of Knowledge for Theories of Reading." *Journal of Reading Behavior* 1 (1969): 11–29.

18. Loban, W. D. *The Language of Elementary School Children.* Champaign, Illinois: National Council of Teachers of English, Research Report No. 1, 1963.

19. Melmud, P. J. "Black English Phonology: The Question of Reading Interference." *Monographs of the Language-Behavior Research Laboratory.* Berkeley: University of California, 1971.

20. Ruddell, R. B. "The Effect of the Similarity of Oral and Written Patterns of Language Structure on Written Comprehension." *Elementary English* 42 (1965): 403–10.

21. _____. "Psycholinguistic Implications for a System of Communication Models." In *Theoretical Models and Processes of Reading,* edited by J. Singer and R. B. Ruddell. Newark, Delaware: International Reading Association, 1970.

22. Serwer, B. L. "Linguistic Support for a Method of Teaching Beginning Reading to Black Children." *Reading Research Quarterly* 5 (1969): 449–67.

23. Shuy, R. W. "Some Conditions for Developing Beginning Reading Materials for Ghetto Children." *Journal of Reading Behavior* 1 (1969): 33–43.

24. Simon, H. "Reading Comprehension: The Need for a New Perspective." *Reading Research Quarterly* 7 (1971): 338–63.

25. Smith, E. B.; Goodman, K. S.; and Meredith, R. *Language and Thinking in the Elementary School.* New York: Holt, Rinehart, & Winston, Inc., 1970.

26. Smith, F. *Understanding Reading: A Psycholinguistic Analysis of Reading and Learning to Read.* New York: Holt, Rinehart, & Winston, Inc., 1971.

27. Stauffer, R. G. *The Language Experience Approach to the Teaching of Reading.* New York: Harper & Row, Publishers, 1970.

28. Stauffer, R. G., and Hammond, W. D. "The Effectiveness of Language Arts and Basic Reader Approaches to First-Grade Reading Instruction Extended into Third Grade." *Reading Research Quarterly* 5 (1969): 468–99.

29. Stewart, W. "On the Use of Negro Dialect in the Teaching of Reading." In *Teaching Black Children to Read,* edited by J. C. Baratz and R. Shuy. Washington, D.C.: Center for Applied Linguistics, 1969.

30. Strickland, R. G. "The Language of Elementary School Children: Its Relationship to the Language of Reading Textbooks and the Quality of Reading of Selected Children." *Bulletin of the School of Education, Indiana University* (1962): 1–131.

31. Thorndike, E. L. "Reading as Reasoning: A Study of Mistakes in Paragraph Reading." *Journal of Educational Psychology* 8 (1917): 323–32.

32. Venezky, R. L. "Non-Standard Dialect and Reading." *Elementary English* 47 (1970): 334–45.

33. Weber, R. M. "First Graders' Use of Grammatical Context in Reading." In *Basic Studies in Reading,* edited by H. Levin and J. P. Williams. New York: Basic Books, Inc., 1970.

CHAPTER 7

Reading Readiness: Preparation for Reading

All of the language and cognitive abilities acquired during the first years of life help prepare children for reading. The previous chapters have analyzed language growth and its relationship with reading. We turn now to instructional procedures which promote the learning of certain skills that have been found to be helpful in the beginning of reading.

Instruction in specific prereading skills traditionally takes place at the end of the kindergarten year and/or at the beginning of first grade in a period of instruction called reading readiness. In this chapter, various questions concerning preparation for reading are discussed. The first section of the chapter considers briefly the question of the best time to begin reading instruction, while the second section provides an overview of important skills needed for preparation in reading, and instructional activities are suggested.

Before turning to the first question, however, review of some background material will help to put some of our present concerns in an objective light. Attitudes toward instruction in reading and reading readiness during kindergarten vary considerably. Occasionally, educators overuse one theory without full awareness of the value of other approaches or of research which has direct implications for the classroom. Therefore, knowledge of various theories and related classroom approaches ought to facilitate objectivity, an important goal for teachers.

One important trend in early childhood education dates back to work begun in the 1930s. During this period, Gesell *(19)* examined in detail the motor, cognitive, and social development of children from birth through adolescence. From the observational records of children seen at various chronologically determined intervals, the researchers searched for common growth patterns which they then combined into descriptions of typical behavior of children at each interval. As a result of this study, childhood was described as a period of natural movement from one discernible stage to another. Children would be "ready" to learn new skills when genetically determined growth developments allowed new learning to take place, not when they had mastered prerequisites. Gesell's work influenced educators for many years and is still considered important; however, researchers and educators alike accepted this approach, particularly in reference to reading readiness, more than empirical study and classroom experience justified.

During the 1950s—especially at the end of the decade when the launch of Sputnik redirected their attention—educators began to look more closely at environmental influences on learning. As a result, educators and psychologists outlined alternate approaches to curricula matters during the late 1950s and 1960s. For example, Bruner *(7)* stated that by closely analyzing the conceptual framework of a field, it was possible to find hierarchically arranged material which could be adapted appropriately to the learning level of all students. Learning experiences then would be based on the essential features of the content; each new concept learned would prepare the student for more and more complex learning. In other words, it was thought that the material could be suited to any level and taught so that children would be prepared to move into the next level.

The assumption behind the curricular developments of the 1960s was that environmental factors played a prominent role in the education of children. While the development of the "new curricula" of the 1960s was applied more successfully to mathematics and sciences than to reading and reading readiness, the shift in approach did influence reading readiness. As a result, some educators now advise teachers that, although maturation is important, we must carefully prepare children to read instead of just waiting for a child to be ready to read (11), (28). On the other hand, Furth *(15)* recently stated that reading instruction should be delayed for all children.

Thus, the area is replete with opposing instructional theories. Often, the advocates of one approach hold on to it with emotional as well as intellectual commitment. The influences of these various approaches can be seen in the reaction to research, teacher attitude, and teacher instruction described in the following pages.

READING READINESS DESCRIBED

The term *reading readiness* was first used in the 1920s to describe the instructional period which prepared children for reading. From this period until the end of the 1950s, research studies were undertaken to find answers to the questions: When is the best time to begin reading instruction? How can an individual's readiness be determined? Although it may appear that the following discussion applies only to instruction which occurs *before formal reading instruction,* many of the readiness skills described here continue to be useful to children *after they have begun to read.* In fact, it is often difficult to know whether training in the association of sounds and symbols, for example, is a readiness or a beginning reading activity. Thus, readiness instruction begins well before reading and continues afterwards.

Determination of Children's Readiness for Reading

From the discussion of the diagnostic nature of the instructional program recommended in Chapter 4, it should be clear that we will focus on techniques which judge an individual's readiness through informal assessment procedures. However, educators in the 1920s, 1930s, and later used standard methods to determine achievement levels of groups of children. During the '20s, large-scale testing of school achievement and of intelligence uncovered reading problems among American children. Since the thesis which stressed actual ripening within the child influenced how these test findings were interpreted, it was thought that failure to read well in first grade must be due to the imposition of reading instruction before children were ready (*24*).

In order to prevent further reading problems, researchers believed that they should find a Mental Age (MA) at which reading would be most effectively taught. Morphett and Washburne's (*29*) 1931 study supplied an answer, but not conclusive evidence, to this question. Based on the first-grade reading achievement in one school system taught with one approach, this study found that those children who had achieved a mental age of 6.6 were more successful than those whose MA was below this point. Morphett and Washburne stated that teachers should wait until children had a mental age of 6.6 before beginning reading instruction. This one study influenced reading instruction more than was warranted, particularly since Gates *(16)* reported that postponing reading for all children without a mental age of 6.6 was not necessary. In a later study, the effectiveness of the teacher and the method he used was found to be far more crucial to reading success than was a 6.6 MA *(17)*. The Gates and Bond studies were virtually ignored though, while textbooks *(19)*, *(22)* continued to inform readers that reading instruction should be delayed until children achieved a mental age of 6.6. Fortunately, educators today are quite willing to accept the idea that teacher skill does matter in developing successful beginning readers. In fact Bond and Dykstra *(4)* recently found that instruction is a major factor determining first-grade reading success.

Reading Readiness Tests

An important development begun in the 1930s and continued later was the production of standardized tests used to gauge reading readiness. The *Lee-Clark Reading Readiness Test* (California Test Bureau), the *Monroe Reading Aptitude Tests* (Houghton Mifflin), and the *Gates Reading Readiness Tests* (Teachers' College) all originally date from the '30s era but have been revised in recent years. The popular *Metropolitan Readiness Test* (Harcourt, Brace, Jovanovich) was developed in 1950. These tests are given at the end of kindergarten or the beginning of first grade. Usually they are group paper-and-pencil tests, although the Gates and Monroe Tests have individually administered subtests of visual discrimination ability (the ability to differentiate among pictures, shapes, letters, and words), and oral comprehension as well as a subtest on auditory discrimination ability (ability to hear differences in the sounds of words). The Monroe Test also includes subtests of auditory blending, motor coordination, visual memory, and maze tracing.

Since readiness tests require paper-and-pencil responses, they pose problems for young children who have not had practice in following complex directions on paper. Further, they require that children understand the distinction between *same* and *different* so that they can *circle the the one which is the same* or *find the one that is different*. Venezky, Calfee, and Chapman *(39)* have suggested that understanding of *same* and *different* is by no means secure at age five, so when, for example, children are asked to draw a circle around the pictures, shapes, letters, or words in a row which are the same as a stimulus presented to the left, they may not be able to understand the directions. Thus, performance on tests of this sort may be a better indication of ability to comprehend complex directions than ability in the skills presumably being tested.

Research data on the effectiveness of readiness tests to predict reading success have not been very encouraging. Gates, Bond, and Russell *(18)* have pointed out that only if the tests represent the method of instruction to be used in teaching reading are they useful diagnostic instruments. Comparisons of readiness tests with teachers' judgments indicate that teachers are at least as good as readiness tests in predicting which children will have success in beginning reading. Kottmeyer *(26)* compared teachers' ability to predict with that of intelligence tests and readiness tests and found that teachers' judgments were not significantly improved when the scores from intelligence and readiness tests were added. Those teachers who had been teaching for ten years or more were better predictors of reading success than were less experienced teachers. Annesley, *et al. (1)* and Koppman and Lapray *(25)* also have reported that teacher assessment of children's probable success in reading is as good a predictor as is a readiness test. Spache and Spache *(35)* have stated that helping teachers judge children's competency in language and readiness through the use of informal techniques of assessment will increase determination of readiness. That training of this sort is beneficial also has been shown by Myklebust *(31)* who found that classroom teachers trained in the use of a simple checklist instrument could successfully find children who needed further diagnosis for possible learning disabilities.

While later discussion will analyze major areas of skill to be included in readiness assessment procedures, some general comments are applicable at this point. For example, Spache and Spache *(35)* recommend use of an informal listening comprehension test to help determine reading preparation. Boney and Lynch *(5)* and Durrell *(12)* have shown that ability to retain words after initial presentation indicates readiness for reading. In addition, as Farr *(14)* has stated, oral language facility—both ability to retell a story and the ability to describe an event—should be examined. Further, Durrell *(12)* has shown that when children can name letters they are able to engage in successful beginning reading. A number of reading-like prereading skills—naming of letters, recall of visually presented words, ability to comprehend stories heard, ability to tell stories, and auditory and visual discrimination skill—are part of the assessment procedures recommended for classroom use.

The Effect of Training on Readiness

The question of whether readiness training in kindergarten or first grade really helps children learn to read can be answered affirmatively by the available data. In fact, Teegarden *(37)* and Pratt *(33)* have shown that attendance at kindergarten alone is helpful for first-grade reading, whether a planned readiness program has been included or not. However, Morrison and Harris *(30)* have shown that inner-city children who did not attend kindergarten are equal to their classmates who attended kindergarten in reading by third grade. However, if the language experience method was used, a residual gain for the kindergarten children remained in third grade. Blakely and Shadle *(3)* and Ploghoft *(32)* have also shown the beneficial effects of planned readiness programs.

One particular question of importance is whether delaying reading instruction for children deemed "not ready" will improve their chances for reading success in the long run. Bradley *(6)* delayed instruction up to a half-year for some children and studied the effects in comparison to a control group. Her conclusions, based on tests made at the start of third grade, were that the children whose instruction had been delayed were better readers. Spache *et al. (36)*, using a far better research design, found that at the end of first grade, the children in the experimental groups where reading instruction had been delayed if warranted were not significantly superior to the children of the control groups who were all taught reading at the beginning of first grade. The experimental black children in this study, though, did show gains over the controls as a result of delayed reading and extended readiness. This study indicates that some children who do not receive readiness experiences before first grade profit by provision of further readiness before beginning readiness instruction.

In nursery school and kindergarten classrooms, a planned readiness program should be provided for those children who need it. It is surprising that not all kindergartens provide a regular readiness program. In a survey by LaConte *(27)*, 57.3 percent of the kindergarten teachers who responded disagreed with the statement that reading had no place in kindergarten classrooms. Nonetheless, planned instruction was found to be minimal. Teachers did provide instruction in naming letters, writing words, word discrimination, and reading words, but they did so only occasionally.

LaConte also found that teachers depend on popular reading readiness workbooks which accompany basal reader sets far more than they did a decade earlier. Allen [this work was reported by Spache and Spache *(35)*] found that these workbooks are quite similar; they include "reading" of pictures, some visual discrimination exercises, and some auditory discrimination exercises. Although Ploghoft *(32)* found no difference in the preparation of children taught with and without workbooks, Blakeley and Shadle's *(3)* study indicates that teacher-planned activities and language experience both are superior to workbooks in helping children get ready to read. Hillerich *(23)* also found language experience better as readiness training than workbooks. Although a workbook program was better than none, it appears that use of workbooks should be supplemented with other teacher-planned activities.

Governmental agencies have recently become interested in early childhood education and have funded many programs. The first such program was, of course, Head Start. Head Start was not designed specifically for readiness training, but the findings of the Westinghouse-Ohio study of 1970 indicate that full-year Head Start children do approach the national norms on the Metropolitan Readiness Test *(34)*.

READING READINESS SKILLS

For many years, educators have debated the value of various kinds of reading readiness skills. The most important factors which appear from many studies to be related to reading success are those in the auditory sphere, in the visual sphere, and in language and listening. *Auditory discrimination* is the ability of young children to hear significant phonemes in words. For example, if children can tell that *bat* in the sequence *bet, bat, bet, bet* is different when the words in the sequence are spoken, they can discriminate auditorily the vowel phonemes. Other auditory skills support the development of auditory discrimination. *Visual discrimination* is the ability to distinguish one visual form from another. When children can tell which letter is different from *b* in the sequence, *d,b,b,* they can visually discriminate *b* and *d*. We will look at a number of readiness skills and at how each relates with reading success, how the skills are used in beginning reading, and what the instructional procedures are for these skills.

For each of the areas of prereading training described below, there are suggested assessment items and instructional activities. Assessment is needed to measure readiness for reading, to plan for specific instructional needs, and to test attainment of instructional objectives. Whenever possible, there has been an attempt to include assessment items and instructional activities which are conducive to group testing and teaching. There also has been an effort to include activities for informal instruction so that classroom variety and individual needs can be met in an open yet task-oriented atmosphere. Teachers should expand the assessment items and activities in ways that suit various classroom situations.

Auditory Skills

It is important for teachers to discover if auditory impairment will hinder reading. Acuity, the ability to hear varying pitch (high and low), and loudness may affect children's ability to discriminate, although this is not necessarily true. Spache and Spache *(35)* recommend that teachers test children's *discrimination* of sounds and use the results of the test as determinants of possible reading difficulty. Some children learn to read quite easily in spite of acuity problems; others have slight acuity difficulties which cause considerable confusion. Unusual difficulty in auditory discrimination may indicate need for referral for more testing for possible auditory impairment.

There are different methods for testing auditory discrimination. The *Wepman Auditory Discrimination Test (38)* presents pairs of words; some of these words have different phonemes, while others are identical. The child responds *same* or *different* after presentation of each pair. Another test is the Goldman, Fristoe, Woodcock *Test of Auditory Discrimination (21)* which requires that the child associate a spoken word with the correct picture from a group of four pictures "with names differing by only one phoneme."[1]

Auditory discrimination subtests in reading readiness tests have been analyzed by Dykstra *(13)*. He found that in seven such tests, there were six ways of testing discrimination and that most of the subtests were very poor predictors of reading success. However, if the test measured the ability to hear the beginning sound, then the test could predict reading achievement to some extent. IQ tests were better predictors than all the auditory discrimination tests though. Dykstra's study may indicate that auditory discrimination ability is not a very important predictive factor even though other studies have shown a strong positive relationship between high auditory

---

[1] R. Goldman; R. Fristoe; and R. W. Woodcock, *Test of Auditory Discrimination* (Circle Pines, Minnesota: American Guidance Service, Inc., 1970), p. 6.

discrimination and reading success. For example, the Spache, *et al.* *(36)* study shows auditory discrimination to be a very good predictor of reading success.

The importance of auditory skill to reading ultimately depends on the amount of dependence on sound/symbol correspondences that is present as an aid to word recognition in the beginning reading program. Duggins *(10)* has shown that auditory discrimination training at the start of first grade resulted in superior reading achievement. If a school stresses phonics or a linguistic approach during the first and second grades, strong auditory discrimination is probably important. On the other hand, if visual techniques are stressed in the beginning reading program, auditory discrimination will be of lesser importance. Chall's *(8)* analysis of studies which examined the effect of various kinds of phonics programs has shown that a heavy phonics program has a salutory effect on reading achievement. And editions of basal reader sets published since 1968 reflect a greater amount of sound/symbol correspondence instruction than did earlier basals. Partly because of these developments toward increased use of sound-/symbol correspondences in beginning reading, it is important to include a strong auditory discrimination component in the readiness program.

Before discussing auditory discrimination skills, we will analyze an auditory discrimination lesson to find what kinds of knowledge children need to perform well. Imagine a teacher working with the initial consonant sound /b/. He may ask children to listen to a group of words which begin with /b/—*big, bat,* and *boy*—and then ask them for other words which begin the same way. In order to respond, they need to be able to *isolate the beginning sound of a word* and then find another /b/ beginning word in their own vocabularies. The teacher may then ask children to tell whether or not the words in the list *bat, top, boat, dog* begin like *big.* The children need to be able to isolate a new sound from the one presented and *compare the two initial sounds* to tell if they are the *same or different.*

Other lessons will concentrate on rhyming words or the end sounds of words. For example, the teacher may ask children to tell what is similar about these words: *fat, pat, mat.* They must then be able to *hear the end component of words* to be able to provide such other rhyming words as *sat, Nat.* Again, children may be asked to tell which of the following words rhyme with the presented words: *bat, song, flat.* Accomplishing this task requires that the end components be *compared and likenesses and differences identified.*

Later, these exercises are combined with the visual presentation of the letters and words so that sound and sight correspondences are built up. Depending upon the method used, additional auditory perception may be needed. For example, many phonics programs require *blending of separate sounds together,* while other programs require *substitution of one sound* for another in a known word to make a new word. Basic concepts and skills needed for auditory discrimination training are listed below. After each skill, activities to use to assess achievement and to teach each skill are described.

I. The following skills should be developed before discrimination of sounds:

    A. *Identification of gross sounds* (door slamming, car motor, footsteps).

      — Children close their eyes and "guess" what is making a sound as a door is slammed, water is turned on, a ball is bounced on the floor.

      — In connection with learning to control their voices according to the situation, small groups learn to identify *loud* and *soft* voices. The children can then take turns using either a loud or soft voice while the others close their eyes and guess who is speaking.

    B. *Identification of less obvious sounds.*

      — The children are asked to identify common animal sounds.

      — The children can distinguish whether a series of musical sounds is going up or down.

II. Children must have an awareness that words are made up of distinguishable sounds.

    A. *Knowledge that beginning sounds are the first ones heard as one says a word.*

    B. *Knowledge that ending sounds come last as one says a word.*

      — In order for phonics training to be of service to children while they are learning to read, they must be able to

perceive the *time sequence of sounds in words* and later
to associate time with *placement of letters in left-to-right
direction.* Assessment of this ability must be made individually. The teacher *slowly* pronounces words with distinct emphasis on initial and final single consonants *(pat,
cap, pan).* After each word, the teacher asks the child to
say the sound that came first; then he asks for the sound
that came last. If the child repeats the word himself, he
will find it easier to respond. Further practice of this sort
in groups will help children to develop a sense of sound
order.

— For those children who are unable to hear the sequence
of sounds in words, sound blending exercises are warranted. In these exercises, the teacher illustrates how *p
... a ... t* becomes *pat.* He and the children practice
together. The sequence concept develops as the process is
often repeated.

III. Children should learn that many different words have the same
beginning sounds and that many different words have the same
ending sounds.

A. *Knowledge that different words have the same beginning
sounds.*

B. *Knowledge that different words have the same ending
sounds.*

— At this level, it is important that children understand
that the same sounds are used over and over again. Although later experiences will present phonemes system-
atically for discrimination, brief informal attention to
this concept is very appropriate at this point. The teacher
can slowly pronounce B ... o ... b ... b ... y with an
emphasis on initial /b/ and ask, "Does anyone else's
name begin like this? Listen, *B ... obby ... Bill.*"

— Awareness of similarity in ending sounds comes from
repetition of rhyming words from poems *(swish, dish,
fish).* The teacher can ask if the words are alike in the
first sounds or in the ending sounds.

— The rhyming concept is built up when children have
many experiences *hearing poems.*

IV. Specific skills of discrimination.

A. *Ability to supply new words that begin with a certain presented sound in words.*

— A recommended instructional order is: /p/ in *pick,* /s/ in *sick,* /m/ in *met,* /t/ in *top,* /f/ in *fat,* /g/ in *go,* /b/ in *boy,* /l/ in *lot,* /n/ in *not,* /d/ in *dot,* /j/ in *joy,* /k/ in *cat,* /v/ in *vat,* /r/ in *rat,* /w/ in *way,* /h/ in *hat,* /z/ in *zoo,* /y/ in *yes,* /kw/ in *queen,* /ks/ in *box,* /š/ in *shut,* /θ/ and /ð/ in *the* and *this,* /č/ in *church.* The sounds which are most distinguishable should be presented first and also kept separately from sounds which are very close like /m/ and /n/.

— At this point, children should supply like examples in a systematic way. Children's names are an appropriate place to begin with this exercise. The teacher can hold up a ball, ask for it to be named, and then ask everyone whose name begins in the same way *ball* does to stand up. He can refer later to the: *ball* boys and girls (Bobby, Bill, and Betty) and the *sock* boys and girls (Sammy, Sally, and Sue).

— Alliteration games are fun (see activities listed in Chapter 5).

— Classification and initial phoneme production is appropriate for this activity. The teacher can say at lunch, "Look we have cookies for lunch. What other foods begin like *cookie?*" (The children might answer with *cake, candy* etc.)

B. *Identification of words which do not begin in the same way as a presented group.*

— Assessment of phoneme discrimination can be made formally with the standardized tests described earlier. If the standardized tests are not available though, teachers can make their own assessment instruments. The teacher should make sure that children understand the concept of *same* and *different* by using practice examples before testing for discrimination.

— Testing children on their ability to discriminate will identify those who need more instruction. Some good commercial materials for these children are: *Building Pre-Reading Skills* (Waltham, Massachusetts: Ginn and Co.), *Sounds for Young Readers Series* (Baldwin, New York: Educational Activities, Inc.), *Auditory and Visual Discrimination* (Plainwell, Michigan: Richards Research Associates, Inc.), and *Elementary Phonics Program* (Chicago: Bell & Howell Co.).

— Learning activities designed for very young children are best done with objects. The teacher places a set of objects before a small group of children (a dollhouse *bed*, a *cup*, a *sock*, a toy *goat*, a *rock*, a *mitten*, etc.) and asks the children to find something that begins like *boy*, for example. After each choice, the teacher and children say the stimulus word and name of the object together slowly to check if the choice is correct.

C. *Discrimination of medial vowels.*

— To develop ability to discriminate medial vowels, the teacher places objects (or pictures if the children are older) before the children in pairs to correspond to such words as these:

Dick (a toy boy)	*dock*
pill	*pal* (a toy child)
ball	*bell*
cup	*cop*
pin	*pen*
cap	*cop*
cap	*cup*
bin	*bun*
knot	*net*
bell	*bull*

The teacher should have named these objects previously; he then names one word of the pair and the child selects that object. The teacher and children then repeat the stimulus and named object to check if the pair is, indeed, the same.

— Soon after discrimination of common phonemes is established, association with letter names begins.

D. *Ability to supply new words which rhyme with presented ones.*

— Initial assessment can be made with quite young children since many will have a sense of rhyme from previous experiences. Rather than depending on children's understanding of the word *rhyme,* however, the teacher can simply name a few rhyming words (e.g., *cat, hat, bat*) and then hesitate. If there is no response, he might say, "Can you give me a word which belongs here? With *hat, pat, fat,* _____?" Children who respond favorably should be told that these words *rhyme.*

— Instructional activities to develop perception of rhyme can include participation in and sharing of poems, riddles, and jingles. The teacher reads each poem or jingle with stress on the rhyming word. When the children develop favorites among the poems, the teacher hesitates at the ends of lines for children to say the rhyming word.

— At this point, *all* of the children should learn to use the word *rhyme.* The teacher can hand each small group an object (such as *sock*) and ask them to think of a word that rhymes with their object. After the children are familiar with this process, the teacher can ask each child to supply a rhyming word for a pictured or real object. When each child presents his pair (the teacher should make sure the child will be successful before he participates in such a group presentation), the rest of the class tries to think of other words that rhyme.

Object	New Word	Other Word
fish	wish	dish
pot	not	got
hand	band	sand

Language Production and Listening Comprehension

In Part I of this book, the language development of young children was discussed, and in Chapter 6, it was stated that general language ability appears to relate to reading success. Consequently, teachers must be conscious of the great importance of the language aspect of their readiness programs. Indeed, language should be included not only during prereading stages but also at the start of reading acquisition and throughout developmental reading. A summary of some important areas of oral language follows.

I. Language Production.

A. *Syntactic development.* The following syntactic structures will have been acquired by all but a few children during the years before reading instruction begins: use of complete sentences when appropriate, occasional conjoined and embedded sentences, use of inflectional endings which are present in the home language environment. Chapters 4 and 5 described assessment and instructional activities in this area.

B. *Vocabulary development.* At the start of reading instruction children should already have indicated that they possess a large passive vocabulary, that they are using in their spontaneous talk the new words introduced in class, that they have an understanding of opposites and important prepositions, and that they are able to use descriptive words in storytelling. Again, Chapters 4 and 5 describe assessment procedures and activities for expansion of vocabulary.

C. *Storytelling.* A point of direct relationship between language and reading is storytelling. Children's oral storytelling should be encouraged very much.

D. *Story dictation.* When children's oral stories are written down by the teacher, they become the bridge from oral to written language.

— For this area, on-going assessment of growth is important. For example, teachers can keep a copy of the dictated stories so that sentence structure and vocabulary development is monitored. A carbon copy provides the child with the original and the teacher with a copy for the file. Once real reading occurs, this filing system becomes extremely important since it contains the reading vocabulary of each child. But even at the prereading level, teachers can look for evidence of conjoined and embedded sentences, use of inflections, and appropriate use of new vocabulary words. Important to the implementation of these language experiences is stimulation of output.

— Storytelling, oral descriptions of observations, and retelling of past events.

1. There are a number of stimulants to storytelling: pictures which show action, objects to be described, walks around the school, animal behavior to be observed, scientific experiments to be recorded, stories which have been read and must be completed, lists of things which are needed for class activities, classroom news, and retelling a favorite story. (A more complete list of these stimulants is found in the final chapter.) It is important that teachers encourage the description of objects and retelling of past events since these activities stimulate abstract use of language.

— Writing preserves oral language.

1. In helping children to perceive that their oral words can be represented by printed symbols, the teacher should immediately reread their stories to them asking if he has written the story as it was said. The words are read as the teacher slowly moves his hand in a *left-to-right direction* across the page. He can ask, "Is this what you said? See this word. It is *umbrella.* Look at how long it is on the paper." The sentences should each begin a new line and the teacher can point this out by saying, "You started a new idea here."

— Experiencing the communicability of printed language by sharing stories with friends.

1. Another important understanding is that stories can be shared. The teacher can encourage this idea by asking a child with whom he wants to share his story. Then both children listen to the story and, perhaps, even illustrate it together. Or two or three children who have *written* (dictated) a story about the same event can listen to all the stories and talk about how they are different and alike.

— Developing the concept of spoken and written words.

1. Finally, children need to understand what a *word* is, both the spoken word and the written representation.

After they have had experiences in dictating and hear‑ ing the stories, the children can be asked to count how many words are in a sentence (a short, clearly spoken sentence) which the teacher *says.* Then, the teacher writes the sentences and asks the children to point and count the printed words. Assessment is accomplished in this way: Each child has a card with a sentence written on it and at the bottom of which are three numbers. The children simply count the words in the sentence and circle the correct number.

II. Listening Comprehension.

Ability to comprehend what one hears is similar to comprehend‑ ing what one reads; both require analysis in terms of one's own language knowledge. Various listening experiences will help children develop ability in skills which will be stressed later during reading instruction.

A. *Recall of important details in a story.*

— Assessment of this ability can be accomplished with the whole group. The teacher can prepare a ditto to be used after reading a story. For example, if Ezra Keats' *The Snowy Day* is used as the story, the format shown in Figure 4 will indicate how well children recall details.

Ditto   *Teacher Questions*

(Identify all pictures first. Look at the pictures next to the circle: Draw a line around the one picture that shows what Peter used to mark the snow.

Look at all the pictures next to the box. Draw a line around the picture that shows where Peter put his big snowball.

Look at the pictures next to the tree. Draw a line around the picture that shows what Peter did the next morning.

FIGURE 4

— Instructional activities for recalling details include discussion after reading the story, discussion of details from a story the children dictated the previous day, and discussion of past events. Occasional assessment may help determine how much attention is warranted in this area of listening comprehension.

B. *Recognition of the main idea.*

— Again, assessment of this ability can be made with *The Snowy Day,* as children are presented with a dittoed copy of the material in Figure 5. Of course, the teacher will want more than one example to assess ability in this area.

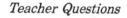

Ditto   *Teacher Questions*

Put an 0 in the picture that shows what the story about Peter is mostly about.

FIGURE 5

— Instructional activities designed to improve identification of a main idea will come largely through discussion of poems, other stories, and dictated stories ("What's the most important idea in your story?") the teacher has read to the children. Since young children often do not want to continue to sit still after hearing a story, the teacher can form little groups of children to discuss a story later in the day. This practice has the advantage of promoting memory and of encouraging more opportunities for each child to talk.

C. *Recall of sequences of events.*

— Assessment can be accomplished in a large group by using a ditto which requires that children put the numbers one, two, and three next to the pictures in the order they occur in the story. This task may require practice by teacher and child together before assessment becomes reliable.

— Instruction occurs in discussion of material read and in telling the order of events in, for example, the child's household during the mornings before he comes to school.

D. *Following one- and two-step directions.*

— Assessment can be accomplished with the large group in the following way:

Ditto	*Teacher Questions*

A	B	Look at the square marked A. Put a box in it. Look at B. Draw a tree in it. Look at C. Draw a box. Now draw a circle on top of the box. Look at D. Draw a circle. Now draw a box *in* the circle.
C	D	

— It is important that the activities with young children to promote following directions be mostly in the realm of physical activity even though the assessment is a paper-and-pencil affair. (Use of paper and pencil enables many children to be assessed at one time.) Practice in both following and giving directions is important. Play with objects on a table, marching around the room according to simple directions, organizational procedures, cleaning up—all these provide opportunity for following and giving directions. The teacher can also have a child give directions for others to follow.

Visual Abilities

Before the children begin formal reading instruction, most teachers expect them to be able to name letters. Our task is to consider how these abilities are learned and how to best provide appropriate experiences.

In order to have learned each letter, children must have acquired enough perceptual knowledge to distinguish the differences among letters which have fairly similar construction. For example, the lower case *i* and *l* are similar, as are *b, d, p,* and others. Further, children are expected to respond to a letter in all its forms, so that, for example, *a* is recognized in its printed form, its manuscript form *α* , and upper case form *A*. In order to do this, children need to be able to perceive both the total form and the critical features within the whole. In other words, children need to know that the *stick* and *circle* placement of *b* helps them distinguish it from *p* or *d*. The placement is the feature which differentiates these letters; it is therefore critical.

Barrett *(2)* has studied the predictive value of visual discrimination in reading success and found it generally to be highly significant. The abilities to name letters and numerals, to copy patterns, and to match words are very closely related to reading ability. On the other hand, the ability to discriminate pictures and geometric shapes is not highly correlated with reading. This last finding is interesting in light of the fact that for some time, many commercial workbooks have concentrated on picture discrimination exercises rather than on letter and word discrimination. Durrell *(12)* also has found a significant relationship between children's success in first-grade reading and their ability to name letters before reading begins. Thus, as was noted in the discussion on reading readiness, the ability to perform readinglike tasks before reading instruction begins predicts success. But in order to know how to help children name letters, we must look into what they naturally attend to as they look at those letters.

A study by Gibson, Gibson, Pick, and Osser *(20)* indicates that children can perceive features of letters which are critical in differentiating like forms as early as age four. The authors were interested in the developmental ability to perceive critical features of letter-like forms. The forms were designed so that the features which differentiated them were like the features which distinguish letters. Children from age four to age eight participated. Apparently, the critical features which the youngest children responded to were features which matter in determining the differences among solid objects. The features tested which even the four-year-olds understood well were whether the lines of a form had been closed or whether they had been broken. In other words, they had little difficulty distinguishing between ⊥ and ⊓ or ⊥ and ⊤. The reason they had little difficulty is that the solidity of objects in the real world depends on these features, too. However, it was more difficult for the four year old to differentiate among forms which were rotated or reversed to the side or up and down. Thus, tested

forms which caused difficulty were changes from $\vdash$ to $\dashv$ and

from $\perp$ to $\top$. The critical features here are similar to those required in distinguishing *b* and *d* and *p*. The authors' explanation in this case was that whether solid objects are rotated or reversed in position is not important in the world of objects and so had not yet been learned as a critical feature. By age eight, when literacy is underway, this feature becomes critical; the eight-year-olds had almost no difficulty with rotated or reversed forms. Another feature tested, the change from line to curve, also is acquired during these years. Thus, children first attend to features which are salient in their world; later, over time, they achieve awareness of features which are common to printed symbols. The authors of this study suggest that children be helped to attend to critical features which may cause difficulty in learning letters.

The results of this study affect the order for instruction in naming letters. In developing the following list, adaptation was made so that lower and upper case letters are combined and so that initial presentation of letters does not present similarly formed letters simultaneously. Later, if confusion among letters becomes evident, teachers can put the troublesome letters side by side in order to help some children understand critical features as they learn to print letters. The teacher should take care that they learn the difference between manuscript and printed letters, too. The letters in Table 7 are sequenced by instructional groups so that letter discrimination is stressed.

In order to learn the names of letters and to distinguish words made up of different letters, children must be able to differentiate among the letter forms. A good deal of visual and manipulative practice will be necessary before all letters are named.

Once children have gained some familiarity with letters, auditory discrimination activities should be combined with the letter or letters involved. In other words, after experiences in supplying words which begin with a sound to match presented words (/t/, for example), the printed symbol *t* should be associated with the word. Thus, auditory discrimination and visual identification are united and children begin their phonics training.

TABLE 7

h	H	i	I	o	O
a	A	c	C	x	X
i	L				

Note that in this first group are some like letters (*o* and *c, A* and *H*). The distinctive feature, whether the line is closed or not, is not difficult for four year olds. Review these letters before moving to next group.

s	S	t	T	y	Y
b	B	e	E	g	G
k	K				

Review all letters.

j	J	r	R	m	M
f	F	d	D	z	Z
q	Q				

Review all letters.

n	N	u	U	v	V
w	W				

Note the confusion inherent in these final letters. Review all letters.

A list of the visual skills follows with suggestions for assessment and instructional activities.

II. Discrimination of Letters and Numbers.

    A. *Discrimination among objects.*

        — Ability to discriminate objects is not highly related to *reading;* however, ability to distinguish objects may indicate the presence of the important *cognitive* ability to categorize objects. I recommend assessment to find those children who need work in grouping objects. Assessment can be quickly accomplished by using pictures of common objects, one of which is different from the others. Examples of exercises are plentiful in readiness workbooks.

        — Children should first learn to discriminate real objects by finding the one that does not belong; thus, measurement of discrimination is not confused with understanding of the task. Rather than asking for the one that is different or does not belong, a teacher can show a picture of an object and direct children to find the one that is the *same* in a given array. One can begin instruction with three-dimensional objects—blocks, clothing, candy, etc.

— Once children can group like objects, paper-and-pencil practice will prepare them for practice with more sophisticated discrimination tasks.

B. *Discrimination of abstract shapes.*

— This skill is closer to the behavior used in recognizing and naming letters than is discrimination of objects. Assessment can be informally done with workbook pages or simple exercises dittoed for each child. The following figure illustrates such an exercise.

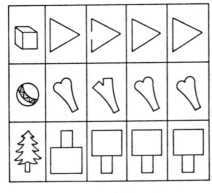

Ditto

Teacher Directions

Look at the pictures next to the box. Draw a line around the one that is different from the others.

Now look at the pictures next to the ball. Draw a line around the one that is different.

Etc.

FIGURE 6

— In instruction, the teacher can make two different shapes and ask the children to try to copy them. If the critical features are similar to those that distinguish letters (broken lines, curves and lines, rotations and reversals), the activity will be much more relevant to the objective. For example, the teacher can ask children to copy these shapes and tell how they differ. (One must remember that triangles are difficult to draw.)

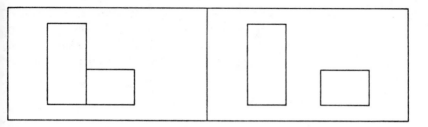

FIGURE 7

C. *Discrimination among letters and numbers.*

— Assessment involves arranging letters in rows and then asking the children to draw a circle around the letter that *does not belong* or *is different.*

M   M   Ⓞ   M

— Another way of assessing this skill is to ask children to draw a circle around a letter in a row which is the *same* as a stimulus.

ⓑ   c   g   p   b

Whatever the task, the assessment instrument should include both upper and lower case letters, discrimination among grossly different letters and numbers, and discrimination among more similar letters and numbers.
— Instruction will also move from working with grossly different letters to those which are more similar and, finally, to those which may be confused.
— Instruction should include visual practice in conjunction with tactile experiences. Tracing sandpaper letters, tracing grooved letters in alphabet blocks, matching written letters with printed letters, and copying printed letters are some experiences children will need to develop discrimination.

— Letter and number naming may be learned during this time since some children will continue to have problems discriminating letters such as *b* and *d* even after most other letters can be named and words are being acquired.

III. Naming of Letters and Numbers.

— Since discrimination can be presumed if letters are recalled and named and since children have many experiences with letters through watching *Sesame Street* and home instruction, it is sensible to test this ability for *all* four, five, and six year olds. Assessment must be done individually by randomly placing all lower and upper case letters on one index card and numerals on another. During the testing, the teacher should mark each unknown letter on a separate paper for instructional planning.

— Durkin *(11)* has suggested that learning of letter names in conjunction with learning to write letters is beneficial. Teachers should focus children's attention on the critical features of letters as they write them. Developing the concept that the upper case, lower case, and printed forms of the letters have the same name demands additional practice. Children enjoy learning how to make letters in the context of words so teachers might teach the letters in words of objects and people in a room.

boy   table

— Letter naming should be associated with beginning sound once auditory skills are developed and some letter names have been learned.

— Various senses should be involved in practicing letters and numbers. Three-dimensional letters are helpful if children match the three-dimensional and the two-dimensional. In this way, the transition to the two-dimensional world of literacy is eased as letter naming is practiced.

— Letter lotto games can be devised or bought. The matching of cardboard letters with their printed forms facilitates the transition to a two-dimensional sphere.

— When further practice with letters and numbers is needed, Bingo is a common activity.

— Another practice game involves placing letters and numbers on paper fish to which a paper clip is attached. The "fish" are put in a "pond," and a magnet is used as the "fish hook." Children then name the letters of the fish they catch. It is important to indicate the mouth and eye of the fish for direction. (These games and others, such as Climbing a Ladder, can be used for practice with sight words, too.)

FIGURE 8

— Motivational devices may help the learning process. For example, every child can be given a card on which the letters named are attached to a piece of yarn which is tied to his chair or coat hook. Or once a letter is named and is maintained, the child may keep it in a Letter Bank. Each named letter can be pinned to his jacket for him to wear home.

A. *Recitation of the alphabet sequence.*

— To be able to recite the order of the alphabet is not necessary for beginning reading instruction; instead, it is a beginning dictionary skill. The Alphabet Song or ABC books will help in developing this skill.

IV. Words.

A. *Discrimination among words.*

— For assessment purposes, the teacher prepares dittoes with rows of words. The children are asked to draw a circle around a word in the row which is the same as the stimulus word. The exercises should include discrimination among grossly different words and among more similar words. The rows should be perceptually clear; the task should be practiced before testing.

cat	house	man	cat
cat	can	cap	cat

— Instruction for children who have difficulty with this skill will begin with discrimination of individual letters and then continue with activities which concentrate on the specific distinctive letters which differentiate words. It may be a good idea for those few children who have difficulty even after work with letters to do tactile activities with words that are formed with cardboard letters and placed in this way.

cat

cap

The teacher shows the two words and names them. The children trace each letter of the word *cat,* then each letter of the word *cap.* The letters *c* and *a* are then placed over each other to show that they are the same. Finally, *p* and *t* are identified as different.

— Further practice occurs when children write over (directly superimpose) with a pen the printed words and then write under the words:

cat	*cap*
cat	*cap*

B. *Identification of a few common words.*

— Assessment is important since children are exposed to words in many ways early in life. Many preschoolers have sufficient visual memory and discrimination to learn these words from frequent exposure. The teacher presents each child individually with a list of words at the preprimer level and other salient terms carefully printed on an index card. Dittoed copies of the list have already been prepared to record each child's correctly recognized word.

stop	*see*	*the*	*go*	*play*	*cat*	*of*
look	*in*	*boy*	*and*	*run*	*has*	*to*
make	*mother*	*father*	*do*		*is*	*a*

If a child recognizes fifteen or more words, he should be given an Informal Reading Inventory to find what his reading level is.

— Children should learn to recognize their own names in print for practical as well as educational purposes. Teachers in preschool use name labels for many purposes: jobs, coathooks, supply drawers, etc. Small photographs of each child can be attached to their names at first and then removed when each child is able to find his name among the others.

— To teach the words *stop* and *go,* which have practical importance, a Musical Chairs game is fun. When the *go* sign is up, the children march about the room; when the *stop* sign appears, the children must find a chair.

— Teachers often label room furniture and learning centers. After these labels have been displayed, they can be removed, placed in a pile, and identified by the children.

— The dictated stories described in the section of this chapter on storytelling include many words that are used frequently in the language. As the teacher rereads a dictated story, he can ask children to "read with him." This practice may be sufficient to allow some children to find words they can recognize alone. (The use of these stories as reading material is described in detail in the next chapters.)

— When children can identify a few words they have experienced previously, they are ready to begin reading instruction. Some readiness activities should be continued, especially those that encourage the development of sound/symbol understanding and of other visual/perceptual activities.

Directionality and Eye Coordination

There are other areas of visual development which should be of concern during the reading preparation period. We have discussed form perception, but according to Spache and Spache *(35),* directionality and eye coordination are also important visual factors in reading. In Chapter 6, we discussed the habitual left-to-right eye movement which occurs as adults read. Nonreading children have the muscular ability to move their eyes in left-to-right direction, but they are not practiced in it. In fact, many children are not even aware of consistency in the direction of print. For example, a five year old told me that he could write the word *eel.* I encouraged him to show me, but before he began, he asked, "Do I start with the *e* or with the *l?*" A very few words of explanation about how placement is coordinated with the sounds one hears in words was sufficient for him to proudly write *eel* for me.

Our language-reading program includes exercises designed to develop a sense of left-to-right and return sweep movements so that directionality is acquired partially before reading instruction begins. Further, some exercises meant to help children develop coordinated eye movements (movements in which both eyes focus together) are included.

It is important for teachers to help detect eye problems which might exist and should be corrected. Unfortunately, not all schools provide adequate testing for visual defects and not all parents are able to make provisions for such testing themselves. In addition, since visual screening tests used in school vary in effectiveness (Spache and Spache, *35*), children need the attention and diagnosis of specialists whenever possible. Knox (as reported by Spache and Spache, *35*) has found that besides screening with visual tests, teachers provide additional information helpful in finding children with visual problems through their observation. Symptoms which may indicate difficulty include: facial contortions, tilting of the head, indication of tension during close work, consistently holding close material near the eyes, and rubbing of the eyes. It is critical that kindergarten teachers attend to the matter of visual difficulty before reading instruction begins so that, if possible, all children can be free of visual distortions.

I. Binocular Coordination.

— It is important that children's eyes move *together.* Not all children will need training to develop this behavior; the best method for teachers to use in determining which ones do, in the absense of good eye screening measures, is observation in classroom situations. If children show consistent inattention, squirming, squinting, rubbing of the eyes when doing near-point work, they are candidates for training. If older, beginning readers seem unable to relinquish use of fingers or markers when reading, they too are candidates. Forms of practice recommended by Spache and Spache (*35*, Chapter 7) include engaging a child's eyes on a slowly moving ball, following finger movements with the eyes, following flashlight movements, and encouraging movement of the eyes from near-point to a greater distance. It is wise to include hand movements with binocular training at first.

II. Directionality.

— It is the teacher's responsibility to stress the left-to-right direction whenever possible. He points to the sequenced picture a child is using to tell a story; he uses a left-to-right movement of his finger when rereading a dictated story; he *occasionally* traces the movement of reading to one or two children who are *sitting next to him;* he emphasizes and explains the movement when reading a chart story.

— All young children need practice to develop consistent left-to-right and return sweep eye movements. This is particularly true of those children older than first grade who always seem to lose their way as they read or who have reversals (*was* for *saw* or *much* for *chum*). In order to assure full participation in practice activities, whole-class involvement in paper-and-pencil exercises can be devised to promote directional behaviors. The follow-the-dots game can be adjusted for this purpose. Children draw a line from one point to another in the left-to-right direction. First, on large newsprint and later on smaller dittoed sheets, the children quickly draw from *A* to *B* in unison and under teacher direction.

$$A \qquad B$$

Then, with increasingly wider spaces, they follow *A* to *B,* and then *C* to *D.*

$$A \qquad B$$
$$C \qquad\qquad D$$

These exercises should be done more and more quickly, and after some practice, the children can begin to con-

tinue the pattern to include the oblique movement required in the return sweep:

$$A \quad B \quad C$$
$$D$$
$$E$$
$$F \quad G \quad H$$
$$I$$
$$J$$

Spache and Spache (*35*) have additional exercises to encourage the development of directionality.

III. Eye-hand Coordination.

— As support for binocular coordination and directionality
practice, children should be encouraged to use their hands so
that hand movement initiates eye movement. Many other
activities involve hand and eye coordination. For example,
when children work puzzles, paint, learn to print, trace letters, and build with blocks, hand and eye coordination is
being developed. Reading readiness training should *never*
mean that these important activities are being neglected
during the nursery school, kindergarten, and primary-grade
years.

CONCLUSION

It is very important that the teacher create a task-oriented atmosphere so that these readiness activities have a positive effect. Small
groups can be isolated from the more boisterous activities of the
room by creating a work space with screens and toy cases. The
teacher should explain carefully that the behavior required in the
little room is different from that of play time. He himself should
illustrate this difference by using a quieter voice and manner.

The instructional activities should be brief and to the point. It is
important that children never be required to attend to tasks for very
long. At first, some children may only be able to sit and participate
for a few moments. The teacher should praise inattentive children
for even brief periods of attention and let them return to the larger

room as soon as they show signs of distraction. Continual reinforcement of on-task behavior will ultimately extend everyone's attention span. Large-group activities should also be brief and as gamelike as possible. We turn now in Chapter 8 to beginning reading instruction.

REFERENCES

1. Annesley, F.; Odhner, F.; Madoff, E.; and Chomsky, N. "Identifying the First Grade Underachiever." *Journal of Educational Research* 63 (1970): 459–62.

2. Barrett, R. C. "The Relationship between Measures of Prereading Visual Discrimination and First-Grade Reading Achievement: A Review of the Literature." *Reading Research Quarterly* 1 (1965): 51–76.

3. Blakely, W. P., and Shadle, E. M. "A Study of Two Readiness-for-Reading Programs in Kindergarten." *Elementary English* 38 (1961): 502–05.

4. Bond, G. L., and Dykstra, R. "The Cooperative Research Program in First-Grade Reading Instruction." *Reading Research Quarterly* 3 (1967): 5–142.

5. Boney, D., and Lynch, J. E. "A Study of Reading Growth in the Primary Grades." *Elementary English Review* 19 (1948): 370–75.

6. Bradley, B. E. "An Experimental Study of the Readiness Approach to Reading." *Elementary School Journal* 56 (1956): 262–67.

7. Bruner, J. *The Process of Education.* Cambridge: Harvard University Press, 1960.

8. Chall, J. *Learning to Read: The Great Debate.* New York: McGraw-Hill Book Co., 1967.

9. Dolch, E. N. *Teaching Primary Reading.* Champaign, Illinois: The Garrard Press, 1950.

10. Duggins, L. A. "Auditory Perception in the Beginning Reading Program." *College Bulletin Southeastern Louisiana College* 113 (1956): 1–45.

11. Durkin, D. *Teaching Young Children to Read.* Boston: Allyn & Bacon, Inc., 1972.

12. Durrell, D. D. "Success in First-Grade Reading." *Journal of Education* 140 (1958): 1–48.

13. Dykstra, R. "Auditory Discrimination Abilities and Beginning Reading Achievement." *Reading Research Quarterly* 2 (1966): 5–34.

14. Farr, R. Untitled speech read at Chicago Area Reading Association meeting. May, 1972.

15. Furth, H. *Piaget for Teachers.* Englewood Cliffs, New Jersey: Prentice-Hall, Inc., 1970.

16. Gates, A. I. "The Necessary Mental Age for Beginning Reading." *Elementary School Journal* 37 (1937): 497–508.

17. Gates, A. I., and Bond, G. L. "Reading Readiness: A Study of Factors Determining Success and Failure in Beginning Reading." *Teachers' College Record* 37 (1935–1936): 679–85.

18. Gates, A. I.; Bond, G. L.; and Russell, D. H. *Methods of Determining Reading Readiness.* New York: Bureau of Publications, Teachers College, Columbia University, 1939.

19. Gesell, A. L. *The First Five Years of Life,* New York: Harper, 1940.

20. Gibson, E. J.; Gibson, J. J.; Pick, A. K.; and Osser, H. "A Developmental Study of the Discrimination of Letterlike Forms." *Journal of Comparative and Physiological Psychology* 55 (1962): 897–906.

21. Goldman, R.; Fristoe, M.; and Woodcock, R. W. *Test of Auditory Discrimination.* Circle Pines, Minnesota: American Guidance Service, Inc., 1970.

22. Harrison, M. L. *Reading Readiness.* Boston: Houghton Mifflin Co., 1936.

23. Hillerich, R. L. "An Interpretation of Research in Reading Readiness." *Elementary English* 45 (1968): 359–64; 372.

24. Ilg, F. L.; and Ames, L. B. *School Readiness.* New York: Harper and Row, Publishers, 1965.

25. Koppman, P. S., and LaPray, M. H. "Teacher Ratings and Pupil Reading Readiness Scores." *Reading Teacher* 22 (1969): 603–08.

26. Kottmeyer, W. "Readiness for Reading, Part I and Part II." *Elementary English* 24 (1947): 355–66; 528–33.

27. LaConte, C. "Reading in Kindergarten" *The Reading Teacher* 22 (1969): 116–20.

28. Monroe, M., and Rogers, B. *Foundations for Reading.* Chicago: Scott, Foresman and Co., 1964.

29. Morphett, M. V., and Washburne, C. "When Should Children Begin to Read?" *Elementary School Journal* 21 (1931): 496–503.

30. Morrison, C., and Harris, A. J. "The Craft Project: A Final Report." *The Reading Teacher* 22 (1969): 335–40.

31. Myklebust, H. R. *The Pupil Rating Scale: Screening for Learning Disabilities.* New York: Grune and Stratton, 1971.

32. Ploghoft, M. H. "Do Reading Readiness Workbooks Promote Readiness?" *Elementary English* 36 (1959): 424–26.

33. Pratt, W. E. "A Study of the Differences in the Prediction of Reading Success of Kindergarten and Nonkindergarten Children." *Journal of Educational Research* 42 (1949): 525–33.

34. Smith, M. S., and Bissell, J. S. "Report Analysis: The Impact of Headstart." *Harvard Educational Review* 40 (1970): 51–104.

35. Spache, G. D., and Spache, E. B. *Reading in the Elementary School,* 2d ed. Boston: Allyn & Bacon, Inc., 1969.

36. Spache, G. D.; Spache, E. B.; Andres, M. C.; Curtis, H. A.; Rowland, M.; and Hall, M. "A Longitudinal First-Grade Reading Readiness Program." *The Reading Teacher* 19 (1966): 580–84.

37. Teegarden, L. "Clinical Identification of the Prospective Nonreader." *Child Development* 3 (1932): 346–58.

38. Wepman, J. M. "Auditory Discrimination Speech and Reading." *Elementary School Journal* 60 (1960): 325–33.

39. Venezky, R. S.; Calfee, R. C.: and Chapman, R. S. "Skills Required for Learning to Read." In *Individualizing Reading Instruction: A Reader,* edited by L. A. Harris and C. B. Smith. New York: Holt, Rinehart, & Winston, Inc., 1972.

CHAPTER 8

Beginning Readers
and Beginning Reading

At some point during the span of years between age three and seven, most children become ready and show interest in learning to read. After they begin reading instruction, children ought to continue with oral language development so that vocabulary continually expands and so that growth toward increased language complexity is assured. If teachers neglect these language activities, long-term growth in reading may suffer, since reading achievement ultimately depends on vocabulary and general language facility. Thus, the total program should include reading instruction as well as on-going instruction in language. Reading instruction is presented here with the realization that although many children do begin to read at the first-grade level, some are ready earlier, while a few will profit from delayed reading.

No area is as replete with advice to teachers, research data, commercial interests, and varying instructional systems as is beginning reading. Since analysis of various approaches to beginning reading is needed in order to make critical judgments, this chapter reviews various reading systems. Some reference to research is made to support the statements made. The content of this chapter will be a review for many readers who have experience with reading instruction, but it also will serve as a general introduction for those who have never before studied beginning reading. The concern here is with beginning reading in general; specific instructional recommendations and procedures are described in Chapter 9.

The first section of the chapter attends to the question of early preschool reading. For many years, teachers were either strongly in favor of early reading instruction or, more commonly, strongly opposed to reading before first grade. However, in recent years, educators in general have altered their thinking somewhat and their classroom instruction to include earlier reading. This section will attempt to answer the questions: Does early reading instruction have any place in the program for four and five year olds? Will early reading affect children adversely or will it, in the long run, help them?

The second section of the chapter focuses on instruction in beginning reading. Questions answered in this section are: What are the various instructional systems for beginning reading? What data is available that will indicate which systems are best? Suggestions for setting up and conducting a beginning reading program follow in Chapter 9.

EARLY READING AND EARLY READERS

Under the influence of the theorists who hold that one should wait for natural development for reading readiness, for many years some educators have advised against a structured reading program in kindergarten or even encouragement of young children's reading interests (24). A number of reasons for this advice have been given, one of which is that the visual immaturity of young children might prevent adequate learning. Furthermore, parents were advised against teaching their children because they might unknowingly use confusing methods of instruction. In addition, it was feared that children who learned to read before first grade might become bored when placed in the regular first-grade program. Finally, the most often cited reason for delaying instruction until first grade was that formal instruction in reading during kindergarten would hinder the major kindergarten goals of social, motor, and cognitive development. Durkin's study (13) shows that mothers of young children during the 1950s were conscious of these reasons for delaying reading. Although some of these mothers ignored the advice they heard, others discouraged their children's growing curiosity about spelling and reading. New evidence and the demands of changing times have altered this picture somewhat. For example, newer study has shown that children's visual growth is quite sufficient for them to read at age five (16).

"The Cooperative Research Program of First-Grade Reading Instruction" by Bond and Dykstra *(4)* demonstrates that beginning readers learn to read through teaching that employs widely varying instructional systems. No known method is inherently wrong. Most educators now advocate finding a method which suits the individual; any method which works well with a child is an adequate one. Because of these widespread attempts to individualize all programs to suit all pupils, teachers are now much less concerned about boring advanced first graders.

Finally, while it is very important that day care centers, nursery schools, and kindergartens devote their energy to helping children grow in social, motor, and cognitive abilities, these goals do not exclude reading readiness and beginning reading, for small children do not think in terms of separate content areas. The idea that reading is taught in a "reading period" and that children must sit still in designated places for a long period of time to learn to read is an artifact of our institutional structure. Both reading readiness and beginning reading can and should be incorporated into traditional preschool activities. In addition, some of the conventional reading materials used in structured first grades can be used with young children as long as they are used wisely. Reading readiness and reading instruction for all ages can and should be conducted in a relaxed, natural setting.

Longitudinal studies of early readers provide insight into one of the questions raised in this section: Are there long-term advantages accrued from early reading? If children benefit from early reading, we will want to include an early reading component in the language-reading program. Otherwise, the argument over reading before first grade is pointless.

Durkin *(12)*, *(13)* explored the long-term effects of early reading. Her early readers were children who had learned to read without school training before the first grade; they could successfully read eighteen out of thirty-seven common, easy words, and they could obtain a raw score on the Gates Primary Reading Test. In the first of two studies she reported, early readers were compared through the sixth grade with children who were not early readers. Since some of the early readers had been double-promoted (and clearly had benefited from double promotion), adjustments in the comparison of the groups were made. The results clearly indicated that children who had learned to read before first grade maintained a reading advantage through elementary school. "The average achievement of early readers who had had either five or six years of school instruction in reading was significantly higher than the average achievement of equally bright classmates who had had six years of school instruction but were not early readers."[1]

In the second study, early readers were matched by IQ with subjects who were not early readers and studied through the third grade. Again, the early readers indicated significantly higher reading achievement than did the others. Parent interviews revealed a greater tendency for the early readers to prefer quiet activities and solitary play than was true of those who did not read early. Apparently, a favorable environment for early reading was provided by the interest of the mothers because, in general, the mothers of the readers responded favorably to their children's questions about spelling, letters, and words; on the other hand, the other mothers tended to put off such questions. In another report on the same studies, Durkin *(12)* showed that early readers were superior to their matched classmates in mathematics and social studies as well as in reading achievement. The advantage in reading, which continued through elementary school, meant that children who read early could assimilate more information more quickly than did the nonreaders. While it is true that early readers had very high IQ's (in the first study, the range was from 91 to 161 with a mean of 121; in the second, there was a range from 82 to 170 with a mean of 133), some of the early readers had low-average IQ's. Generally, if they are interested, some bright children learn to read with very little instruction, but a few children with low-average ability are able to read early, too. The implications of these studies are far-reaching.

The Denver Early Reading project (Brzeinsky, *5)* also made a longitudinal examination of children who read early. However, these children were *taught to read* in kindergarten. After participating either in an experimental kindergarten where reading activities were provided for twenty minutes a day or in a conventional kindergarten, children were placed either in an "adjusted first grade program" which continued the approaches used in the experimental kindergarten rooms or in a conventional first grade. This type of mixing continued through the fifth grade when comparisons were made. At the end of kindergarten, the children in the sixty-one experimental classrooms were better at naming letters and recalling words than were the controls. By the end of the first grade, the original experimental children were still making better achieve-

---

[1]D. Durkin, *Children Who Read Early* (New York: Teachers College Press, Columbia University, 1966), p. 41.

ment scores in spite of the mixed classroom assignments. By the end of the fifth grade, there was no difference between the two groups except in the case of the experimental subjects who had continued in "adjusted" programs; these children were significantly better readers.

We might interpret these two studies as an indication that early reading is profitable only if children are highly motivated to read— so motivated, in fact, that they ask questions of their willing mothers. Otherwise, early reading is not helpful over the long run. However, another interpretation is possible. Durkin's work may demonstrate that children who are stimulated consciously in a favorable environment which duplicates the home environment of the early reader will have long-term achievement benefits.

Durkin's *(14)* follow-up two-year study of the reading preparation for nearly forty four and five year olds indicates that sensitive instruction results in early reading development. The forty children were in a special program she designed to replicate the environment provided in the homes of the early readers. Her school program began at age four, an age when most of the subjects of the previous studies had begun asking questions about letters, spellings, and words. Initial instruction emphasized writing since that was a common entry into literacy for the early readers. Because the other children had not learned from commercially produced materials in the past studies, few such materials were used in the training program. Furthermore, more emphasis was placed on recognition of whole words from memory rather than on the use of phonetic principles. Oral language activities, reading of stories to children, and learning to name the words and numbers used in play activities were emphasized. The goals were to teach children to print, name letters and numerals, and to recognize a number of words. No standardized testing was done, but criterion-based tests revealed that by the end of the first year, children could identify an average of fourteen numerals, thirty-eight letters (lower and upper case), and twenty-nine words. At the end of the next year, the average child could identify forty-seven numerals, fifty letters (out of fifty-two), and 124 words. At no time were more than twenty minutes a day spent on academic work. This child-oriented beginning reading program, which Durkin *(15)* has described in detail in a recent book, appeared to be successful in achieving program goals.

In summary, although early reading is still a somewhat controversial topic, it generally is accepted that early reading is not harmful. If some children want to learn to read and have help, they can become successful readers early and maintain that lead in reading and in other reading-dependent content areas through the elementary years. If children are placed in a reading program before first grade, we cannot be sure that they will continue to be superior to children who do not read early, but for the first years they, too, will have an advantage. There are further indications from Durkin's more recent study *(14)* that careful reading preparation training and some reading for four and five year olds results in achievement growth. Therefore, I recommend that reading be taught to all children, no matter how young, who demonstrate interest and who can name letters, remember a few words, have auditory discrimination ability, and whose oral language and vocabulary development is sufficient. Furthermore, it is the school's job to promote reading preparation and to stimulate reading interest for all young children.

BEGINNING READING

Before turning to the various approaches used in teaching beginning reading, we should note that there is a difference between an *instructional system,* a generic term for approaches to reading instruction, and a *reading program,* a term for the materials used to implement the systems. It would be impossible to discuss in these short pages the wide variety of reading programs; instead, we will describe here major instructional systems briefly. We will also discuss major instructional goals, assumptions about the reading needs, and data from important research studies which compare various systems.

Although much research has been done in the area of beginning reading instruction, it is well to note that such research has inherent difficulties which are rarely completely overcome. These difficulties include the effect of the *teaching* rather than *instructional systems* on achievement outcomes, the variety of student ability in comparative groups, and even the differential effect of using a familiar instructional system compared with the effect of using an innovative program in experimental groups. When there is an attempt to control these factors, research data is more reliable. Attempts were made to control these variables in the "Cooperative Research Program in First-Grade Instruction" by Bond and Dykstra *(4)*. Twenty-seven government-sponsored studies of instruction in first grade reading had similar research design, statistical procedures, and other important research characteristics. Therefore, we will devote much attention to these studies in the next pages.

Instructional Systems Based on Vocabulary Control

There are a number of ways various systems can be classified but none of them is entirely satisfactory. The attempt has been made here to group systems so that their differences are stressed *(20)*. Thus, in this first reading system, control of the vocabulary introduced to the beginning reader is an important distinguishing characteristic. Although there is more than one kind of vocabulary control, this first group of programs introduces new words in terms of the frequency of their use. Vocabulary studies dating back into the 1920s resulted in compiled lists of words grouped by difficulty and frequency of use *(32)*, *(35)*, and *(9)*. The authors of instructional systems based on high frequency vocabulary feel that gradual increases in the words which can be recognized on sight is the major goal of beginning reading. Another major goal of the vocabulary control instructional system is that comprehension of a passage must be attained, even at the beginning of the instruction. The beginning readers' task is to recall words which already have been introduced and repeated often and to understand these words when they are combined in the context of a story. After pupils have achieved a small sight vocabulary, they must learn a number of word recognition techniques. An important word recognition skill is phonics, which helps pupils to relate the sound of oral words to the written symbols. Thus, early memorization of a stock of basic sight words, meaning attainment, and later introduction of a variety of word recognition skills are the characteristics of this instructional system.

Among the many major programs which follow high frequency-based vocabulary are: *The New Basic Reading Program (P)*[2] *Ginn Basic Readers (Q)*, *The Reading for Meaning Series (L)*. More recent additions to this group are: *The Bookmark Reading Series (H)*, *Reading 360 (F)*, and *The Houghton-Mifflin Readers (G)*. Although there are variations among these basal reading series, especially among the newer ones, all consist of readiness workbooks, two or three paperback books called preprimers for the beginner, and at least one hardcover text for the first-grade program. Accompanying the pupils' texts are extensive teachers' guidebooks which present in-

---

[2]Reading programs are listed separately at the end of the chapter by letter.

structional guidelines. For each reading selection, the guidebooks describe techniques for introducing new words and practicing old ones, suggestions for preparing pupils for the reading, a guide to the reading with questions to focus on, and, of great importance, a system for introducing and teaching necessary word recognition and comprehension skills. There are also pupil workbooks which reinforce these skills. In addition, there are other helpful teaching aids, such as word cards, charts, etc. Some teachers find the guides and other paraphernalia very helpful, while others find them confining. This latter group usually adapts the texts to their own classroom needs.

The story content in the first books of the basal series of the early 1960s usually centered on the activities of the family members of one white, middle-class, suburban family. During the early 1960s, there was considerable criticism that these books were irrelevant to the lives of many American children, especially urban, minority-group children. As a result, the publishing companies included black families in revised editions published in the mid 1960s. In the primer, *The Little White House (Ginn Basic Readers, Q)*, one finds two families—one white and one black—whose life patterns are indistinguishable. Macmillan Company's *Bank Street Readers (C)* and Follett Publishing Company's *City Schools' Reading Program (I)*, on the other hand, were written to appeal to inner-city children while maintaining the characteristics of the other vocabulary controlled programs. Many people continue to feel that the multi-ethnic character of our society is absent in reading materials. However, the most recent basal series have responded to continuing criticism by including fantasy stories with urban, rural, and foreign settings as well as some non-fiction material.

In the programs with vocabulary control by high-frequency usage, words are introduced slowly and repeated many times. As a result, in the first preprimers, the story events occur in the illustrations and the words are commentary on the pictured action. Gradually, as vocabulary increases, this process is reversed. But partly because of the repetition of vocabulary, the language of the preprimers has been criticized as being very stilted and unrepresentative of the rich language of the beginning reader. When the language of the texts does not parallel the language patterns of the reader, it is somewhat difficult to promote use of context and language cues as word recognition devices. Thus, this criticism has merit, and changes in the newer basal series indicate that it is possible to have more representative language structures while still introducing vocabulary gradually. One change has been the introduction of *more* words at an earlier point; this change is in line with the recommendations of Chall *(7)* whose research has indicated that children can acquire a vocabulary more quickly than the vocabulary load of the earlier basals.

In nearly every study of "The Cooperative Research Program in First-Grade Reading Instruction," an innovative instructional system was compared with a pre-1965 basal series. Although pupil preparedness (ability to name letters, particularly) was most crucial in determining results, whenever there were significant differences between instructional systems, they usually favored the innovative program over the basal series. Bond and Dykstra *(4)* found that the basal programs with control by high frequency vocabulary were simply not as effective as instruction which also included a strong sound/symbol component. This conclusion is supported by Chall's *(7)* study which indicates that early training to decode printed words into oral equivalents is important in the first grade. Specifically, Chall has found that early inclusion of heavy phonics in the first year of reading instruction results in higher word recognition than when phonics instruction comes later in the year and is not strongly emphasized.

Phonics is a method of associating *sounds with symbols* in order to unlock unfamiliar words. Of the different approaches to teaching phonics, one is synthetic in that pupils sound out words by blending letter/sound by letter/sound. The *Phonovisual Method (R)* is one example of this approach. Other programs teach pupils to substitute a sound associated with an initial letter or letters in a word context. For example, a pupil who does not recognize *brat* but knows *cat, fat,* etc. as well as the consonant cluster /br/ in *broke* learns to place /br/ in the context _____ at. In addition, generalized rules are used when appropriate. A well-known example is the rule that states that in words of the consonant-vowel-consonant final *e* pattern, the first vowel has a long sound and the *e* is silent. Sometimes, these rules are taught deductively; sometimes, pupils are encouraged to state the rule in their own words. There are many phonics generalizations; some are more productive than others. The final chapter of the book will list phonic elements which are the most useful for the beginning reader.

Many of the revisions of basals and series written since 1969 have a stronger phonics program in the first grade than did previous basal series. This is a shift not only in emphasis; adaptation also has been made to reflect findings from linguistic study. Thus, rules and procedures which are not consistent with the language are excluded while terminology and methods reflect linguistic concepts. For example, the *Reading 360 (F)* has a unique sound/symbol component which combines analytic phonics with linguistically sophisticated knowledge.

Some caution about phonics instruction must be indicated. Phonics, or any system which relates sound to symbol, is only beneficial in so far as it helps the beginning reader to increase his ability to unlock words. The reader's own language must be the oral base for application of phonics principles. The teacher must take care that phonics instruction helps rather than confuses the beginning reader. For example, if the words *told, old, mole,* and *toll* are all rhyming words in a child's dialect, expectations that he will hear and isolate *told* and *old* from *toll* and *mole* without supportive instruction are unrealistic *(8).* Whatever the dialect, the sound/symbol program must be a sensible, workable aid in the acquisition of reading.

Some adaptation of the phonics program for speakers of Black English is needed. Since initial consonants vary little by dialect, they are useful beginning sound/symbol skills to be learned and are the features most used by mature readers. Increasing awareness of initial consonant letters as cues to words is useful for speakers of all dialects; however, work with final consonants and, especially, consonant clusters can result in confusion if the teacher does not relate the phonics principles with children's speech. The teacher must ascertain whether pupils articulate these sounds, whether they fail to discriminate them *(des* and *desk),* or whether both situations are true. If the children fail to discriminate the sounds, it is best to develop auditory discrimination before initiating instruction of clusters as word clues. Another area of difficulty is with short vowel sounds *(a* in *rat, o* in *hop, i* in *pin, e* in *bed, u* in *up).* Because the effort required to develop discrimination prior to instruction is extensive, because these sounds vary considerably by dialect, because they are often placed in medial position in the word, and because they are, therefore, less useful clues to words than letters in initial position, it may be best to delay introduction of short vowel sounds until after there has been considerable development of relationships between written consonants and their oral counterparts.

In turning again to instructional systems, we find a number of adaptations to the high-frequency control. For example, *Basic Reading* by McCracken and Walcutt *(K)* uses a combination of approaches. While many phonic programs [for example, *Phonetic Keys to Reading, (J)*] have vocabulary control based on high-frequency words, *Basic Reading* controls the vocabulary in terms of how closely the spelling parallels the sounds heard, although a few necessary function words which do not have a close sound/symbol correspondence are introduced separately from the other words. Because most of the words for the beginning program are selected according to the similarity of spellings with sounds, many *more* words are introduced than in high-frequency vocabulary controlled programs. There is also less repetition of vocabulary. Thus, the *Basic Reading* series, introduces about 2000 words by the end of the first year while the more conventional series introduces approximately 350 words *(7)*. Apparently the increase in vocabulary due to the sound/symbol relationships results in higher initial reading achievement than does use of the more conventional basal series *(4)*. There are other programs which control vocabulary by sound/symbol correspondence, but these must be grouped separately from the phonic programs.

Beginning in 1963 with *Let's Read: A Linguistic Approach,* the Bloomfield and Barnhart program *(D)*, a new word analysis approach emerged on the reading scene. In response to earlier work by Bloomfield *(3)*, the linguistic programs for beginning reading during the early 1960s began to stress earlier and more extensive efforts to help pupils "break the written code." In linguistic programs, the major thrust of the first stages of reading is to teach pupils to decode words. Word decoding is achieved by structuring the vocabulary so that pupils *induce* a system of sound/symbol correspondences for themselves. That is, words are presented in groups so that individual words vary only by one phoneme/grapheme *(fat, sat, mat, pat);* later, words are presented in more varied patterns. The stories in the first texts are based on these words and are somewhat limited in their content and style. Not all such linguistic programs are alike, but they share an emphasis on early decoding, control of vocabulary by sound/symbol correspondences and learning by induction; there is little emphasis on comprehension of the material read. Two examples of linguistic systems are: *Merrill Linguistic Readers* by Fries, Fries, Wilson, and Rudolf *(I)*; *Basic Reading Series* by Rasmussen and Goldberg *(O)*. According to the Bond and Dykstra study *(4)*, use of the linguistic programs results in a slight advantage over conventional basal programs in word recognition but a disadvantage in rate and accuracy of reading. Otherwise, there are no differences.

Thus, within the vocabulary control instructional systems category, there are several subgroups; some programs base the vocabulary control on words most frequently used, emphasize meaning, and have some sound/symbol relationship training. Others emphasize phonics as the important word recognition technique. And still others base the vocabulary control on words which deductively teach rules for attacking new words; such linguistic programs help children induce a system for themselves. Generally, it appears that the combination of a vocabulary controlled program with special training in phonics during the first year of instruction is better than use of one system alone.

Instructional Systems Based on Programmed Learning

Programmed learning is a result of study done in laboratories on the acquisition of discrete skills. The theory emphasizes the positive effects of successful learning; therefore, the material is structured in very small steps so that previous learning leads to correct responses in the next step. Because immediate reinforcement is considered necessary for further progress, programmed material provides pupils with evaluation just after their response is made. Furthermore, because individuals are known to learn at a variety of speeds, the programmed materials are self-paced.

A popular reading program which is based on this instructional system is *Programmed Reading* by Buchanan and Sullivan Associates *(E)* which combines the principles of the linguistic approach to word decoding with programmed learning principles. Workbook pages are sectioned off and a colorful picture and corresponding sentences or questions to which pupils are to respond are placed within each section. The correct answer is printed in a column to the side and is masked by a paper marker until the student responds. Comparative study of programmed instruction with use of basal texts indicates conflicting results. Burkott and Clegg *(6)* found no differences, but Rogers and Fox *(25)* found significantly better word recognition in children taught with programmed material. Some programmed materials are machine-based; some have prescribed materials while others such as O.K. Moore's Responsive Environment (see Chall, *7)* allow for more self-discovery in reading acquisition.

Instructional Systems Based on Alphabet Reform

Under the assumption that the traditional orthography (t.o.) of written English consisting of twenty-six letters with lower and upper case forms is inadequate for representing the varied sounds of the English language (which contains approximately forty-four phonemes), educators have made use of Sir James Pitman's augmented alphabet as an instructional tool in initial reading. This alphabet, called i.t.a., *initial teaching alphabet,* has forty-four characters, each of which corresponds to a phoneme. Upper case letters in t.o. are eliminated in i.t.a. in favor of enlarged lower case forms. With this instructional system, children are introduced first to the augmented alphabet and continue to read in i.t.a. for a period of about a year to eighteen months. At the end of this period, they go through a transition period. During transition to t.o., the i.t.a. characters are gradually replaced by traditional letter forms. The major argument for use of i.t.a. is that when each phoneme has an equivalent grapheme, the written language corresponds closely to the oral forms. In other words, i.t.a. orthography is a reliable representation of oral language during the decoding stage.

The i.t.a. instructional system was first introduced in England. These programs did not recommend a change in teaching methods, although there was generally a heavier phonics emphasis than in other British programs. Downing *(11)* has reported that i.t.a. children performed better than t.o. children when each group was tested with the orthography with which they had learned. It should be noted though that some i.t.a. children did suffer during transition to t.o.

Mazurkiewicz and Tanyzer have adapted i.t.a. to American standard dialect. Their *Early-to-Read: i.t.a. Program (N)* encourages changes in method in the direction of consciously increased training in sound/symbol relationships. Five of the "Cooperative Research Studies of First Grade Reading," which examined comparative use of i.t.a., showed that it did not result in significantly improved reading achievement except in word recognition. In this case, according to Fry *(17),* the i.t.a. pupils were better than pupils taught with conventional basals. The high cost of buying story books and content materials in i.t.a. and possible confusion for children who move from one school to another during the program are practical disadvantages of i.t.a. In addition, since i.t.a. is written to represent standard dialect, speakers of nonstandard dialects are at a disadvantage. These children will not receive the possible benefits from the close sound/symbol correspondence inherent in i.t.a.

A less drastic adaptation of the traditional alphabet to oral language is the Diacritical Marking System. The traditional letters are maintained in this system but are marked to indicate pronunciation. This alphabetical change does not require the period of transition which i.t.a. demands. Nonetheless, a three-year way comparison of i.t.a., Diacritical Marking, and t.o. has indicated no differences in the three-systems *(18)*.

The Language Experience Instructional System

For years, teachers of primary-grade pupils have on occasion helped their pupils produce experience charts. The teacher recorded children's dictated comments on a specified topic; then, the teacher, the teacher and pupils, or the pupils themselves (depending on the reading level) read the dictated story. The teacher often used key words from the story later in a vocabulary lesson. This procedure was used to record special events such as a new animal in the class, a class trip, or an important school happening. In recent years, this use of group experience charts has been extended as an instructional system for beginning reading.

With the language experience system, children dictate many stories to the teacher even before they are ready to read. Some are individual stories; some are group stories; some represent an effort by the whole class. Teachers use the printed story as a focus for training in prereading skills. Thus, pupils learn to recognize letters within the context of words; they learn to recognize their own names, etc. Words which begin with the same initial letter are isolated and become the material for auditory-visual discrimination. Children learn that spoken words have written equivalents and that the spaces mark off printed words. When each sentence occupies a separate line, they become conscious of how punctuation parallels intonation. Once readiness skills are underway, children who have dictated many stories, have heard those stories read, have identified words which begin with the same letter, have learned to name letters within words, and have learned to distinguish different words which have similar form usually begin to recall words which they have used often or which are critical to a story. (For example, *elephant* may be recalled two days after a story about a trip to the zoo.) Once children begin to recognize such previously used words, Stauffer *(30)* recommends that the teacher initiate a *word bank*. A pupils' word bank is a collection of words which he can recognize on sight. This collection is used as the material for development of skills. Children also are encouraged very early to write stories themselves. Dictated and self-written stories on an individual and group basis are continued, but, once reading is underway, group reading experiences from tradebooks or basal texts become important components of the reading program *(30)*.

Advocates of the language-experience system, such as Stauffer *(30)* and Lee and Allen *(23)*, believe that children's learning is enhanced by inductively and independently using language knowledge as a crucial aid in reading acquisition. Because these educators think requirements for accurate spelling are inhibiting to beginning writing, they contend that learning the idiosyncracies of the English spelling system can be postponed until children have had a good start at literacy. When we read the samples below of children's self-written stories, it is obvious that communicability is seldom lost because of the unconventional spellings. Because the writer and reader share the phonological structure of English, there is no difficulty in deciphering these uniquely spelled words. Furthermore, as children listen to word sounds and translate them into printed code, they acquire awareness of sound/symbol relationships which will serve them in decoding unfamiliar printed words.

My dog's name is Furry. I like my dog. I love my dog to peasis.

Brad[3]

My Mother and Father won't let me and my sister have a dog. Becose if I had a dog I wood haff to take caer of it and evry day I wood haff to take if for a walk and I wont have time to take it for a walk. Becose I have two cats.

Maura

My dog's name was peper. My dog was playful. He likes to be peted n' played with n' pated on the head.

Philip

My dog awos jumps on my bed and he awos wake me up.

James

From a theoretical viewpoint, this instructional system has a good deal of linguistic support. When learning to read with printed forms of his own oral language, the beginning reader finds no mismatch between his syntactic knowledge and the written structures. Furthermore, there is no lack of conceptual background, as the material consists of the reader's unique experience with the world. In addition, even when there exists a variety of nonstandard dialects in a class, each pupil can learn to read with material which represents

---

[3] These stories were written in September, 1972, by second graders at the Dogwood School, Park Forest, Illinois.

his language. From a human point of view, this instructional system encourages and requires—when properly applied—one-to-one contact between teacher and pupil as the pupil shares his important ideas and experiences. Not only will the teacher closely share communication, he can use the dictated story to gauge the pupil's conceptual level and oral language skill. Sylvia Ashton-Warner's vivid and compelling book *Teacher (2)* demonstrates clearly the social and human interaction which occurs when a sensitive teacher begins to communicate with his pupils' real level of thinking and experience.

Research data from studies comparing this instructional system with others is fairly encouraging. Allen was one of the first modern proponents of language experience and his early study *(1)* revealed that language experience resulted in achievement gains that were at least equal to those of a basal reader program. Bond and Dykstra's "Cooperative Research First-Grade Programs in Reading Instruction" demonstrates few differences between language experience and basal systems *(4)*, but a long-term comparative study by Stauffer and Hammond *(31)* shows more positive effects from language experience. After three years, the pupils trained in this integrated system were better than the basal group in content area subjects, in rate and accuracy of reading, on an individually administered word recognition test, and on a measure of creative writing.

Serwer's analysis *(27)* of data from a longitudinal examination of reading achievement of New York City inner-city children is of particular interest. When the achievements of pupils from a basal plus phonics program were compared with language experience trained pupils, the basal plus phonics pupils did better during the first and second year *(19);* however, by the end of the third grade, the language experience students were significantly better in comprehension than were the other students. Apparently, positive effects from this system become evident only after two or three years of instruction.

Some writers in the field of reading, such as Heilman *(21)* and Spache and Spache *(28)*, point out that facilitation of the language experience system is difficult. There are classroom management problems, and there are difficulties associated with initiating and extending decoding training. There is also a need to constantly stimulate pupils' inventions and creative expression. Stauffer *(30)* and Lee and Allen *(23)* have described instructional techniques for managing the system. Chapter 9 outlines other possible procedures.

Although the instructional system used depends on pupil output, there are commercial materials available. The Encyclopedia Britannica Press produces the *Language Experience Program (B)* by Allen and Allen which helps to establish a framework within which to work. Scott Foresman's *Reading Systems* by Aaron et. al. *(A)* is a meaning-emphasis basal program meant to support children's language experience. Martin's *Sounds of Language* series *(M)* is an excellent adjunct to the language experience system. Oral reading of poems, songs, folk tales, and fantasies beautifully illustrates rhythm, rhyme, and repetition of language forms. The author presents no prescribed instructional program. Group experiences with these texts can enhance the beginning reader's oral language store and stimulate his own dictated and written stories.

The Individualized Reading System

Individualized reading is interpreted in different ways by different educators. In a totally individualized reading program, pupils read independently for the most part. Direct teaching occurs during independent conferences with the teacher *after* periods of independent reading. Comprehension questions and vocabulary review give teachers information about each individual pupil's progress.

The system is based on the assumption that learning rates and styles are so varied that grouping children obscures these critical differences. It holds that the best way to approach learning is to encourage each pupil to develop his potential in his own unique way. Some teachers view their role in an individualized system as that of a facilitator and are reluctant to limit their pupils' choice of books and reading levels. Others carefully guide their students' choices of books so that they read different kinds of books at their instructional reading level. This second group of teachers is apt to have a separate word recognition skills program, while the first group may include word recognition training as needed during the individual conferences.

Although Sartain *(26)* reported no significantly positive effects of use of an individualized reading system over use of basals, Johnson's *(22)* study of three years of individualized instruction showed strong positive effects. Spencer's *(29)* study demonstrated higher scores for individually taught pupils who also had experienced a heavy phonics program. It appears that when combined with phonics and when done well, an individualized reading system is of benefit to students. Teachers report observation of increased interest and independence among pupils taught with this system.

Another type of individualized instruction in reading reflects the adaptation of a general individualized system used in all content areas to reading instruction. In this program, reading skills are specified and placed in sequence. Instructional objectives help to determine the assessment of preinstructional achievement and post-instructional growth. In some programs, the instructional techniques are predetermined; in others, teachers plan their own instruction. An example of the former type of program, in which the teacher is primarily a facilitator of a total program, is the Individually Prescribed Instruction; an example of the latter is the *Wisconsin Design for Reading Skill Development (S)*. The Wisconsin plan is designed to identify clearly skill development needs and to provide a system to meet these needs. Pupils are engaged in a skill program as well as in developmental reading activities.

Thus, even more than with the other major instructional systems, programs within the individualized system vary widely. Some are quite open, while others are highly structured in terms of the predetermination of diagnosis, sequencing, and content of lessons. The common element is the conscious effort to focus on individual student ability and to design a program to suit each individual. This is, of course, the goal of teachers using every system, but it is the major thrust of the individualized reading system.

SUMMARY AND RECOMMENDATIONS

The diagram of the beginning reader which was introduced in Chapter 6 is repeated at this point to provide the focal point for a summary of the instructional systems discussed in this chapter. The vocabulary controlled system based on *high-frequency words* includes instruction in all seven aspects of the diagram. Initial introduction to reading establishes a base of sight recognition by *feature discrimination*, or recognition of letter and word shapes. During the first year of instruction, pupils learn to use substitution and phonics rules to relate the oral equivalents, or *words sounded*, to printed words. Use also is made of contextual and picture clues to develop *contextual meaning*. Pupils are encouraged to achieve understanding of the *meaning* of the story content. The supplement of a strong phonics program increases pupils' ability to unlock the *words*

FIGURE 9

The Beginning Reader[4]

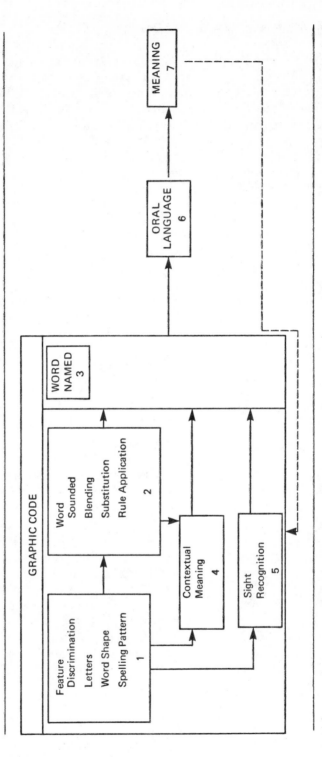

[4] Inspired by and changed from K. S. Goodman, "The Psycholinguistic Nature of the Reading Process," in *The Psycholinguistic Nature of the Reading Process*," ed. K. S. Goodman (Detroit: Wayne State University Press, 1967), pp. 17 and 19. Copyright © 1967 by Wayne State University Press. Reformulated by permission of the publisher and the author.

sounded by means of sound/symbol relationships early in reading acquisition.

When vocabulary is controlled by *sound/symbol correspondences,* as in many linguistic programs, instruction is almost exclusively concentrated on *feature discrimination,* on spelling patterns and oral-written equivalents, *or words sounded,* so that pupils can *name words.* Thus, pupils have a limited repertoire of word recognition skills. *Meaning* is *not* an important goal and, as a result, relatedness between the written message and oral language may be by-passed. Popular examples of the *programmed system* also emphasize *feature discrimination, words sounded,* and *words named. Alphabet reform systems* are intended to help pupils make efficient use of these three components, while clues from *contextual meaning* are also used. *Meaning* is achieved by direct reference to the *oral language* code.

The *language experience system* offers pupils a variety of alternative techniques for unlocking words. Use of *contextual meaning* is one critical tool, but teachers can include in their instruction a phonics skill program to help pupils use *feature discrimination, words sounded,* and the *words named.* The word bank is the expanding collection of *sight words.* This system assures explicit use of *oral language* to achieve *meaning* because the material is dictated oral language. In this way, the testing and providing aspects of reading behavior are stressed.

The *individualized reading system* neither stresses one aspect of beginning reading behavior nor does it ignore any other. However, a highly systematic individualized program tends to center instruction around each of the possible word recognition techniques as isolated elements unless teachers help pupils develop an overview of the entire process.

Some important points which have been made about beginning reading acquisition in this chapter are:

1. Reading is a meaningful process. Communication between reader and writer is necessary for reading to occur.
2. To be able to achieve comprehension, beginning readers have to process the individual words they name through their language knowledge systems.
3. Beginning reading materials should reflect the language structures commonly used by children so that the children can use their language facility in learning to read.
4. Children should learn a number of methods for decoding words which are in their oral but not their reading vocabulary.
5. Beginning readers appear to benefit from training in sound/

symbol correspondences during the first two years of reading instruction.

6. Children also use context to figure out unknown words. Explicit instruction in use of context with associated sound/symbol awareness may hasten the development of skilled reading behavior.

7. There are a number of systems for beginning reading instruction. Successful beginning reading is dependent more on teaching effectiveness than on the characteristics of different instructional systems.

8. The most common system controls vocabulary in terms of the frequency of word usage. Many basal reading programs published since 1968 show increased vocabulary, a stronger phonics program, and a greater variety of subject matter than did earlier basals. It should be noted that when using this system, teachers must take care that individual needs are met.

9. Another system for reading instruction is control of vocabulary in terms of sound/symbol correspondence. Sometimes, children in programs based on this system are explicitly taught how to *sound out words;* in other programs, children are encouraged to induce their own methods for relating symbol to sound. Since the first stories in programs of this nature are likely to have little meaning, teachers must take care that children develop the idea that reading is a meaningful process.

10. Another system, the language experience approach, promotes use of children's dictated and written stories as reading material. Teachers need to include sound/symbol correspondence instruction and early reading of published materials deliberately to expand reading ability if they use this system.

11. Another system is individualized instruction either by use of programmed materials or by student choice of reading material. Attention to individual learning styles is required on the part of the teacher with this system.

12. Another system adapts the printed symbols to provide one-to-one correspondence between sound and print. Use of such a system requires a gradual adjustment to conventional orthography.

13. There are combinations of these systems, a notable one being DISTAR[5] which is a highly structured decoding approach to reading.

---

[5]S. Engelmann, E. C. Brunner, S. Stearns, *DISTAR Instructional System* (Chicago: Science Research Associates, Inc., 1972).

14. Whatever the system used, teachers must diagnose entry ability, monitor growth, and attend to individual needs whenever possible.
15. Whatever system is used, teachers must plan for stimulating, varied, and logically developed lessons. Well-planned lessons can occur in formal or informal situations.

In spite of these recommendations, the reader who is given a program which is not his or her preference should be reminded that no one reading system has been found to be the best, that children learn to read under a wide variety of systems, and that teacher expectation and skill remain the critical aspects of reading achievement. Specific instructional techniques intended to promote teacher skill are the concern of Chapter 9.

REFERENCES

1. Allen, R. V., and San Diego Public Schools. "Three Approaches to Reaching Reading." In *Challenge and Experiment in Reading: Proceedings of the International Reading Association* (1962): 153–54.
2. Ashton-Warner, S. *Teacher.* New York: Simon and Schuster, Inc., 1963.
3. Bloomfield, L. "Linguistics and Reading." *Elementary English Review* 19 (1942): 125–30; 183–86.
4. Bond, J. L., and Dykstra, R. "The Cooperative Research Program in First-Grade Reading Instruction." *Reading Research Quarterly* 3 (1967): 9–142.
5. Brzeinsky, J. E. "Beginning Reading in Denver." *The Reading Teacher* 17 (1964): 16–21.
6. Burkott, A. P., and Clegg, A. A. G. "Programmed vs. Basal Readers in Remedial Reading." *The Reading Teacher* 21 (1968): 745–48.
7. Chall, J. *Learning to Read: The Great Debate.* New York: McGraw-Hill Book Company, 1967.
8. Channon, G. "Bulljive-Language Teaching in a Harlem School." *The Urban Review* 2 (1968): 5–12.
9. Dolch, E. W. "A Basic Sight Vocabulary." *Elementary School Journal* 36 (1936): 456–460.
10. _____. "A Basic Sight Vocabulary." *Elementary School Journal* 37 (1936): 268–72.

11. Downing, J. A. "Initial Teaching Alphabet: Results after Six Years." *Elementary School Journal* 69 (1969): 242–49.

12. Durkin, D. "The Achievement of Preschool Readers: Two Longitudinal Studies." *Reading Research Quarterly* 1 (1966): 5–36.

13. ———. *Children Who Read Early.* New York: Teachers College Press, Columbia University, 1966.

14. ———. "A Language Arts Program for Prefirst-Grade Children: Two-Year Achievement Report." *Reading Research Quarterly* 6 (1970): 534–65.

15. ———. *Teaching Young Children to Read.* Boston: Allyn & Bacon, Inc.: 1972.

16. Eames, T. H. "Physical Factors in Reading." *Reading Teacher* 15 (1962): 427–32.

17. Fry, E. "I.T.A.: A Look at the Research Data." *Education* 88 (1967): 549–53.

18. ———. "Comparison of Beginning Reading with I.T.A., D.M.S., and T.O. after Three years." *The Reading Teacher* 22 (1969): 357–62.

19. Harris, A. J., and Serwer, B. L. "Comparing Reading Approaches in First-Grade Teaching with Disadvantaged Children." *The Reading Teacher* 19 (1966): 631–42.

20. Harris, L. A., and Smith, C. B. *Reading Instruction through Diagnostic Teaching.* New York: Holt, Rinehart, & Winston, Inc., 1972.

21. Heilman, A. W. *Principles and Practices of Teaching Reading,* 3rd ed. Columbus, Ohio: Charles E. Merrill Publishing Co., 1972.

22. Johnson, R. H. "Individualized and Basal Primary Reading Programs." *Elementary English* 42 (1965): 902–04; 915.

23. Lee, D. M., and Allen, R. V. *Learning to Read through Experience.* New York: Appleton-Century-Crofts, 1963.

24. Micucci, P. "Let's *Not* Teach Reading in Kindergarten!" *Elementary English* 64 (1964): 246–51.

25. Rodgers, P. R., and Fox, C. E. "A Comparison of McGraw-Hill Programmed Reading and the Scott-Foresman Basic Reading Program." *Illinois School Research* 4 (1967): 45–47.

26. Sartain, H. W. "The Roseville Experiment with Individualized Reading." *The Reading Teacher* 13 (1960): 277–81.

27. Serwer, B. L. "Linguistic Support for a Method of Teaching Beginning Reading to Black Children." *Reading Research Quarterly* 5 (1969): 449–67.

28. Spache, G. D., and Spache, E. B. *Reading in the Elementary School,* 2d ed. Boston: Allyn & Bacon, Inc., 1969.

29. Spencer, D. U. "Individualized versus a Basal Reader Program in Rural Communities—Grades One and Two." *The Reading Teacher* 21 (1967): 11–17.

30. Stauffer, R. G. *The Language Experience Approach to the Teaching of Reading.* New York: Harper and Row, Publisher, 1970.

31. Stauffer, R. G., and Hammond, W. D. "The Effectiveness of Language Arts and Basic Reader Approaches to First-Grade Reading Instruction —Extended into Third Grade." *Reading Research Quarterly* 5 (1969): 468–99.

32. Thorndike, E. L. "The Vocabulary of Books for Children in Grades Three to Eight: I." *Teachers College Record* 38 (1936–37): 196–205.

33. _____. "The Vocabulary of Books for Children in Grades Three to Eight: II." *Teachers College Record* 38 (1936–37): 316–23.

34. _____. "The Vocabulary of Books for Children in Grades Three to Eight: III." *Teachers College Record* 38 (1936–37): 416–29.

35. Thorndike, E. L., and Lorge, I. *The Teachers Word Book of 30,000 Words.* New York: Teachers College, Columbia University, 1944.

READING PROGRAMS

A. Aaron, J. E., et al. *Scott Foresman Reading Systems.* Glenview, Illinois: Scott, Foresman and Company, 1971.

B. Allen, R. V., and Allen, C. *Language Experience Program.* Chicago: Encyclopedia Britannica Press, 1966.

C. Bank Street College of Education. *The Bank Street Basal Reading Program.* New York: The Macmillan Company, 1966.

D. Bloomfield, L., and Barnhart, C. L. *Let's Read: A Linguistic Approach.* Bronxville, New York: Clarence L. Barnhart, Inc., 1963.

E. Buchanan, C. D., and Sullivan Associates. *Programmed Reading.* New York: McGraw-Hill Book Company, 1963.

F. Clymer, T., and Gates, D. *Reading 360.* Boston: Ginn and Company, 1969.

G. Durr, W. K.; Lepere, J. M.; and Austin, M. L. *The Houghton Mifflin Readers.* Boston: Houghton Mimin Company, 1971.

H. Early, M.; Cooper, Ely K.; Santeusanio, N.; Adell, M. *The Bookmark Reading Series.* New York: Harcourt, Brace, Jovanovich, Inc., 1970.

I. Fries, C. C.; Fries, A. C.; Wilson, R. G.; Rudolf, M. K. *Merrill Linguistic Readers.* Columbus, Ohio: Charles E. Merrill Publishing Co., 1966.

J. Harris, T. L.; Creekmore, M.; Greenman, M. *Phonetic Keys to Reading.* Oklahoma City, Oklahoma: The Economy Company, 1966.

K. McCracken, G., and Walcutt, C. C. *Basic Reading.* Philadelphia, Pennsylvania: J. B. Lippincott Company, 1963.

L. McKee P., et al. *The Reading for Meaning Series,* Boston: Houghton-Mifflin Company, 1963.

M. Martin, Bill. *Sounds of Language.* New York: Holt, Rinehart, & Winston, 1970.

N. Mazurkiewicz, A. J., and Tanyzer, H. J. *Early-to-Read: i. t. a. Program.* New York: Initial Teaching Alphabet Publications, Inc., 1963.

O. Rasmussen, D., and Goldberg. L. *Basic Reading Series.* Chicago: Science Research Associates, Inc., 1964.

P. Robinson, H. M.; Monroe, H.; and Artley, A. S. *The New Basic Reading Program.* Chicago: Scott, Foresman and Company, 1965.

Q. Russell, D. H., et al. *The Ginn Basic Readers.* Boston: Ginn and Company, 1966.

R. Schoolfield, L. D., and Timberlake, J. B. *Phonovisual Method.* Washington, D.C.: Phonovisual Products, 1961.

S. Wisconsin Research and Development Center for Cognitive Learning. *The Wisconsin Design for Reading Skill Development.* Madison: The University of Wisconsin, 1970.

T. Writers' Committee of the Great Cities School Improvement Program of the Detroit Public Schools. *City Schools Reading Program.* Chicago: Follett Publishing Company, 1962.

CHAPTER 9

Instructional Procedures for Beginning Reading

In the three sections that follow, the emphasis is on teacher deci-sion-making for instructional needs, planning, and the development of materials. Of course, a multitude of published materials for read-ing instruction is available, but this chapter is not intended as a source list of materials. Instead, the suggestions in this chapter ought to serve as guidelines for the teacher for choosing published materials.

Because of the emphasis on teacher decision-making, there is an absence of reference to highly structured *teacher-proof* programs. The omission is intentional for the underlying instructional ap-proach in this book is alien to teacher-proof materials. Although many teachers and administrators look for *materials* which will upgrade instruction, the history of research in reading indicates that improvement depends on teachers—their knowledge and instruc-tional ability. Even with a teacher-programmed system, effective instruction occurs only when teachers thoroughly understand the program assumptions. In contrast to teacher-proof programs, the recommendations of this book require that teachers be the decision makers and planners for instruction.

Based on the analysis and discussion in previous chapters, the recommendations for reading instruction that follow include use of the language experience approach, word recognition techniques, and extension of reading into basal texts and trade books. The preread-ing period initiates language experience activities and word recognition readiness; the transition from readiness to actual reading instruction should be gradual.

LANGUAGE EXPERIENCE

In Chapter 7, the basic concepts of language experience were introduced. In Chapter 8, we examined the language experience approach as a beginning reading system and found its most salient features included:

1. Use of children's oral language for reading material; the child's written language therefore parallels his spoken language.
2. Built-in provision for dialect and experiential variation.
3. A personalized instructional approach; the teacher and child share important thoughts, experiences, and observations.
4. A natural means for an integrated language arts program; reading, writing, listening (to others' stories), and speaking (dictating) are all involved in the production of language-experience stories.
5. An open enough system to encourage creativity in children and in teaching.
6. Ease in combining the system with other methods of teaching reading.

Before children actually begin to learn to read, they have acquired the following prereading understandings from their readiness work with dictated stories:

1. Writing preserves oral language. Written language communicates to readers.
2. Speech and writing are made up of words.
3. Sentences are made up of words and express thoughts.

Instructional Sequence

Once children are ready to learn to read, the language experience activities should follow a regular sequence so that maximum use is made of children's stories. The following sequence is slightly amended from one by Stauffer *(27)*.

Day 1: On the first day of the sequence, the child dictates a story to the teacher who reads it back immediately to check it to see if it is *correct.* The child is then asked to identify any words he knows in the story, and those words are underlined. Then, the teacher and child reread the story; the teacher reads and hesitates before each underlined word so that the child can respond.

When taking children's dictation, the teacher should observe a number of conditions. He should encourage free-flowing language as much as possible. That is, it is important that the teacher not interrupt or slow down the story dictation process unless this is necessary. For the unresponsive child, some prodding may be needed, but even in these circumstances, the child's words only are recorded—even if these words are not in complete sentences. For the child who is long-winded, the teacher may need to suggest alternatives because of time constraints. At a good stopping point, he might suggest that they discontinue dictation and continue the following day. He also might suggest that the child's parents complete the story that night. Under no circumstances though should the exuberant child be discouraged.

If the teacher has a primary typewriter available, the dictation process is facilitated. The typed words and spacing are more consistent than in hand-printed stories and are, therefore, perceptually clearer. But if there is no primary typewriter, the teacher should be very sure to have a *very neat, consistent* manuscript form and use a black pen for clarity.

Whether a typewriter or pen is used, a carbon should be made of each story and filed in the child's folder. The files then are used for informal assessment of progress. The file of dictated stories contains data about the size of a child's reading vocabulary (underlined words), the span of his interests (the variation of story content), his ability to observe the world around him, the complexity of his sentence structures, the development of his conceptual understanding, and the extent of his oral vocabulary.

Teachers are often perplexed about taking dictation from nonstandard-speaking children; however, since the goal of this technique is to preserve each child's language and unique experiences for reading acquisition, I think the solution is clear. I suggest that the child's sentence structure be preserved as the teacher writes the story but that conventional spelling be used. That is, I would not hesitate to write double negatives, insert a subject pronoun after a topic name, use nonstandard pronouns or immature or nonstandard past tense verbs, but I would spell each word in the traditional manner. Just as children will learn later new ideas and new ways of expressing ideas from reading other's writings, so too will they learn to understand alternative sentence structures.

Day 2:   The previous day's story is reread and, again, the teacher hesitates before each underlined word. If the words underlined previously are identified again, they are underlined again. The reading activity is followed by more sight practice with these words. Twice-underlined words are listed in random order or isolated from the story context by a window card so that clues are minimized and the newly underlined words are practiced.

Day 3:   On rereading, those words still recognized in and out of context are printed on small cards by the teacher (so as to maintain model print) and are placed in the child's word bank. A new story can be produced on the second or third day for the active, excited learner, and the sequence begins again.

Development of Sight Vocabulary

The *word bank* can be made from a child's size shoe box which has been decorated and labeled by the child (*e.g., Jim's Word Bank*). When there are only a few words in the bank, the cards can be arranged haphazardly. A block can be used to hold the cards upright. There should be ample room for continual growth—a highly motivating factor for beginners. Since all known words are deposited in the word bank, the word bank is the store of the child's sight vocabulary for the first weeks and months of reading acquisition. Therefore, the word bank is very important; it is the source for sight word practice and for other word recognition learning. In addition, the word bank has an emotional appeal to the child; each child saves his *known* and therefore *important* words just as adults save money in the bank. By contrast, a common classroom procedure is to give children cards with words they do *not* know. With the word bank, positive learning is reinforced; in other systems, negative learning is reinforced.

At first, the word bank words will be the words of heavy critical content in the dictated stories, but because the child's stories will include the most frequent words of the language, prepositions, articles, conjunctions, and auxiliaries will soon be acquired as well. The teacher should make certain that the frequently used words are being learned so that the transition to reading in basals and easy-to-read trade books is eased. Words listed on the Dolch Basic Sight Word List *(4)* or in a recent modernized version by Johnson *(16)* should be the source for frequent words. Individual assessment of the growing vocabulary comes from the child's file or word bank; the teacher matches the child's acquired vocabulary with the word list. When there is a dearth of high-frequency function words, the teacher should point out one or two of these words in each story, explain that they are very important to learn, and then underline them *with a wavy line.* When the child recognizes the words on rereading, the wavy line is erased and replaced by a straight line. Since these words are so common, children will use them again and again in their own stories where their contextual meanings—the only meanings these function words have—are clear and learn them with relative ease.

In order to provide sufficient practice and additional skill work with the word bank words, the following independent activities are recommended:

1. Children enjoy finding their first word bank words in newspapers and magazines. They can cut these words out and paste them on the back of their cards.
2. Two children can share their words to see how many similar words they have. New acquisitions are often made this way.
3. Once a child has acquired ten or so words, he probably can make a new sentence by arranging the words in order. Then, when he copies his "new" sentence, the child has practice in manuscript writing and early creative writing as well.
4. Two or three children can combine their words (after initialing their own words) to devise a whole story by placing the word cards and sentences on the floor. Again, the copying procedure reinforces handwriting skill as well as the concept of preservation by writing.
5. After illustrating a story or observation, children should look through their word banks for appropriate words for a title, arrange the word cards in order, and copy the title onto their illustration.
6. In some British schools, teachers teach manuscript writing by having the children trace over the words printed by the teacher. When the child's pencil moves far from the model, he immediately knows his form is inaccurate. After he has developed skill in tracing, the child learns to copy the story words. Later, he copies the story on a new sheet of paper.
7. Once children have learned to look through their word banks for words to use in their titles or for sentence words, they will learn that if the words are in some kind of consistent order, it is easier to find them. This is a natural moment to introduce

the idea of *alphabetizing*. A sample chart can be devised which the children can use as a model for alphabetizing their word banks once they know the sequence of letters in the alphabet. As the teacher explains the chart illustrated in Figure 10 below, the children sort their own cards. (Note that the words are alphabetized at first only by initial letter.)

FIGURE 10

8. Once the words of the word bank have been alphabetized, picture dictionaries are introduced in such a way that the children understand that the same alphabetizing principle is used and that the dictionary serves as a source for even more words. With alphabetized word banks and picture dictionaries in use, beginning readers are well on their way to becoming independent readers and learners.

9. If the teacher provides many opportunities to practice and use word bank words, most children will recognize these words on sight with ease, but informal testing is needed, too. The words should be listed in random order on a sheet of paper and the child directed to name each word quickly. Words not named should be studied again in story context and further practice with word games provided.

10. Practice games with sight words are simple to devise. For example, Bingo is easily adapted to sight word practice. Teachers also can make a long ladder on a sheet of paper with a prize at the top. As soon as each word written between the ladder steps is named quickly, the prize is won. Or a cut-out train engine can reach the station when each word written on the tracks is quickly named.

11. The work with word bank words will not be sight recognition practice alone. These words provide the basis for much of the

development of the other word recognition learning which will be described in a later section of this chapter.

When the size of the word bank has increased so that children are able to read nearly every word of their dictated stories, the teacher should underline only the *unknown* words. These words, once learned, are added to the word bank. At this time, too, children will be reading in texts and trade books (see the last section of the chapter) and will be writing many of their own stories.

Beginning Writing

Writing as a mechanical skill really begins as children learn letter forms, trace over the teacher's print, copy under the teacher's print, and copy on separate paper. Writing as a creative experience begins with the first dictated story. The mechanical and creative components are united when children form sentences and stories with their word cards and copy their results.

The language experience system encourages early writing as a total activity. Stauffer *(27)*, Hall *(10)*, and Lee and Allen *(20)* offer a number of specific suggestions about how to stimulate and extend writing experiences. I would suggest that whole-story creation in written form by the child begin when he has the mechanical skills (formation of letters with ease and some legibility), when he has a workable word bank with fifty or more words alphabetized, and when he shows signs of eagerness to begin.

The teacher should respect the child's every attempt at early writing. It is crucial that children feel successful when they are applying their vocabulary directly, exploring their own thoughts, and expressing them in writing. Some children will be more creative than others; some will be better at the mechanics; some will have a wider vocabulary upon which to draw. These differences should not be used to differentiate the children, however, since critical comparisons will inhibit development. Nonetheless, differential reinforcement can be used to extend these beginning experiences. This reinforcement is directed to individuals in such a way that the children are praised and shown which aspects of their work are strong and which need attention. For example, with a child whose ideas are good but whose mechanical skills are not consistent, the teacher might say, "What wonderful ideas you have in your stories, John, and look at how well you are beginning to write with big, clear letters. The words on the top line here are especially clear." With a child who has difficulty getting her ideas across clearly, the teacher might say, "Yesterday's story about your family, Clare, was so well done. You told us first who is in your family and then what your apartment is like. Today try to tell us first one idea and then another in a new sentence."

One way in which a teacher of language experience encourages early independent writing is by acting as a facilitator of spelling rather than as a speller. Conventional spelling should not be one of the initial goals of early writing for emphasis on it will interfere with the more important goal of communicating ideas. Children should learn to use their word banks, picture dictionaries, and displayed word charts (color words, weather words, clothing words) to find words they need and cannot figure out themselves. Often, however, a child will ask, "How do you write . . . ?" The teacher ought to respond, "Well, say it again to yourself. What sound do you hear first? What letter do you think you should write? Good. Now, what do you hear next?" Children are encouraged to relate their growing sense of the relatedness between sound and writing to their efforts. By so doing, they are developing an actively induced system of sound and symbol which will reinforce both reading and writing success.

Many teachers and parents have expressed fear that early writing which encourages children to write words as they hear them rather than with memorized, correct spellings will result in the acquisition of bad spelling habits. However, with experience, the transition to conventional spelling does occur independently. Many words which have been spelled unconventionally are changed to the conventional form after the children have realized for themselves that their word *luv* is written *love* in books. The teacher can juxtapose the child's word and the conventionally spelled word to hasten this change. Formal spelling usually begins in the second grade and ought to complement the growing sense of spelling accuracy by emphasizing the difficult words which have little sound/symbol correspondence.

Although many of the first self-written stories are brought home by the young author, it is a good idea to collect stories and illustrations on a theme into a book once the newness of the school experience has worn off a bit. Some techniques for bookmaking are:

1. A three-hole punch is used on each sheet, the holes are reinforced, and brass fasteners (or wide yarn) are used to hold the book together.
2. For more permanent books, it is a good idea to glue each sheet on oaktag, laminate each reinforced page, attach the pages to each other by strong masking tape, and bind with oaktag. Card-

board covered with bright material makes an attractive book
cover.
3. Two or three stories can be glued to a single large chart, a cut
   paper cover made and attached to thick yarn in order to make
   a *huge* book.

Of course, some books should contain dictated stories which will
continue to provide opportunity for full expression of ideas. Other
books of self-written stories indicate clearly that the children's
efforts are valued. These books should become part of the classroom
library. Children delight in finding their stories and reading them
to friends. On occasion, a child's self-written story should be dated
and filed with his dictated stories to provide a source for evaluating
growth of writing skill.

Classroom Organization

Classroom organization is another area of concern, especially for
inexperienced teachers. While the focus of language experience is on
the individual, group management can be applied to this approach.
For example, children can be placed in groups according to their
story output. In this case, while members of two groups of children
are engaged at their seats in independent work, one group can be
seated around a table together. The same story stimulant can be
introduced to the whole group by having the other members of the
group practice with their underlined words, match their words with
those in newspapers spread out before them, illustrate their intended or just completed stories, create sentences with their word
bank words, and match each other's word bank words while the
teacher takes individual dictation. After each child has dictated and
reread his story, the group can listen to each other's stories. Sometimes, the group together will produce one story which is written on
a large chart. Experience charts are treated much as individual
stories are. When the children have collected between seventy-five
and one hundred words in their word banks, they will move into
basal text reading.

If the teacher is able to develop interest centers which serve as the
content of dictated and/or self-written stories, grouping is done by
interest rather than achievement. When the teacher is working with
each group, he takes dictation, reads with each child, and provides
direction for further word practice or supplementary activity associated with the topic. Group organization is facilitated by stimulat-

ing activity. When children are excited by a proposed experience, it becomes much easier to organize them for on-task involvement than when a monotonous routine is followed. When student teachers complain about discipline difficulties and disorganization, what is needed is usually an additional planned motivating experiences.

Suggestions for Language Experience Activities

Teachers using language experience need to be creative in stimulating both the dictated and the self-written stories and observations. The more the teacher relates the language experiences with on-going classroom units and other activities, the more relevant the program will become. The general categories of stimulants which are discussed here are personal experiences, scientific observations and learning, nature, picture storytelling, role-playing through words, and folk and family stories. Stauffer *(27)*, Lee and Allen *(20)*, Herrick and Nerbourg *(15)*, Hall *(10)*, and Allen and Allen *(1)* offer many more such possible stimulants.

Personal experiences: Sharing of personal experience should be handled with care. The teacher should never expose a child's personal difficulties, but he and the others in the class should delight in a child's joy. Some suggestions for sharing personal experiences in the context of the language experience approach are:

1. By introducing the word *me* on the first day of first grade, the teacher, from that beginning, can carry out introductions in dictated stories which can be collected later into a book of self-portraits [see *A Day Dream I Had at Night (9)* for ideas on how to make books].
2. Illustrated and accompanying stories about the family.
3. Personal lists of "Things to Do."
4. Stories beginning with the following titles: "My Favorite Animal," "What I Hate to Do at Home," "My Favorite Relative," "The Most Beautiful Place I've Seen," "My Favorite TV Program," "My New Baby Sister," "What I Look Like," "My Mother," and "Our Trip."

Scientific observations and learnings: Any simple experiment performed *by the children* can be translated into an experience story. On-going notes of observations are a good idea. Some suggestions in this area are:

1. Descriptions of how an electrical circuit is made.

2. Asking the question, "Which objects floated and which did not?"
3. Keeping a weather chart to record seasonal change.
4. Asking, "Which objects are attracted by magnets and which are not?"
5. Asking, "Which of these foods have seeds inside and which do not?"
6. Asking, "What would have happened to our plants without water, without sun, with water, with sun, etc.?
7. Since measurement is an important mathematical concept, it is important to develop the concept of measurement of size determined by strings, of weight determined by a simple frame, of temperature, and of measurement of liquids.
8. Descriptions of what happens when oil and water, sugar and water, and detergent and water are mixed.
9. Descriptions of the effect of freezing and boiling water.

Nature: The world around the school environment is available to stimulate language experience no matter where the school is located. A few activities which can be related to language experience follow.

1. Descriptions of the difference between how people move around outside on a snowy day and on a warm day. The teacher can ask how grown-ups and children differ in how they move.
2. Descriptions of the construction (or demolition) of a nearby building.
3. Comparison of the school neighborhood with a contrasting one.
4. Listing all of the foods eaten by the class gerbil or guinea pig.
5. Descriptions of how the class animal cares for her young.

Picture storytelling: This activity is an almost too common way of eliciting stories from the children. Therefore, the teacher must take care in selecting the pictures. As a criterion for choice, he might think of what story *he* could tell from any given picture. A few suggestions to develop this activity follow.

1. Asking, "How would the children in the picture live differently from the children in the class?"
2. By looking at the workers in these pictures, telling what tools each one uses.
3. Beginning to develop a sense of people's diversity by looking at pictures of people from different cultures.

4. Drawing pictures of a classmate, describing him in writing without naming him, and participating in a classroom guessing game to name him.
5. Dictating a story to accompany picture books that have no words. [These books are reviewed by Bissett (2)].

Role-playing through words: In order to maximize the development of abstract language, the teacher should encourage the children to imagine themselves in a new situation. Much motivational introduction is needed before asking the following questions:

1. What would it be like to be an inchworm on the stem of a plant?
2. What would it be like to be a pencil?
3. What would it be like to be the school secretary?
4. What would it be like to be a mother?
5. What would it be like to be a Christmas tree?
6. What would it be like to be a worm in an apple?

Folk and family stories: In *A Day Dream I Had at Night (15)*, Landrum describes how older children of diverse backgrounds collected family stories which were used as reading materials. Some suggestions for similar activities follow.

1. Each child's asking for a special story about his family to be retold and written at school. In a class of children of immigrant parents, the move to America would be a productive source of story material. How each family celebrates Christmas also might provide material, as might the move of the family to a new area.
2. Thinking up a folk tale after hearing the teacher read a number of folk tales and discussing with the teacher their common characteristics.
3. Planning fables to be written by the children after listening to *Aesop's Fables.*

Whatever techniques are used to stimulate language experiences, the teacher should be sure to allow interests to develop naturally from the stimulation that children bring to these programs. And although language experience is important to the beginning of reading, other components are also needed.

WORD RECOGNITION

While the word bank encourages development of a sight vocabulary and early writing offers opportunity for inductive analysis of sound/symbol awareness, children need further techniques for unlocking unknown words if they are to become independent readers of their own and others' writings. In addition to the acquisition of a sight vocabulary, the specific abilities in word recognition that should be developed during the first year of reading instruction are: initial single consonant phonemes; initial consonant clusters (two phonemes); single consonants and consonant clusters in phonograms (*-an* in *pan, fan,* and *can;* and *-est* in *best* and *vest*); inflections on nouns and verbs; other word changes such as abbreviations, contractions, and possessives; vowel sound/symbol correspondences; and use of context. Since this book discusses the *initial* stages of reading acquisition, the list of word recognition skills includes only those usually taught during the first year or so of reading instruction. The list is modified somewhat by personal preferences which emphasize those sound/symbol correspondences which are most productive and which can easily be associated with use of context.

There are a number of excellent sources for more in-depth reading on teaching word recognition techniques than is provided here. Among these are Spache and Spache *(24)* and Heilman *(11)*. Some excellent suggestions for teacher-produced materials can be found in Durkin *(5)*. Commercial materials for instruction abound. The *Phonics We Use (13)* workbooks and accompanying games are an old favorite in a new edition. Durrell and Murphy's *Speech-to-Print Phonics (6)* is also excellent. Garrard Press supplies many inexpensive games to reinforce skills taught in class. Still other old favorites are the Level A and B *Using Sounds* books *(3)* since these combine phonics skills with contextual analysis. In these few pages, it is not possible to describe fully the materials available to the teacher; however, in judging the merit of phonics materials, identification of the approach used and its relevance to the classroom program, clarity of the presentation, the amount of reinforcement and practice provided, and the motivational quality of the material should be considered.

In contrast to the instructional procedures used in the language experience part of the reading program to teach word recognition skills, we are interested in specific achievement of those skills; consequently, the instruction we advocate is more structured.

Initial Single Consonant Phonemes

This area includes instances when one grapheme or letter corresponds with one phoneme and instances when *two* graphemes represent one phoneme. Therefore, it includes both the sound made by *s* in *sick* and the sound made by *sh* in *shut,* although the single grapheme/single phoneme situation is taught first. Readiness training will provide information for initial assessment since the prerequisite understandings are perception of sounds and identification of letters. Once these have been acquired, children are ready to associate initial single consonant letters with sounds. It is important to note that in the instructional steps below, use is made of known word bank words.

Instructional Steps	*Lesson for p/p/*
1. Review of sound of initial position.	1. Teacher asks children to listen to *pat, pick, Peter, Patty;* he then asks how these words are alike.
2. Recognition of letter in initial position.	2. Teacher writes *pat, pick, Peter,* and *Patty* on chart; he then asks if the words are alike and, if so, where and how.
3. Supplying of new examples by children.	3. Teacher asks children to look in their word banks for words that begin like *pat.*
4 Differentiating which words belong and which do not.	4. Children write *P* on a worksheet for each picture that has the phoneme /p/ in initial position.
5. Application of new concept to new words. Nonsense words can be used to test application if children understand that the words are *not real ones.*	5. The teacher writes sentences on a chart with new words beginning with *p* (e.g., "Bobby *put* the toy away.").

These instructional steps form a framework which should be amplified in creative ways. Planning may include a new single consonant sound/symbol correspondence each day for three days. The fourth day can be used for review of the three letters. Practice books can be used or children can create their own. On each page of the child-made book is the target letter on which children paste pictures representing the sound; these pictures are then labeled accordingly.

The sequence of letters introduced needs to be attended to since confusion may arise. For example, since /p/ and /b/, /t/ and /d/, /g/ and /k/, and /f/ and /v/ differ only by the presence of absence of *voicing* (caused by vibrations of the vocal cords), these elements should not be presented next to each other. Furthermore, the instances when two graphemes make one sound should follow the single grapheme/phoneme correspondences. A recommended order is: p = /p/, s = /s/, m = /m/, t = t/t, f = /f/, g = /g/, b = /b/, l = /l/, n = /n/, d = /d/, j = /j/, c and k = /k/, v = /v/, r = /r/, w = /w/, h = /h/, z = /z/, y = /y/, qu = /kw/, x = /ks/, sh = /s/, th = /θ/ and /ð/, ch = /č/, and -ng = /ŋ/. The last six phonemes should be taught only after children have done some work with phonograms.

Initial Consonant Clusters

This area includes situations in which *two consonant graphemes* are heard as *two consonant phonemes:* for example, *st* in *stop* and *cl* in *cluster.* (The word *cluster* also has the *st* cluster in the middle.) Study of phonograms will include final consonant clusters, but we are concerned first only with initial clusters. The instructional steps are similar to those already presented, but they also include review of each single consonant first.

Instructional Steps	*Lesson for cl - /cl/*
1. Review of initial sound.	1. Teacher asks children to identify the initial sound in *can, cup.*
2. Review of other phoneme.	2. Teacher asks children to identify the initial sound in *loud, lap.*
3. Auditory experiences with combined consonant phonemes.	3. Teacher asks children to listen to the combined sound in *cloud, clam, close,* etc.
4. Visual identification.	4. Teacher presents children with written words *cloud, clam, close,* etc.,

and they identify graph-
ic similarities.

5. Children find *cl* words in
   their word banks.

5. Supplying by children of
   new examples.

6. Teacher presents new *cl*
   words in sentence con-
   text.

6. Applying of new con-
   cepts to new words.

Some early important consonant clusters to present are: *st, bl, sp, sn, sk, sl, pl, fl* (*r* clusters in *gr, br, dr, tr, fr,* and *str* are more difficult). Instruction should involve a number of review lessons. Achievement is examined on the auditory level and, more importantly, in use in new words presented in sentence context.

*Single Consonants and Consonant
Clusters Substituted in Phonograms*

As soon as the children are relatively familiar with the initial single consonants, they can be exposed to some familiar phonograms. At first, teachers help children to substitute a single consonant in a phonogram to make a new word; later, the children are encouraged to make their own substitutions with these phonograms so that many new words can be formed (e.g., *-an, -et, -og, -ig, -ed, -ag, -ay, -in, -at, -op, -ell, -all*).
The following list contains some word families with single consonants:

pan	bed	big	pay	cat
man	Ted	dig	may	bat
tan	fed	fig	day	mat
fan	red	jig	bay	sat
can	Ned	pig	say	fat
ran		wig	hay	hat

Once initial consonant clusters have been learned, the following words (and others) can be added:

span	bled	stay	flat	stop
plan	sled	play	skat	flop
	Fred			

And when the phonograms themselves include final consonant clusters, these are some more additions to the list:

pest	past	hand	sold	sent	melt
test	fast	sand	told	tent	felt
best	last	land	fold	bent	belt
nest	vast	band	gold	dent	
vest		stand	bold		
			cold		
			hold		

Prerequisite to any inductive use of phonograms must come understanding of rhyme; this concept should be thoroughly developed during the readiness period. An instructional procedure for developing independent substitutions of consonants in phonograms follows.

Instructional Steps	*Lesson for -ay*
1. Presentation of known words in a pattern.	1. Teacher reminds children that they know the words *say* and *day*.
2. Recognition of rhyme and graphic similarity.	2. Teacher encourages children to identify two common elements of: *-ay* rhyme and letters.
3. Making a new word.	3. Teacher writes *pay;* children identify graphic similarity; they use rhyming and pronounce word.
4. Supplying new and additional words.	4. Children suggest *may* and *hay* and then hunt for more examples from their word banks.
5. Making application to new words.	5. Each child pronounces new words: for example, *bay* and *way*.

In a class where Black English is spoken, words presented in phonograms often rhyme, even if the final consonant sound is weakened. That is, when the teacher pronounces *sold, told, fold,* etc. in Standard English, these words also rhyme when repeated by a Black English-speaking child. Words may be suggested as additions which rhyme in a child's dialect but not in Standard English. For example, a Black English speaker may add *bowl* to his list that includes *fold, cold.* In this case, the teacher will be positive in reinforcing the sound similarity but will show that the words differ graphically. In addition, auditory discrimination of final consonant clusters should be developed in rhyme and jingle practice.

Inflections on Nouns and Verbs

Because children use inflections in their oral speech and can understand the meanings associated with inflections when decoding speech, it is a relatively simple matter to teach understanding of these forms when they are met in print. Most language experience stories and beginning basal stories will have these inflections. *Noun plurals: -s, -es; verb endings: -s, -ed, -d, -ing* (spelling changes on verbs may include doubled consonants as in *stopping* and *stopped* or deletion of *y* in such words as *stories* and *easier*). When a child has used a plural noun *pots*, for example, the root word is presented separately *(pot),* and the child pronounces it. The teacher then asks the child to say the word he uses "when there are two of them." The child can then be directed to listen for the last sound heard when he says "pots." The identified *letter for sound* is added to the printed singular form, and he is told that when more than one is meant, people usually write an *s* at the end of the word. The same procedure can be used for the other inflections. When inflections have resulted in doubled consonants or a deleted *y,* children usually have little difficulty *reading* the words; confusion arises in *spelling,* a matter for more advanced training.

For speakers of Black English, some inflections will not be present in speech, and the inductive approach will not be effective. In this situation, the teacher can simply explain deductively the meanings attached to the various endings. Most children who do not realize all inflections in their oral speech understand the associated concept nevertheless in their basic language knowledge. If the teacher suspects that this is not so, a simple test in which the child matches an appropriate picture with a stimulus sentence will indicate comprehension. For example, the concept of plurality is shown when a child matches the sentence *Billy was playing with the dogs* with a picture of Billy with two dogs rather than the picture of Billy with one.

Other Word Changes

Children will need to learn that simple abbreviations such as *Mr.,* *Mrs., Miss,* and *Ms.* and contractions (which can be taught inductively, with possessives taught first) have special meanings when words are written down.

Vowel Sounds in Predictable Spelling Patterns

This area has been placed late in our list of sound/symbol correspondences deliberately. One reason is that vowels are included in the phonograms presented earlier in the instructional sequence. Another is that vowels are more difficult to learn than consonants. A third is that vowel sound/symbol relationships are less important to word recognition than consonants because fewer words begin with them and because attention to initial letters is often enough to recognize a word when met in context.

Most reading programs introduce the so-called short vowel sounds first. In Ginn's *Reading 360,* the term *unglided* is more correct linguistically speaking.

$a = $ /ae/ in *hat*
$e = $ /e/ in *set*
$i = $ /i/ in *thin*
$o = $ /a/ in *hot.*
$u = $ /u/ in *put*

Children need to recognize the differences among these sounds first; then, they need to identify the sounds in known words, and, finally, they need to associate each printed pattern with the associated sound. Some of this process will occur in teaching the phonograms; the rest must be made explicit in the instruction at this point. Children should build up the expectation that words which have a consonant-vowel-consonant pattern have an unglided vowel sound. Next, children should be exposed to *long* or *glided* vowel sounds, although some glided vowel sounds, such as those in *spoon, how,* and *toy,* are not as common, and instruction can be postponed for a time.

$a = $ /ey/ in *hay*
$e = $ /iy/ in *beat*
$i = $ /ay/ in *sight*
$o = $ /ow/ in *coat*
$u = $ /yew/ in *use*

As these sounds are first distinguished, a sense of expected spelling patterns common to these vowels develops; finally, use is made of the sound/symbol expectations when new words are met. Children should build up the following generalizations for the spelling patterns of words which have glided sounds: when words have a single vowel following a single consonant, the vowel is often glided; when words have a consonant-vowel-consonant pattern, -*e*, the first vowel is usually glided and the -*e* is silent. At this point, too, the following vowel patterns can be learned since they usually present a glided vowel pattern: -*ight, oa* + consonant, *ai* + consonant.

Once the above word recognition skills have been acquired, children will be able to decode many words met in print for the first time. The whole focus of the word recognition program is to help children make use of these decoding skills in the context of the reading material.

Contextual Clues to Word Recognition

In Chapter 6, it was observed that children naturally use context to figure out words *(25)*. Explicit instruction in use of context plus sound/symbol awareness will increase the efficiency of contextual use and will also provide experiences which may promote the development of skilled reading behavior. Instruction begins with oral activities. The teacher asks for all possible words which could fit into the sentences:

> The boy jumped over the _____.
> The man walked into the _____.
> The _____ cat ate his supper.

When language-experience reading is underway, the teacher can extract sentences from the children's dictations, write them on the chalkboard leaving out a blank, and proceed as in the above cases. Once the children have become accustomed to this procedure, they can make sentences from the word cards in their word banks leaving a space on the table for a word. Another child tries to find a word card in his bank which will sensibly complete the sentence. Activities to promote use of context proceed to those which more closely resemble the behavior which occurs in reading. Again, using sentences dictated by the children, the teacher can offer two words from which to choose to better complete a sentence. At first, the correct responses will be obvious as in:

> We looked under the _____ (tree, run).

After practicing with sentences like these and emphasizing what makes sense, the children should realize that the choices should be words which have more graphic similarity.

Once children understand the concept of choice of words which are grammatically sound, the instruction should proceed to incorporate sound/symbol correspondences with context. A way of showing children how use of initial single consonants will help them to figure out an unknown word is to first present a sentence with no graphic clues:

My sister likes to wash the ———.

All the possible nouns which fit should be elicited from the child. Then, the teacher should say that he will give a hint and add the grapheme *d* at the left of the blank. The children should choose which of their possibilities now fits. They then would be encouraged to describe the help given by the initial consonant. After a number of these kinds of experiences, initial consonant clusters can become the clues. Finally, the teacher might want to devise situations in which initial letters would not be sufficient clues. Thus, in the sentence, "I put on my c———," *clothes, cape,* or *coat* might fit in the blank. The teacher could then add *ape* to complete the experience, and the children would learn to use the graphic content at the *end* of the word. The children will eventually learn to ask the following questions when meeting an unknown word in their reading: What word do I know that would make sense here in this sentence? What word do I know that makes sense and begins with an———? The children then learn to read the sentence with the chosen word in order to evaluate their hypotheses themselves. If the sentence still does not make sense, use is made of the sound relatedness of the letters at the end of the word.

Systematic Record Keeping of Word Recognition Skills

Since the instruction in word recognition will have most relevance when it matches the children's needs, a consistent, easy method for recording achievement in the various skills is needed. When a group of children are presented with a specific lesson, differential understandings always occur. When a few children have failed to achieve understanding during the initial exposure, a follow-up lesson or additional practice with games is required so that the children can be kept together in a group for ease of management. The various skills to be taught can be listed in a column with the names of the members of each group in a row across the top. Whenever the teacher finds that children have acquired the skill and have used it in application with new words, he can make a check in the appropriate place. Continual progress thus can be monitored. By these means, the teacher is providing individualized instruction based on on-going diagnosis of progress within a manageable grouping arrangement.

TEXTS AND TRADEBOOKS

The final but by no means least important component of a beginning reading program is the reading done in textbooks and/or tradebooks. Expansion of concepts, exposure to new vicarious experiences, and learning a variety of expressions all occur as children read material written by others. Just as children gain language understandings and reading comprehension ability from stories read to them *(21)*, the opportunity for cognitive and language growth is just as limitless when they read alone. Children who have experienced the joy of learning and the pleasure associated with listening to a good story—and all should have—look forward to independent reading with positive anticipation. For example, one six year old I know said enthusiastically as she was acquiring a store of sight words and techniques for unlocking new ones, "Now I don't have to wait for you, my mother, or my father to read me a new story; I can read it myself as many times as I want!"

When children have learned the basic concepts which are acquired with language-experience, have acquired seventy-five to one hundred sight words, have mastered techniques for unlocking new words, they are ready for a planned program of reading in texts and/or tradebooks. The children will continue *writing* and *dictating* stories on occasion, but a major portion of the structured reading program will come now from this component. We will now discuss practical suggestions for use of basal texts and then describe possible activities for use with tradebooks.

Use of Basal Texts in Beginning Reading

While the reader may conclude that instruction with use of tradebooks is preferable to instruction with basal texts, there are reasons for moving into group reading of basal text stories, especially for inexperienced teachers. A teacher who has designed and executed a creative series of language experiences and who has developed a word recognition program will find it difficult to implement an individualized reading program as well. In any case, group experiences with reading during the acquisition process are quite helpful. When children share ideas about their reading material, they learn a great deal from each other. Generally, in classroom group reading situations, the instructional sequence includes the following components: discussion of story setting, introduction of vocabulary, development of purposes for reading, silent or oral reading, discussion of story meaning, rereading, and enrichment activities. In keeping with the declared goal of promoting independent, self-evaluating readers who comprehend the material and the author's message and who are developing skill in making and verifying predictions, we will make some adaptations to the conventional procedures for group reading.

Story setting: It is important that children become acquainted with the setting and important concepts of a story before reading. Pictures and reference to related stories and experiences are used to establish an understanding of the concepts and setting of stories.

Vocabulary introduction: Some teacher's guides suggest that every new word in a story be introduced carefully. However, if children are to *use* their word recognition techniques effectively, not all words should be identified before story reading. Those words which have unfamiliar *meaning* should be clarified by use of context and concrete reference whenever possible. Words which the teacher feels the children will not be able to decode should also be identified and placed in context. Only a few minutes should be spent on this vocabulary introduction.

Development of purposes for reading: We all know that our reading comprehension is affected positively by the strength of our purposes for reading. If we are reading a new book by our favorite author, an important article with new information, or a text on which we will be examined, we are apt to read with great attention. In the first case, we read with expectation of great pleasure and new insights. In the second, we expect to find data which will fit into an already developed informational framework. In the last case, although reading under pressure, we read, review, self-test. Children should learn that reading is done for a variety of purposes, and we should help them to develop these purposes. Where the teacher directs children to read a story only for specific details, they will not learn to diversify their reading; however, when the purposes for reading have been set to attain higher understandings, comprehension will be improved *(14)*. Teachers can help by suggesting two alternative stories to a group and letting them decide which story to read. They can suggest that the children read to solve a mystery, to find needed information, to get to know a really weird adult, etc. If children are asked to predict the content or plot of a story from just the information contained in the story title, interest is peaked.

Oral reading: When children first start to read, they usually do so orally. But soon after they move into the text reading component of the reading program they should begin to learn to read silently. Early silent reading is recommended by a number of reading authorities, among them Spache and Spache *(24)* and Heilman *(11)*. There are a number of reasons for early acquisition of silent reading habits:

1. Swift, skilled reading is done silently. When reading orally, children cannot learn the behaviors associated with skilled reading.
2. When children read silently, all must read! By contrast, in typical oral round robin reading, individual children lose interest unless they are the one reading orally.
3. Oral reading may overemphasize word calling to the detriment of comprehension, which is the real goal of reading.
4. Audience-pleasing behaviors, such as speechlike intonation, are needed for successful oral reading and are very difficult to acquire.

Silent reading: To introduce children to silent reading, the teacher should first point out that older children and adults cannot be heard as they read. This "grown-up" reading behavior then motivates the children. The teacher then suggests that children try to whisper (and many will need to be shown what this means) their story. After this whispering has been practiced, the children are asked to read without making a sound. After a time, the teacher tells the children to read without moving their lips at all. While these behaviors are being acquired, the children should occasionally read material which is very easy for them. It is important to remember that it takes considerable time for children to acquire silent reading behaviors.

Follow-up discussion: The follow-up discussion should expand children's literal, interpretive, and evaluative understanding of the story. Good questions ask children which person in the story they liked best, why an event occurred, whether the story was true, what someone meant when they said _____, what the child would have done in a similar circumstance, and what _____ meant in the sentence _____.

Guszak *(9)* has shown that teachers tend to ask questions dealing with detail contained in the content of the stories far more often than they ask the kinds of questions which elicit reasoning and analysis of the structures of the story. In his study, primary grade teachers were more inclined to ask detail questions than were intermediate grade teachers. Guszak believes that primary teachers are responding to the simple content of the stories found in primary-level readers. Spache and Spache *(24)* have pointed out that children read to fulfill the kinds of questions they have come to expect their teachers to ask. Yet it is possible for teachers to learn to ask questions which encourage interpretive, critical, and creative thinking *(19)*. Since reading comprehension ability requires more than recall of story details, teachers must learn to ask children questions which promote important comprehension skills. These skills include the ability to draw inferences from the content, to recognize the writer's purpose, to understand the organization of the material read, and to understand word meaning *(25)*. Sanders *(22)* is one source for learning to ask good questions.

Rereading of a story: This activity is not always necessary, but it provides an opportunity to practice *oral* reading if the story is first read silently. Rereading is good practice if done with a purpose. Oral rereading is effective when children read a story again to prove a point raised during a discussion, when they practice to prepare for reading aloud to parents, and when they read to younger children. However, it is not necessary for the teacher to listen to children read orally every day.

Enrichment activities: Extension of the content or topics of stories should often accompany group reading experiences. Further reading on the same topic, reading of other stories by the same author, play reading, dramatic improvisation, oral poetry reading, illustrating the story setting, and writing or dictating an alternate ending are just a few follow-up activities possible.

Sequencing textual reading: It is not necessary to read every story from a basal as long as no difficulty with vocabulary emerges. Nor is it necessary to read only from one text if other materials are available and if interest indicates that in-depth reading of a topic at one level would be beneficial.

Alternative group reading structure: The Directed Reading-Thinking Activity (DRTA) described by Stauffer *(26)* encourages active positive reading experiences. With the DRTA, children constantly make predictions about story content—first, from the title and pictures alone; then, from the information of the first paragraph; then, from the first page; and so on. As the reading progresses, predictions are tested and verified and further predictions are refined. As children disagree about predictions and discuss the reasons for their predictions, they attend to the author's organization, the development of the characters, significance of the setting, and the details described in the setting. With this method, the teacher acts only as a guide to the strategies of prediction and verification used by the children.

Use of Tradebooks in Beginning Reading

In recent years, a number of books have been published which have a low vocabulary load but also have a varied content and are appealing to beginners [see Guilfoyle *(8)*, Spache *(23)*, and Groff *(7)* for lists of easy-to-read books]. While some of these books are available in paperback and can be bought in quantity for group reading experiences like those just described, some reading should be individualized to provide for personalized interests and growth.

When children choose a book, read it, and enjoy it, they should share their reactions with their classmates. Some activities to promote sharing include:

1. *Book Salesman:*   In order to win a ticket which allows a child to receive another book from the class library, each child must "sell" his book to a classmate.
2. *Book Recommendation Period:*   Children display their books and suggest why a classmate would or would not enjoy them.
3. *Book Tree:*   Children write the titles of their books on green paper leaves. After reading the title to the class, each child says one thing about his book and attaches the leaf to an upright leafless branch.
4. One child prepares to read the first page of his favorite book aloud to the others but refuses to tell what happens in the rest of the book.
5. *New Words:*   Children add new and interesting words to a large chart entitled *Words from Good Books.*
6. *Book Categorization:* The children display their library books. In discussion, the children decide into what groups they could

put the books. For example, one class might have *Real* and *Not Real* as categories. Another might find *Animals, People,* and *Earth Books* an adequate system for grouping.

7. *Favorite Books:* In this activity, both self-read and teacher-read books are displayed. The children write the title of their first, second, and third preference.

8. *Jackets:* Covers of popular books are placed on a bulletin board. The authors' names are masked, but an envelope holds cards with each author's name. The children attach all the cards to the books and then check to see if they have named the authors by lifting the masks.

9. *Dictated Stories:* When children are very familiar with one author, the teacher suggests a topic similar to the content of the author's books. As a group, the children dictate a story like the author's.

10. *Illustrating Books:* There are, of course, a number of ways for children to demonstrate their pleasure in books through art; for example, they can make new book jackets, design a diorama, illustrate a previously unillustrated scene, etc.

As children share their books in a variety of ways, they continue to add new words to their word banks. By this time in the beginning reading program, the word bank does not represent all the words the children can identify, but when the new words are written on cards (by the children now), they still are reinforced and practiced. The word bank becomes an effective source for follow-up activities.

In conclusion, the beginning reading program ideally allows for both pupil and teacher creativity. Children approach and learn important reading concepts and initial vocabulary through language experience. The more structured word recognition program provides them with techniques for becoming independent readers, while in the group and individual reading of texts and tradebooks, they apply their ability to read independently as they grow in vocabulary, language, and experiential knowledge.

REFERENCES

1. Allen, R. V., and Allen, C. *Language Experience in Reading.* Chicago: Encyclopedia Britannica Educational Corporation, 1968.

2. Bissett, D. J. "Literature in the Classroom." *Elementary English* 49 (1972): 1016–024.

3. Boning, R. A. *Using Sounds.* Rockville Center, New York: Barnell Loft, 1962.

4. Dolch, E. W. *Problems in Reading.* Champaign, Illinois: The Garrard Press, 1948.

5. Durkin, D. *Teaching Young Children to Read.* Boston: Allyn & Bacon, Inc., 1972.

6. Durrell, D., and Murphy, H. *Speech-to-Print Phonics,* 2d ed. New York: Harcourt, Brace, Jovanovich, 1972.

7. Groff, P. "Recent Easy Books for First-Grade Readers." *Elementary English* 37 (1960): 521–27.

8. Guilfoyle, E. *Books for Beginning Readers.* Champaign, Illinois: National Council of Teachers of English, 1972.

9. Guszak, F. "Teacher Questioning and Reading." *The Reading Teacher* 21 (1967): 227–34.

10. Hall, M. *Teaching Reading as a Language Experience.* Columbus, Ohio: Charles E. Merrill Publishing Co., 1972.

11. Heilman, A. W. *Principles and Practices of Teaching Reading,* 3rd ed. Columbus, Ohio: Charles E. Merrill Publishing Co., 1972.

12. Heilman, A. W., and Holmes, E. A. *Smuggling Language into the Teaching of Reading.* Columbus, Ohio: Charles E. Merrill Publishing Co., 1972.

13. Heilman, A. W.; Helmkamp, R.; Thomas, A. S.; Carselle, C. J., consultants. *Phonics We Use.* Chicago: Lyons and Carnahan, 1968.

14. Henderson, E. H. "A Study of Individually Formulated Purposes for Reading." *Journal of Educational Research* 59 (1965): 438–41.

15. Herrick, V. E., and Nerbourg, M. *Using Experience Charts with Children.* Columbus, Ohio: Charles E. Merrill Publishing Co., 1964.

16. Johnson, D. P. "The Dolch List Reexamined." *The Reading Teacher* 24 (1971): 449–57.

17. Keats, E. J. *The Snowy Day.* New York: The Viking Press, Inc., 1962.

18. Landrum, R., and Children. *A Day Dream I Had at Night and Other Stories: Teaching Children How to Make Their Own Readers.* New York: Teachers and Writers Collaborative, 1971. (Available from NCTE)

19. Lanier, R. J., and Davis, A. P. "Developing Comprehension through Teacher-Made Questions." *The Reading Teacher* 25 (1972): 153–57.

20. Lee, D. M., and Allen, R. V. *Learning to Read through Experience.* New York: Appleton-Century-Crofts, Inc., 1963.

21. Porter, J. "Research Report." *Elementary English* 49 (1972): 1028–037.

22. Sanders, N. M. *Classroom Questions: What Kinds?* New York: Harper and Row, Publishers, 1966.

23. Spache, E. B., and Spache, G. A. *Good Reading for Poor Readers.* Champaign, Illinois: Garrard Publishing Co., 1968.

24. Spache, G. D., and Spache, E. B. *Reading in the Elementary School,* 2d ed. Boston: Allyn & Bacon, Inc., 1969.

25. Spearrit, D. "Identification of Subskills of Reading Comprehension by Maximum Likelihood Factor Analysis" *Reading Research Quarterly* 8 (1972): 92–111.

26. Stauffer, R. C. *Directing Reading Maturity as a Cognitive Process.* New York: Harper and Row, 1969.

27. _____. *The Language Experience Approach to the Teaching of Reading.* New York: Harper and Row, 1970.

28. Weber, R. M. "A Linguistic Analysis of First-Grade Reading Errors." *Reading Research Quarterly* 6 (1970): 427–51.

Index

Index